SPARKLY AND STRONG

SPARKLY AND STRONG

Suing IBM

Surviving Domestic Violence

Thriving as an Entrepreneur

by age 40

Karen Dunning

DEDICATION

For my mother and grandparents,
who demonstrated resilience, bravery, grace, and love.

Disclaimer
Names have been changed for privacy

TABLE OF CONTENTS

INTRODUCTION

I am sharing the lessons and experiences I've collected over the last six decades, in both business and my personal life. My hope is that this book will heal me and others.

The catalyst for finally writing my book was the dire medical diagnosis of cancer, with 6 to 12 months to live on May 19, 2020. On May 20, my mother died at the age of 97, giving me the freedom to share the full story of the abuses I'd experienced without fear that my perpetrators would retaliate against her or that my own safety would be compromised (as my perpetrators lived in the same area as she did). I am grateful to be able to move toward the end of my life with this cathartic act of truth telling.

In my professional life, I have been able to use my natural gifts and talents with confidence and ease. Over the course of my career, I won many awards, including Entrepreneur of the Year at age 39. I also helped create equal pay at IBM by filing a significant legal case at age 27, founded and built several small businesses, attended international trade missions, founded an endowment at age 38, wrote and performed songs, and sang and acted in TV shows and movies. I achieved what many people consider the pinnacle of success. At the end of this book, you'll see evidence of these achievements in a series of articles that were published about my life's work. At age 40 I was officially "retired".

My world hasn't been all puppies and rainbows, though. The truth is, while I was breaking glass ceilings in my professional life, my personal life was fraught with a pain that very few people knew about. The duality was striking. My experience with domestic violence knocked the wind out of me and broke my heart into pieces between the ages of 26 and 39. In essence, I became two separate people. My confident business and public persona was pitted against my petrified private persona.

When I was 34 years old, I was strangled to unconsciousness and almost died. As I hovered between life and death, I saw white light and felt what I can only describe as pure love. In that moment, I saw that everything and everyone is connected. What each of us does affects everyone else. This moment catalyzed a chain reaction of events that would eventually help my "3D" human self catch up to what my spiritual self already knew. It took professional counseling to deprogram the damage and regain my true inner sense of self and reality.

But I did it.

I am proud to have broken the cycle of violence in my life and to have come into a recognition of my wholeness. I would love for other people, especially women, who have been in similar situations, to come to the same recognition. My desire is for them to know they are not broken and that it is possible to move past toxic conditioning and enter into powerful truth telling...so that we no longer hide from the totality of our stories...so that we finally have the courage to change our path—because it is never too late.

I've lived through a lot of significant changes over the last 60-plus years of my life. I've witnessed the struggle for civil rights and equal pay for women and minorities. I've experienced the cultural revolution of the 60s and 70s, and the subsequent redefinition of our social roles and identities. I've recognized the pain and trauma, stifled by generations of women, rising to the surface in the midst of the #MeToo movement. I've also become more acutely aware of the genius of our survival mechanisms, and how easy it is for many people to deny the trauma that has shaped their choices and behaviors.

I have compassion for the many women who are only now coming to a realization of the injustices and abuses they lived through, as well as admiration for their resilience. While women have braved the struggles of their personal lives and the world around them, until very recently, most of us were raised to be "good girls." We were raised to take the open-hearted, wide-eyed naivete of a Girl Scout into the remainder of our lives as daughters, sisters, mothers, wives, girlfriends, and professionals. We were not taught to discern that some people have bad intentions, and that if we are the recipient of those bad intentions, we must stand up and speak out rather than remain passive or wait for a white knight to come save us. For most of us, the white knight never came, and we quickly learned to remain silent about the harms we experienced—even to bury them under denial and the need to keep up appearances. Moreover, if something happened to us that was beyond our control to respond to or transform, we internalized that pain. We blamed ourselves if we were hurt, beaten, raped, degraded, and demeaned.

I am heartened by the fact that so many women are waking up to assess the circumstances of their lives, and to finally put their foot down and say, "This isn't right. And I'm going to fix it." I am also heartened by the fact that young women today are summoning the courage to speak out about the abuses they've experienced, and that the world is beginning to take notice.

Throughout history, women have changed the world through our refusal to be silent. And so, I share my story here in the hope that it will add to the chorus of brave voices that have shed light on our share of the human condition—and in doing so, have inspired others to do the same.

I've learned and grown a lot through my journey, and what I like to refer to as my graduation from the school of hard knocks. At the same time, these experiences have softened me and opened me up to the magic that is always here. I am grateful to the presence of miracles and to the invisible guides that have lit up my path. As I've been told, everything I touch "turns to gold." My goal as a child was world peace, and it still is.

I now know I need to be my own "white knight" and shero. I need to love myself and send love to others to create peace in myself. For when each person has peace, the world has peace.

I hope my journey will inspire you to make sense of your own life story, mine the gifts, and find the peace that is waiting for you.

Much love,

Karen Dunning

CHAPTER 1

LEAVE A PLACE BETTER THAN YOU FOUND IT

I was born in Everett, Washington, at Providence Hospital, on December 3, 1956, to Dorothy and Earl Dunning. I shared my date of birth with my maternal grandfather—a man who was patient and kind, and with whom I celebrated many birthdays (we each got our own cake, of course). I had two older brothers, Steve, born in 1952, and Dave, born in 1954. We lived in Lynnwood, Washington, a small peaceful suburb 16 miles north of Seattle. My dad was a CPA for a Big Eight accounting firm in Seattle. My mom was a former teacher and U.S. Signal Corps decoder who eventually became a full-time stay-at-home mom. Our house was brand-new with gleaming wood floors, a backyard for our swing set and jungle gym, and a stunning view of Mt. Rainier. Dad took the train to Seattle for work, so Mom had the car to drive us on adventures and to swim at Green Lake. In many ways, at least on the outside, we were the picture-perfect all-American family. On the inside, we were much more complex.

My mom didn't find out she was pregnant with me, her third child, until after undergoing major surgery to remove a mysterious mass in her upper right back (which, as it turned out, doctors believed was Mom's "twin" from when they were back in the womb). Mom was incapacitated as doctors cut through her lymph glands, leaving her with limited use of her arms. Throughout the rest of her pregnancy, as she would later tell me, she worried that I would be born brain-dead. She would also note that when I was a baby, I didn't like to be picked up by her. I would push her away with my little arms. It made me sad to know this, but years later, an energy reader told me that children who push people away at an early age often end up harboring a gift of reading energy and healing.

In December 1958, when I was two years old, we moved to Kearney, Nebraska, where my dad was to start a branch accounting office for Phillip G. Johnson CPA's, whose headquarters were in Lincoln. My sister, Linda, who was born in October 1958 (on the same day as my brother Steve), was only six weeks old when we made that cross-country trip with two adults and four children. My grandparents came with us, and together, we drove two cars from Washington to Nebraska. Ever an adventurous spirit, I took this great adventure as an opportunity to roam free. My mother told me that during one of our stops, my parents heard tires squealing and horns honking—which is how they discovered I had wandered out on the highway. A woman stopped her car and carried me to safety when my parents arrived.

When we arrived in Kearney—a small flat town with blazing hot summers and snowy cold winters—it took a little getting used to, but soon, life resumed as normal. I attended A.O. Thomas Preschool, a special program that was part of Nebraska State Teachers College. It had observation rooms for adults, who were invited to examine the latest teaching techniques. My love for music began at an early age. At school, I loved playing all the instruments and singing songs. In addition to my musical ability, I was naturally athletic and loved to run, climb trees, swing high and jump out, and go down slides. I also took ballet from the ages of three to five.

It's possible that some of this had to do with having two older brothers. At the same time, growing up in the 50s and 60s, I received an early education in the gender roles of the day.

I recall my brother Dave informing me that men were better than women. With my four-year-old logic, I declared, "I am going to be a princess."

He went on to tell me he would be a prince—and that was higher. So I said I would be a queen. Well, he would be a king and that was higher than a queen. So what? I would be an Ace.

He scoffed, "There's no such thing as an Ace."

That stumped me. I ventured, "Mommy is a good cook."

He said decisively, "Well, the best cooks are men and they're called chefs."

Defeated, I thought, *Poor Mommy.*

**

Along with many of the other people in our social circle, my family went to a large Methodist church. On Sundays we always went to services, then ate a delicious lunch and popcorn for supper. I remember being afraid of the pastor's sermons, as he roared while delivering them. Paired with vivid images of fire and brimstone, it felt like he was directly putting the fear of God in all of us. I always ran as fast as possible to get to the safety of Sunday School.

From a very young age, music was my chosen religion—something that filled me with a sense of joy, ease, and connection. Mom had a portable electric chord organ that she would play as she sang songs with us. The whole family gathered around to join in, as Mom had a beautiful singing voice. She taught me how to play the organ, too. I always felt most at home with myself when I was singing.

As Mom helped to whet my creative appetite, my father was working every day, sometimes overnight. Occasionally, he took me to his accounting office on Saturdays. I always loved accompanying him and felt very special and important. Overall, being in my dad's presence was like being bathed in warm sunshine. He was joyful and had a powerful laugh. Naturally, he was very popular and social, and he had lots of friends. He was also engaged with a number of community service activities; he was in Rotary and other service and business clubs, and also served as treasurer for our church.

Dad was brilliant and could speak many languages, including Spanish. In fact, he used to read to us in Spanish. (I especially liked his Spanish version of *The Three Bears*.) Overall, Dad inspired a sense of deep trust and security, which were especially welcome whenever

I followed him under the house to the dark crawl space full of spiders and cobwebs. I also recall my sister and I hanging onto Dad as our brothers grabbed our ankles and tickled the soles of our feet until one of us cried. Dad let me and Linda crawl all over his legs, even as he was holding a newspaper in front of his face while smoking a cigarette. He would sit with one foot on the floor and the other foot across his knee, forming a hole we could crawl through to get to safety.

As the two girls in the family, Linda and I did everything together, including swimming lessons and setting up our Barbie dream house. When I got to Kindergarten and Linda was too young to go with me, I informed her that she couldn't come. I guess Mom didn't like my tone of voice because she yelled, "I adored my sister, and she's dead now, so you two had better get along!" From that point forward, I felt a strong sense of responsibility and loyalty toward Linda.

Linda and I usually got matching gifts in different colors. Once, we both got stuffed kittens, shaped like triangles with tails—one black, the other white. We used to hold them by their tails and ring them like bells, saying "Ding dong!" ad nauseam to the annoyed adults.

In my early childhood, Mom stayed home with Linda and me as my brothers went to school and Dad went to work. We did all sorts of projects, from finger painting, to sculpting with handmade clay, to sewing doll clothes. Once, I drew a tree whose trunk had a green ball on top and small red circles for apples.

My mother asked, "Is that what a tree looks like?"

I assured her, "Oh, yes."

She took me outside to examine a real tree and pointed out the separate branches, leaves, and details of the bark. Then, back inside, she showed me how to draw in the branches, leaves, and other details.

Mom wasn't always so patient with me in sharing insights about the ways of the world, and there were times I bore the brunt of her anger and impatience. Once, I washed my hair all by myself with a bar of soap in the sink. I was so proud of my efforts—until my hair dried crunchy, as the soap residue had not been fully rinsed out. Mom was so furious she made me eat what remained of the soap bar.

Another time, I cut the fingernails on my left hand with Mom's pinking shears. When I tried to cut the nails on my right hand with my left hand, the shears were too bulky and unwieldy, so I went to find Mom to help me.

"Mom, will you please help me trim the nails on my right hand?"

Her face turned dark as she looked at the jagged nails on my left hand and asked, "What have you done?"

I exclaimed, "I cut them with the pinking shears!"

Mom was mad about that. Apparently, pinking shears were expensive and were only to be used on fabric—not even paper cutting was allowed. She threatened to tell my father when he got home. That scared me. After cutting down the points I'd so carefully crafted on my left hand, Mom spanked me for using the pinking shears without permission. She used a flat hand for the spanking, which I could barely feel through my clothes, so that made me giggle. Because the spanking didn't seem to be having the effect Mom wanted, she hit a little harder. I played along and let out a fake sob, which seemed to satisfy her. At that point, she sent me outside to play that hot summer day. It really didn't feel like a big deal, and it certainly wasn't much of a punishment compared to the thrill of having all those points on my left hand—even if they were short-lived.

Next time, I decided, I wouldn't show my mom, just so I could keep the points longer. What she didn't know wouldn't hurt her—or me!

**

When I was about four years old, Mom decided she wanted a second family car, so she wouldn't be stuck at home with four children all the time. My dad was adamantly against this, but Mom was determined. When Mom shared my dad's reluctance with me years later, in 2015, I felt upset on her behalf. I also learned that Mom had wanted to go back to school and get a job, but Dad was opposed. "No wife of mine is ever going to work," he insisted.

Mom cashed in a war bond she'd saved from before they were married and bought a large four-door used gray car. This was back before seat belts. When she rounded a corner, we had to hang on to each other to keep from falling out, as the back doors would swing open on the curves more than once!

At some point, my mom had the car repaired, but it wasn't fixed correctly and she drove to the gas station with me in the back seat to complain. Even as a five-year-old, I could tell from his body language that the gas-station attendant didn't take Mom's complaints seriously. As we were waiting in the car for him to come back, I noticed that Mom was talking to herself in low tones.

From the back seat, I asked, "Who are you talking to?"

Mom sighed, "Nobody."

Intuitively, I felt the man had not treated my mom with respect, and I noticed that she hadn't stood up for herself. I was angry, and sad, that he'd gotten away with it. "Are you saying what you wish you would have said to that man?" I softly inquired.

Mom paused for a moment before responding, "Yes."

**

I knew that Mom could get angry and frustrated from time to time, and there were moments when she would take that out on me and my siblings. The moments when I was on the receiving end of Dad's wrath were infrequent in contrast, but when they happened, they were dramatic.

I remember one such occasion. My mom had hand-painted two

ceramic figurines, a woman and man with matching forest-green outfits. The woman wore a crown, and the man wore a sailor hat. Both had dark hair and red lips, and they seemed content to just gaze at each other. The ceramic glaze finish made them look luminous and angelic. As a treat, Mom would sometimes bring them down from the shelf and let me look at them but told me that I was never to touch them. I was obedient.

But once, I climbed on my rocking horse to get a better look at the beautiful figurines. Without warning, Dad grabbed me off the horse, pulled off my pants and underpants, and spanked me as hard as he could—for much longer than I felt I deserved. I cried and yelled for him to stop, stop, stop! I could see others in the room, but no one came to my aid. Dad went on like that for some time until finally he put me down, pants still around my ankles, and pushed me away.

"Go to your room," he ordered. There was no hint of an apology in his voice.

My skin stung and was blistered with welts. My face and eyes were puffy and red. I hurt so bad. As much as I loved and admired Dad, I hated him with a passion in that moment. (Many years later, in 1996, when I was in counseling, I asked Mom if she remembered this traumatic event. She said that she didn't, but some 20 years later, when Mom was in her 90s, she told me she was sorry and had felt bad about the incident all these years.)

Sadly, that experience didn't get a chance to be redeemed by other more loving moments with my father. In August of 1962, Dad died of a massive heart attack from smoking three packs of cigarettes a day. He was only 37 years old.

The U.S. Navy had given Dad free cigarettes when he served during World War II, and like so many others, he quickly got addicted. While Dad survived WWII, he didn't survive the Marlboro Man.

Dad was brought home by our family doctor from an evening

church meeting where he'd fallen ill while giving his treasurer's report. My brothers were visiting our maternal grandparents in Lincoln at the time. Linda, who was only three years old, recalls being on the bed with Dad shortly after his heart attack. I tried to come into the bedroom where he was in bed, with Mom and the doctor and Linda gathered around him.

When Mom saw me come in, she looked flustered. "Get out!" she screamed.

So out I got. At the age of five, as my dad lay on his deathbed, I sat alone crying on the kitchen floor until it became dark. At some point, Dad came out of the bedroom to go to the bathroom.

When I saw him, my last words to my father were, "Are you sick, Daddy?"

His last words to me were, "Yes, honey, I am."

I never saw my father again. I wasn't allowed to go to the visitation or funeral service in Kearney. Although I pleaded with Mom to let me go, she simply retorted, "Well, you can't!" My cousin Kathy recalls that I was visibly and vocally upset about not being allowed to go. Instead, Linda and I were picked up by the doctor's wife and whisked away in our PJs to their home to stay. The doctor's wife helped me dress—which was weird, since I had been doing it by myself for years. I remember how spacious the bedroom was and how soft the light cream carpet felt to my bare feet. It was a beautiful place.

For weeks, it felt like I was sleepwalking, or dreaming. It was a somber time during which I felt I was watching everything from afar. I was totally in the dark. It was certainly a powerful rite of passage. I was only five years old, but I became wise. While I didn't know the whole story, I knew something big and scary had happened—and it was up to me to take care of my mom from now on.

I knew the stress of Dad's sudden death took a toll on Mom, and it made her anger seem even more volatile. Soon after Dad died, Mom got mad at me and my siblings as we watched Saturday morning cartoons.

"Why are you kids watching cartoons? Why aren't you vacuuming?" she screamed.

I recall being bewildered and thinking, I'm only five! I can't even move a vacuum cleaner!

She yelled, "Your father died because he couldn't take you kids!"

Sometimes, Mom would pick up her purse and threaten my brother, Steve, who was only nine at the time. "I'm leaving and never coming back!" she'd say, and would stalk out of the house. Like me, Steve was worried about how he, as the oldest, would be able to take care of the rest of us if Mom didn't return.

I tried to be as helpful as possible from that point on. After all, I was worried that, just like Dad, Mom might end up dying. And then, what would happen to us?

**

Shortly after Dad died, we moved from the brown house to a two-bedroom apartment. Although things were rough, we'd never really loved our Kearney house, which was a rental, to begin with. And while Mom's married friends abandoned her after Dad's death, she seemed to be in a better place overall—perhaps because she now had more agency in her life.

Mom, who was now tasked with being the primary breadwinner, went back to school to renew her teacher's certificate. Right before I was to start Kindergarten that fall, Grandma sent five beautifully tailored dresses for me to wear, one for each day of the week. I also had ruby-red shoes, like Dorothy in *The Wizard of Oz*, my favorite movie—which provided something of a consolation in the midst of all the change.

I went to afternoon Kindergarten at Emerson Grade School, and Linda stayed with a neighbor lady who took in ironing. After school I went there, too, and sometimes she let us help her iron the handkerchiefs.

Overall, there was little adult supervision in those days—and best of all, no spankings from Dad! I also loved the kids and all the bustling activity in the apartment complex. I had a crush on Billy, a classmate who lived in the building next to ours. There was always something going on, and someone to play with. At dusk, Mom rang a bell for the kids to come in.

I roller-skated every day. Mom's sister, Aunt Evelyn, had died the year before, and Uncle Don had sent me her skates with eagle wings over the wheels and ball bearings in them. I could skate faster than anyone. I also rode my bike really fast—so fast I skidded on the gravel as I turned a corner and tore up my knees, leaving tiny pebbles embedded beneath my skin.

We had our swing set behind the apartment, and our Easy-Bake kitchen set up in the hallway outside our apartment. Plus, we had a balcony overlooking the courtyard. Linda and I shared a double bed and Mom slept in a single bed, all in the same bedroom. Steve and Dave shared the other bedroom. For many families, the move from a big house to a small apartment might have felt disruptive but, for me, it was a wondrous adventure.

Throughout it all, Mom made sure that the kids reached all the important milestones, like learning to swim. Mom hadn't learned to swim as a child and regretted it. Linda and I both went to private lessons, and later to group lessons at the public pool. I loved the freedom that came with swimming and being in the water. I could naturally float on my back with my toes out of the water.

Mom also did her best to make learning accessible and fun. One day, when I was five years old, I was trying to count and was having trouble with the order of the numbers. I asked Mom, "How do you count to 100?"

She paused and looked me in the eye. "Would you like to learn how to count to 100 now?"

I smiled eagerly. "Yes!"

Mom took me by the hand and led me to the tiny table in the

cramped kitchen. She sat opposite me at the table—and very quietly, slowly, and patiently, started to count. "One. Two. Three…" And so on, all the way up to 100. From that day forward, I could count to 100. As I look back on that time, recalling how challenging it was for everyone in my family, I admire my mother for the patience she was able to show me, and her willingness to devote time to me when she was going to school to renew her teaching certificate and was simultaneously struggling to support four children.

For years after Dad died, people who didn't know would ask about my father and what he did for a living. I told them he was dead, and they looked uncomfortable. Sometimes I would hear them whisper when they thought I couldn't hear, "She's the one without a father," or "She doesn't have a dad."

After Dad died, Linda and I were playing at my friend Judy's house on her front porch. She'd asked us if we'd join her butt club. She propped up a big piece of cardboard as a screen, and at her prompting, we each took turns dropping our pants and exposing our butts to huge gales of laughter. We were sheltered from the street, but not the dining-room window. Judy's mom came out with her hands on her hips and an angry expression as she snapped, "You girls from the broken home! Get out and never come back!"

We went home, and I asked Mom, "What's a broken home?"

I was the only one in my class without a father. It's possible that my classmate Billy's parents were separated, but most adults back in the 1960s remained married.

At school one day, my teacher instructed, "Draw a picture of how your father looks in the morning." I drew his gravesite with him sleeping under the flower-covered earth. I got in trouble, and the teacher showed my mom my picture. I didn't understand what the big deal was, as I had only followed directions.

When there were father-daughter functions, Linda and I were usually not allowed to go, not even with a substitute. However, on one occasion I invited our minister (a kind one with a gentle demeanor, not the one who yelled his sermons) to my Father Visit Day, and he came. Bless his heart! I remember taking his hand and leading him around my class. My mom later told me as well as my teacher that I'd asked him of my own volition. When I'd suggested it to Mom, she'd warned me not to be disappointed, as our minister had six children of his own to visit that day. I was preparing for the worst, but I remember how happy I was that he'd come. He was a good dad.

While there were some silver linings that would emerge to brighten my day and remind me that there were people who cared and were watching out for me, I looked forward to nap time at school so I could cry without anyone seeing. As I lay there, I would imagine my father gazing lovingly down from a cloud, silently watching over me and offering comfort.

**

Within a year after moving to the apartment complex, Mom saved enough money to buy a brand-new three-bedroom blue house, and we moved from our apartment to a new school district in a new neighborhood. My grandparents came to visit, and Grandpa built two bedrooms in the basement for my brothers. Upstairs, mom slept in one bedroom and Linda and I shared another. The third bedroom doubled as a sewing room and guest bedroom. Mom also bought a piano, and Grandma taught me how to play a C Major scale with proper fingering. I walked to piano lessons every week and loved it. I woke up early and played piano as the family alarm clock, to the delight of my mom.

One of the most important parts of my childhood was our connection to my maternal grandparents, who lived three hours away in Lincoln, Nebraska. After Dad died, we seemed to visit them more often. Mom wanted the kids to experience flying in an airplane, so on one trip we all flew from Kearney to Lincoln. At the Kearney airport, we were amazed at the high ceilings and the big open spaces.

The people who worked at the airport were very kind to us and gave us pins in the shape of wings to wear on our collars. The pilot even let us take turns sitting up front with him in the cockpit.

We took off down the runway and were up in the air in no time. The land below looked like a faraway patchwork quilt, and the people and cars on the ground were just little dots. By the time we landed in Lincoln, my sister Linda was crying because her ears, which had not popped throughout the flight, were hurting. We had to take her to the hospital in Lincoln, where they gave her a shot in her rear end to make her better. We took the bus back to Kearney this time.

Two years after Dad died, in 1964, Mom bought a new Chevrolet Impala, which we lovingly named Greenie, and in 1965 she accepted a teaching job in Lincoln. We sold our Kearney house and bought a house in Lincoln to be closer to Grandma and Grandpa, which delighted me to no end, as I loved them dearly. Linda and I got our own bedrooms. My bedroom had purple carpet, and Linda's walls were painted a robin's egg blue.

Aside from the fact that they were wonderful to spend time with, my grandparents were a deeply loving example of what I thought a couple should be. They were devoted to each other, the best of friends who worked as a team but who also had their own interests and passions. I never heard either say a negative thing about anyone else or lose their temper in any way. They were patient and kind, and they both lived by the golden rule: *Do unto others as you would have them do unto you.*

In their own way, both my grandmother and grandfather showed me how to look at the big picture, while being sure to notice all the details.

From my grandmother, I learned sewing, embroidery, cooking, penmanship, math, resourcefulness, being of service to others, religion, and the piano. Whenever she took me clothes shopping and had me pick out my favorite dresses, she always frowned. Her eyes sparkled with knowing as she pointed out how poorly made the dresses were. After this, we would go to the fabric store and buy fabric, and Grandma would make a better dress—one in which the plaids matched, buttons were secured, hems were invisible, and seams were finished. You'd never know it was a handmade dress. It was Grandma who instilled in me a love for sewing and the craft that goes into making a fine item of clothing.

If I desired to do something, I would ask Grandma, "Can I do such and such?"

She would reply with a twinkle, "I don't know—*can* you?"

I would respond with a giant smile, "Yes, I can!" and off I'd go!

Grandpa took me to the hardware store and taught me woodworking, patience, and kindness. He was a masterful handyman who could fix anything. He had worked maintaining street cars, and he retired from the Goodyear plant in Lincoln when he was in charge of maintenance. When I met the plant manager years later, he still remembered Grandpa fondly.

As loving and kind as my grandparents were, I would later recognize that their way of dropping everything to help Mom had been handed down to Mom, and then to me. In fact, they had unwittingly perpetuated a family pattern in which everyone dropped what they were doing to help others. While such care and selflessness is laudable on the surface, it was my sister Linda who exposed me to the concept of maintaining your own personal power, as well as your boundaries, in the 90s.

While I would come to learn a great deal about personal power and boundaries later in my life, it was a different time back then— one in which old-fashioned family values and dinner at my grandparents' after church every Sunday reigned supreme. The entire family sat around the blond wooden dining table with the extra leaf inserted, seven places set with the fine china. On the table would always be a platter of fresh sliced tomatoes, drizzled with spices and oil and vinegar, from Grandma and Grandpa's garden.

The lucky ones were chosen from the assortment that were lined up on the window sill of the back porch. The room was attached to the kitchen, but it felt more outside than inside. When Mom sliced tomatoes, she always peeled them, but Grandma never did. "Lots of vitamins in the skin!" she would say with authority. I believed her.

My grandparents' garden was their pride and joy. Grandpa's roses filled the back two-thirds of their backyard. They lay in beds with paths of grass between them. He had many varieties, and they all smelled divine. He always brought Grandma cut roses for her bouquets. The other third of their yard was a vegetable garden: peas, lettuce, onions, beans, tomatoes, cucumbers, dill, and peppers. Grandma canned all of it, and their basement was filled with glass jars of chili sauce, pickled beets, peaches, beans, and tomatoes.

I'd learned the importance of industriousness and hard work from my grandparents and both of my parents, so I saved my dime-a-week allowance and birthday money and accumulated $21, enough to start my own bank account, by second grade. Mom took me to the bank, and the employees made a big fuss over my accomplishment. Mom had also taken me to the bank every month ever since Dad died to deposit our Social Security death benefit checks into our respective college funds. I loved going to the bank and dreamed of owning one.

At this age, I was also beginning to discover more about my passion for helping others. In first grade, we read a book about three identical brothers, each with a special talent they used to help other people. One of them could swallow large amounts of water, saving people from floods and putting out large fires. One of them could stretch their arms and legs large distances to save cats in trees, or carry groups of people to safety. The last brother could hold his breath for long periods of time so he could search for food on the bottom of the ocean or save people who were drowning. I loved that story so much that I built a scene based on it. I constructed the brothers from cut-off pencils and pipe cleaners, drawing in their eyes, noses, and mouths with a pencil. Then, I used Styrofoam balls for their heads and yarn for their hair. My mother helped me glue them to a flat piece of cardboard so they could stand up.

I loved how resourceful the brothers were. I read the story over and over, and when it was time to return it to the library, I wanted to keep it, so I asked Mom if she would type the story for me. She stayed up almost all night typing the story of the three magical brothers on her manual typewriter. I kept waking up to the sound of her relentless tapping of the keys. For a moment, I felt a twinge of guilt that she was not able to get a good night's sleep because she was busy helping me. The next morning, she handed me the story, neatly typewritten on the manual typewriter. She had a smile on her face, but the dark circles underneath her eyes revealed to me how tired she was. I had never seen her look that tired before—but in that moment, Mom was my hero.

**

My love of reading and learning was helped along by the entire wall of books that filled our basement, which included two complete encyclopedia sets (a treasure for any child at that time). Both my parents had taken Dale Carnegie training, which offered professional and personal development programs based on the concept that transformation starts within. We had a number of other books that were all about the power of positive thinking. I devoured them. They confirmed my innate belief in abundance and my abhorrence for violence and manipulation. At an early age, I understood that we could use our minds for good and that the sky was the limit, and these books confirmed what I already knew deep down.

One summer I set out to read the dictionary. That was a short-lived project. The first time I used a new word in a sentence, my older brother laughed and said he bet I didn't know the meaning—and that I was using it wrong in any case.

Lincoln was larger than Kearney, so in third grade, I was placed in the middle reading group over my objections. It turned out our former small town was ahead of Lincoln, and soon I was moved up to the highest group. From an early age, though, I understood that being smart wasn't necessarily seen as a good thing. After taking an IQ test in third grade, I purposely marked two answers wrong so I wouldn't appear too smart.

I was also confused by the contradictions and seemingly unexplainable aspects of some of the things I learned at school. I didn't understand why "men" was used as shorthand for "men and women," and why when the generic "he" was used in books and speeches, it referred to both "he and she." If "mankind" supposedly extended to women as well, why is it that women couldn't vote in the United States until the 20th century? Why did the phrase "for the people by the people" exclude so many people? And if the U.S. really believed in "separation of church and state," why did they allow the words "under God" to be inserted into our Pledge of Allegiance in 1956? I never received a satisfying answer. When we were taught about slavery, I was so glad Nebraska had been a "free" state, otherwise I'm not sure how I would have responded!

In that time, there were a lot of gendered restrictions that were a regular part of my life. For example, girls were only allowed to wear slacks on PE days: Tuesdays and Thursdays. Otherwise, we were required to wear skirts or dresses. When we hung from the jungle gym, our skirts went over our heads and our underwear was exposed to the world. It was, therefore, important to have nice underwear.

I didn't let the foolishness of some of these rules get in the way of my dreams. In sixth grade, we had to write down our most desired goal. My goal was world peace. I was practical, so I decided that in order to create world peace, I should be the President of the United States. Never mind that there had never been a female president— in my eyes, the sky really was the limit!

The student teacher gave me a bad grade. She said that dreaming of being president was selfish, but world peace was a good goal.

And I really believed it was possible! As a Girl Scout, I wholeheartedly believed in the concept we had to master in order to get the Girl Scout Way badge; that is, we needed to leave a place better than we'd found it.

Of course, this honorable motto didn't always vibe with friendships at school. A girl in my grade had a gang, but it was by invitation only. Naturally, I wanted to be in the gang. But after I was invited to a slumber party at her house, I saw how she would belittle others in her gang. At that point, I didn't see the purpose of being in a gang with someone who made fun of others, so I decided not to join when she asked me to. After all, Mom and my grandparents were always kind to others, and that's the type of person I wanted to be, too.

The summer before seventh grade, in 1969, Mom bought a new Impala. This one was burgundy with power steering and 350 V8—very fancy for the time. For our summer vacation, we drove to Washington State to visit relatives. Day by day, we were guided by our AAA Triptik road trip planner. Dad had grown up in Pasco, Washington, where we stopped to visit his best friend from grade school forward. Duane was an attorney. He asked my brothers what they wanted to be when they grew up, completely ignoring Linda and me.

I wandered around Duane's office reading his awards and certificates on the walls. *Attorney at Law*, they said in big bold letters. For some reason, that felt good to me. I walked back into the room everyone was in, and I announced, "I want to be an attorney!"

Everyone just stared at me, but Duane seemed to notice me for the first time. "You *do*! That's great!" he said with a big smile.

I felt special and important. I knew that no matter what I ended up doing, it would be something big that had the power to change lives and the world.

CHAPTER 2

MAKE YOUR OWN WAY IN LIFE

My desire to make the world a better place than I left it, as well as my early political dreams, led to my running for Student Council in seventh grade and again in ninth grade. Although I won, I was disappointed to realize it wasn't all it was cracked up to be. While I had hoped to push for massive systemic change, student politics felt pointless after a while. The other council members voted for things that only benefited the people on the Student Council—such as treats and lunch for our meetings—not the rest of the students. In contrast, I was a big-picture kind of person. I wanted to end the war in Vietnam and teach peace. When I asked my fellow council members what our "purpose" was, nobody could answer—not even our faculty leader.

As a child of the 60s and 70s, I still had to contend with the sexism of the time. During PE, girls had to wear baby-blue bloomers, with elastic around each leg. The bloomers were actually quite comfortable, but certainly not flattering. My brother Dave told me that Mr. Fox, the boys' PE teacher, made fun of the idea of girls doing sports—and also laughed at our bloomers.

Some of our class requirements were also unfairly gendered. The girls had to take sewing class, while the boys were required to take woodworking. Since I already knew how to sew (and loved it!), I asked if I could take woodworking instead. I was told no—that was just for boys. I was furious and defiant, and even went to the principal's office to complain—but to no avail. It was only in the 90s that I learned girls attending a different junior high in the area could take woodworking.

In the meantime, my love for music remained robust. When I was twelve, I was invited to compete in piano at the state auditions held at the University of Nebraska–Lincoln. I played "The Firefly" by Anton Bilotti. Most of the other competitors were college students, so I knew it was a big deal to be there. I was also beginning to come into my own musical tastes. At some point in junior high, I asked my piano teacher if I could learn how to play jazz and pop piano instead of always sticking to classical. When she said no, I eventually quit my lessons but joyfully kept up with my piano playing every day.

My love of music extended to my dream of someday singing in a band—but I had no idea how I would manage this. I decided that joining the junior-high chorus would be my starting point. Chorus was a traumatizing experience for many of my fellow classmates when we were all required to sing a solo in front of the class. A lot of them cried; I didn't. The teacher was incredibly harsh and insulting, which I'm sure turned off many aspiring songbirds. I didn't care what she said, though. I knew I enjoyed writing and singing songs. I tried out for a small, elite singing group in chorus class but was replaced by one of my friends at the last minute. I was disappointed and chalked it up to not singing very well. Still, I didn't let it deter me. I continued to belt out my songs in chorus class and at church, confident that I would someday be vindicated.

As I matured into adolescence, conversations about sex and family planning furtively entered the school curriculum. In health class, we studied reproduction for two weeks. Curious about my mother's experience, I went home and asked, "Mom, did you plan all four of us kids?"

She was candid in her response. "We only planned on having two children, your brothers—but we loved you all the same and always held you when we fed you."

I learned that Mom used an IUD, but it failed—twice. I finally understood why Mom had scolded us so many years ago and said that Dad couldn't take us kids. With two extra mouths to feed and souls to care for, I could imagine how overwhelmed my parents had been.

On my thirteenth birthday, Mom made a big deal about my becoming a teenager. She made me feel I had achieved something of great importance and significance just for having a birthday. She sat me down to talk about boys and the importance of abstinence— a conversation that was a rite of passage for many girls my age. She didn't have to worry, though. I had already decided I didn't care about getting married. As a result of what I had learned during my fifth-grade unit on zero population growth, I had already vowed never to have children. Besides, from what I'd seen, men only seemed to slow women down. And despite the sexist notions that women were helpless without a man around, Mom had already proven to me through her actions that women were more than capable of doing pretty much anything.

The summer before high school, I went through another rite of passage: my first job, pouring coffee at a retirement home in the summer of 1971. The impetus: I wanted to buy a Schwinn 10-speed bike. Mom had informed me that I'd have to save my money and buy it on my own, so I went up the street to Clark Jeary Retirement Home and applied for a job. Most of the neighborhood kids worked in the dining room—pouring coffee; preparing and serving breakfast, lunch, and dinner; and cleaning up after each meal. The pay was $1.25 an hour—a modest yet sizable salary at the time. After all, babysitting was only 50 cents an hour.

My first purchase was my Schwinn 10-speed bike for $72, and my second purchase was a stereo receiver, speakers, and turntable for $1,000. Every night before bed, I put on a record at low volume and did a 20-minute stretching routine, complete with sit-ups and boy-style push-ups (that is, body in a straight line without my knees kissing the floor). When we had to do the timed hanging arm in PE, some girls fell off the bar in seconds. I would hang easily for several minutes until the teacher told me to get off the bar.

Being an independent working girl who wasn't scared of push-ups, I was naturally industrious and prone to problem solving. One of the issues that emerged as a problem I needed to solve was my nose. My nose had been broken twice when I was young, and my glasses made it look doubly deformed to me. So at the age of 14 or so, I rode my bike to a plastic surgeon's office and asked if they could fix it. They said yes—for about $1,000. Unbeknownst to me, they sent the estimate to my mom. She sat me down for a serious discussion, in which I admitted that I thought my nose was too big. She assured me it was perfect and, after that, she would cut out articles of models and other celebrities with prominent noses who were proud of what they were blessed with.

Mom often asked me if I felt good about myself. I always replied, "Yes," because despite the situation with my nose, I really did. She squinted her eyes and scrutinized me for a moment, then she asked a few more times. "Are you sure?"

Each time I said yes. Exasperated, I finally asked, "Am I not supposed to feel good about myself?"

She laughed. "Of course you should feel good about yourself." She explained to me that the Lincoln public schools had told teachers that girls sometimes developed poor self-esteem in junior high, so she wanted to be sure I felt good about myself. This was perhaps one of the only times my mother and I got into what approached a "deep" discussion, as we never really touched on personal things like our feelings when we talked. I do feel that having a relative amount of independence as a young girl may have contributed to my sense of self-sufficiency and the feeling that I was capable of anything if I set my mind and heart to it.

By the time I got to high school, I had a large group of friends, made up of both boys and girls. Together, we did many group activities: sledding, sailing, ice skating, and skiing trips to Colorado, which I paid for with money I earned from my job. Several of my friends lived on a lake, and we always seemed to end up there for activities. Once, at the drive-in movies, we were watching *Play Misty for Me*, a suspenseful Clint Eastwood movie (and the first he directed). During one nail-biting scene, there was a knock on the passenger window. We all screamed and cracked the window! The man parked behind us raised an eyebrow and informed us, "You've got your brake lights on." Every time our driver was scared, she stomped on the brake without realizing it, which was interfering with our neighbors' ability to watch the movie.

I was accustomed to doing things and behaving in ways that most other girls didn't. In high school, I finally got to take woodworking, as well as drafting. Predictably, I was the only girl in each class. In drafting, the boys built models out of balsa wood, while I was required to sit at a desk and work on lettering. I wanted to learn how to change the oil in my car, but girls could only take a class called Powder Puff Mechanics, and we only learned about lawn-mower engines. I was so irritated that I didn't bother to pay attention—it may have been the first time in my life I didn't relish learning.

My "non-girly" athletic prowess wasn't exactly helped along, either. In high school, after the passage of Title IX—a federal civil rights law that states, "No person in the United States shall, on the basis of sex, be excluded from participation in, be denied the benefits of, or be subjected to discrimination under any education program or activity receiving Federal financial assistance"—the girls finally got our own basketball team. Unfortunately, female athleticism was still scorned and taunted, and male students made incessant fun of the girls on the team for everything from missing a basket to the way they ran. I didn't try out for the basketball team, but I was on the swim team for a short while. Unfortunately, my job—which I still worked at during the school year—interfered with sports practice.

As I was finding my own path at school, Mom was also moving into a new stage in her life. Mom had been active in Parents without

Partners (an international educational nonprofit that promotes single parents and their children) for years, and had also served as president. One of the dads in Parents without Partners had taught me how to water ski. In fact, in the midst of the general social stigma around being a single parent at the time, Parents without Partners was refreshing—an extended family with lots of kids our ages and kind parents who helped normalize our family structures. We went on group camping trips and other activities, such as bowling and miniature golf. There was a very kind man in particular who adored my mom, but she thought of him as only a friend—nothing more. At the time, I didn't think much about it. My mother seemed asexual to me—almost as if she'd had her children without sex. She didn't date and certainly didn't speak about being interested in men. In my mind, Mom was like a lone bird who could soar as high as she wanted without the shackles of a relationship to hold her down.

**

I don't know where Mom met Walter...just that he charmed her as only con artists can. The first time I met him, I was 16 years old. I walked into my house one Friday night and interrupted him and my mom kissing on the couch. He was on top of her. I had startled them, but I was just as embarrassed. My face was beet red as I ran past them to my bedroom as fast as possible.

He dressed well in slacks and shirts. He had shiny tan skin (I later learned this was known as the "alcoholic glow") and a neat crew cut. He seemed always to be smiling and doting on Mom, opening her car door for her and being charming and attentive in front of neighbors. According to Walter, he was disabled from the war—but he never specified exactly how, and he more or less seemed fine to me. I never knew what Mom saw in him. I never asked, and she never bothered to tell me.

Mom and Walter got married a short time later at a small ceremony at my grandparents' home. I poured punch at the reception, also held at their home. Linda, whom I knew despised Walter, was on a summer trip to Mexico and missed the wedding. I don't recall my brothers being present, either.

After the wedding, Walter moved into our house. Unlike the rest of us, he had little interest in camping or outdoor activities, and didn't have a whole lot of meaningful interaction with us kids. He certainly didn't behave the way a father figure would.

A few times, he, Mom, Linda and I went out for a Sunday drive so I could practice driving on the highway. He kept telling me to stop so he could check the windshield wiper fluid level. At some point, I realized he had replaced it with vodka and was drinking it every time we stopped. Walter admitted to the rest of us that he was a recovering alcoholic but "never touched the stuff." That was another lie.

At some point, Walter traded cars with me, which I had no complaints about. I drove his stylish 1972 fully loaded Matador, and he drove the extra family car, Greenie—a 1964 Chevrolet Impala with no power steering. We had no idea that Walter had been driving without a license due to too many DUIs. My guess is that he'd traded cars with me not out of the kindness of his heart, but because he didn't want to be caught driving something so flashy. The first time I drove his Matador to school, the police pulled me over a couple blocks from my house. The officers looked confused to see me driving, and they let me go.

Walter's propensity for lying and attempting to cover up his tracks with extravagant displays of generosity became clear over time. Like the time he "bought" me a wood lathe for a present. Well, Mom got the bill for $1,000 and back it went to the store.

Another time, I came home from school and Walter and several men were adding a second garage stall onto our one-car garage. He told us they were his friends, but Mom soon received a bill for thousands of dollars from a construction firm. This house was Mom's house, but it didn't seem to matter. He was the man, and everyone naturally assumed it was his house.

Mom was quickly tiring of Walter's schemes. She signed up for a three-week trip to London and told Walter he would have to pay his own way. To her shock, he came up with the money and went on the trip!

Walter's schemes became even more ruinous. It turns out he'd come up with the trip money by forging Mom's name and putting up her house as collateral on a loan—but then he neglected to make any payments. Mom almost lost her house attempting to prove her signature had been forged. Walter was shameless and lied to my mom about my sister on purpose to get her in trouble and take attention off himself. Because Linda hated Walter, he would routinely lie to Mom about my sister disobeying him—which would lead to a big kerfuffle that ended in Mom yelling at and grounding Linda for something she hadn't even done. Linda would later tell me that she was upset about Mom always believing Walter and never her. Although I recall Linda getting in trouble a lot, I didn't know why at the time and hadn't suspected that Walter was behind it. In retrospect, I wish we'd been able to talk about things, sister to sister. But of course, the unspoken rule against discussing our feelings was in effect throughout my childhood and adolescence.

Like all con men, Walter used his charm to his advantage and was well liked by almost everyone he met. But he was rapidly draining our family's resources, not to mention Mom's patience.

Although Walter insisted he went to work every day, Mom was onto him. One day, she followed him and found out he'd spent the day drinking at the Library Lounge, a bar a few blocks away from our house. My mom later told me she always dreaded coming home from her teaching job, as she routinely found him passed out in the front hallway. She was afraid my sister and I would see.

One day, I walked into our garage and saw Walter slide a bottle of vodka into the fertilizer bag. I was shocked as I caught him red-handed. I exclaimed, "Hey, you said you don't drink!"

His eyes were filled with shame and fear as he pleaded with me, "Don't tell your mother." He moved toward me, perhaps in an attempt to convince me to stay quiet about the whole thing, but I was afraid. I ran out of the garage as fast as I could and into the house. I blurted to Mom, "Walter has vodka in the fertilizer bag!"

Naturally, Walter came in and tried to weasel out of his predicament, but the writing had been on the wall for quite some time by now. Mom divorced him soon after. Altogether, the marriage lasted about a year. Years later, Mom would confide that when she told Walter's extended family she was divorcing him, they admitted that they'd debated telling her he was an alcoholic con artist. It turns out they'd chosen not to because they were so relieved to pawn him off on someone else.

Although I wasn't aware of this at the time, I learned that after Mom divorced Walter, he would park in front of her school for hours. He threatened to come back daily and sit outside her class window—and although he promised that if she gave him money he'd never come back, he always broke that promise and continued to pester her, day after day.

Then one day, she came out and said, "No more money!" She never saw him after that.

When we got news that Walter died, not long after the divorce, we were all relieved. The whole ordeal had devastated Mom. She'd always been optimistic and friendly, but now she had lost her faith in her own judgment of others.

After the fiasco of her second marriage, Mom sighed and told me, "You can't count on men. You need to have your own career and make your own way."

Mom had always been open-hearted and easy to befriend, but something in her demeanor changed after her negative experience with Walter. She came to question her judgment of people. After all, if she'd been so easily won over by Walter, what did that say about her? Unfortunately, like many women of the time, she didn't blame

Walter for being a rotten con artist; she blamed herself for being fooled by him.

Walter was quickly written out of our family history book, as if he'd never existed to begin with. Our family soon got back into our old rhythm, secure in our knowledge that things were better without him.

**

As a junior in high school, I had a boyfriend, but our relationship was never serious. We had fun together, and he felt like a good companion and friend. I was my mother's daughter and, while having a boyfriend was nice, it certainly wasn't my life's purpose.

My boyfriend invited me to go to a basketball game at the University of Nebraska–Lincoln Coliseum one night, and he asked if I wanted to meet him afterwards and go to the senior house, which I'd been to several times before. The high-school senior class boys rented a house that was solely used for parties. Alcohol was often served. If there was sex going on at the house, I wasn't aware of it, nor had anyone mentioned it to me. The house mostly seemed like a place to go to socialize and have fun. I'd already been warned by Mom not to have sex until I was married, although she didn't provide any good reasons why. I had even been instructed not to use tampons until then.

When we got to the senior house, it was empty. We were the only ones there. I'd never seen it like this before. He showed me a ladder leading to a small loft I had also never seen before. We climbed the ladder and sat with our legs dangling over the edge. Suddenly, he started kissing me and pushing me sideways. His hands were under my pep-club skirt and trying to wriggle into my underpants.

"What are you doing?" I said, shocked at his insistent hands.

He didn't mince his words. "I want to have sex."

"No," I said, unequivocal.

He didn't seem to hear me. He just ignored me and kept trying. I could feel what I assumed was a penis poking at my thighs.

I kept wiggling away as best I could. "No! I don't want to have sex!" I was so frustrated and shocked by his behavior that I started to cry.

This made him inexplicably angry, so he resorted to the manipulative lie that many a teenage boy has tried: "If you loved me, you would have sex with me."

I had read of that ploy in Ann Landers' book, *What Teenagers Need to Know about Sex*. Despite my tears, he persisted, until to my relief, someone opened the house door and yelled, "Anyone here?"

We quickly scrambled down the ladder. I wiped my tears and tried to put on a smile. Instead of socializing as usual, I sat forlornly on the couch in my pep-club uniform, trying to hold back my tears. All I could think was, *I almost had sex! Mom would be so upset with me!*

My boyfriend and I avoided discussing what had happened...what had *really* happened. Not once did the thought that he'd violated my boundaries cross my mind. I didn't see him as having done something bad. In fact, I was more upset with myself for going there with him in the first place. After all, it was 1974—it was always the girl's fault. Years later, I would recognize the truth: *No means no.* My so-called boyfriend had attempted to rape me. And if others hadn't shown up at that moment, he probably would have succeeded.

Despite what happened that night, I continued to date him. Later that summer, we had a repeat incident when he tried to pressure me into sex once more. This time, I didn't hesitate to say no. "I'm not having sex with you!" I yelled, with such force that he never pressured me like that again. (Eventually, at the beginning of my senior year, I broke up with him. Now that he was in college, I didn't feel comfortable attending college parties while I was still in high school.)

I never told anyone. But 44 years later, as I watched Dr. Christine Blasey-Ford's brave testimony at the Brett Kavanaugh hearings in September 2018, a thought crossed my mind: *I'm so glad nothing like that happened to me.* At that point, the memory of the attempted rape came surging back. It was a revelation. I realized as I looked back on that time of my life just how many experiences I'd taken for granted as "normal"...just how much I had buried.

**

The summer before senior year, I told my mom I wanted to buy myself a car and she offered to match whatever I could save. True to form, I was industrious and quickly saved $1,500. We went car shopping and bought a brand-new car for $3,000. Mom informed me that I was to pay for gas, insurance, maintenance, and any other expense related to the car. It was a bright-yellow Dodge Colt stick shift with black stripes and a black faux-leather interior. It looked like a bumble bee and drove beautifully, even in snow.

Buying my first car with Mom right beside me was an important moment—one that quintessentially involves a dad or a boyfriend. Contrary to all the sexist slights I'd heard growing up, I knew firsthand how capable women were—especially my mom. She raised four children, worked full-time, bought a house, and provided for all our needs. To my mind, she was a multitasking superwoman.

Still, she faced plenty of challenges and the dismissiveness of many more people after that first gas-station attendant who'd treated her so poorly. For instance, there was the time she invested her money with a trusted financial advisor. I overheard a phone conversation with him from the basement extension line. The despair in Mom's voice was palpable when he told her she'd lost all her money that he'd invested in the silver market.

Incredulous, she asked, "All of it?"

There was no trace of empathy in his voice when he curtly responded, "Well, it was a risky investment—you shouldn't have done it."

Then, there was the time Mom tried to get a credit card in her own name when I was in junior high, instead of her deceased husband's (my father's)...and she was denied. She asked, "Who do you think has been paying his bills all these years?"

And then, when she asked for her "head of household" payment from the public schools she worked for, she was informed that this payment was only for men.

When I saw my mother's justifiable frustration with everyone who ever looked down on her, doubted her capability, or dismissed her intelligence just because she was a woman, it made me both angry and sad at the way things were. True to form, we never got into deep discussions around the obvious unfairness of the gender roles that tried to box Mom into the role of Mrs. Such-and-Such, even when she'd been single for years. But I believe it influenced the direction I would take in my own life. I would be the kind of person who ultimately defied people's low expectations of me. I would be a woman of my own making.

**

One memory from my adolescence stands out in stark relief, almost as a cautionary fable about women and the sad roles to which our society will sometimes consign us. Linda and I were banging on the window of our friend Annie's house. The window was by the back door of her family's walkout basement. She lived in the house behind our house, so all we had to do was walk through our backyard and into hers, and up to the door. Their street had big houses. Our street had smaller houses. But altogether, both streets were strewn with middle-class homes that were well taken care of and situated uniquely on the lots in such a way that nobody noticed they all had the same basic floorplan. Annie's dad was the director of a Medical Clinic, and thus, a pillar of the community. But that night, Linda and I saw something that horrified both of us. Something we should never have seen.

We watched, aghast, as this well-respected man hit Annie on the head with a board. Linda and I immediately screamed. We had never seen such an act of violence in our lives before. And the fact that it was our friend who was being hurt made it doubly worse. Upon hearing us, Annie's dad dropped the board and came rushing to the back door. "What is wrong with you girls? Go home!" he screamed.

Despite the fact that Linda and I were frightened out of our wits, we were thoughtful enough to yell at our friend to come with us. Somehow, she was able to slip past her angry, red-faced father—and we all ran as fast as we could to our house, where we told our mother what we had seen. Mom was stony-faced and insisted that Annie stay with us rather than going back home.

At some point, Annie's father came storming through the yard and began yelling at our mother for interfering. She was inside the house on one side of the screen door, and he was outside on the other side of the screen door.

"Let me at my daughter!" he yelled.

Presumably, he was angry enough to do real damage at this point, and there was no way any of us were letting Annie out, or her dad in. My mom stood firm and ordered him to leave her property or she would call the police—and she certainly wouldn't let him hurt his daughter again. We cowered behind her, in awe of her courage and calm. He was so much bigger than she was, but her conviction caused him to back down and go home. Our friend was safe for the time being.

Later, Annie told me her father was taking her to Omaha for a lobotomy. It was a horrible situation, but Linda, Mom, and I were helpless and could do nothing. At that time, as her legal guardian, her dad could basically do anything he wanted short of murder or what may have been considered egregious abuse.

When she came back, Annie was docile. Her normally bright and bubbly personality had undergone a complete change. I didn't recognize her anymore, and she barely recognized me. It was impossible to have a conversation with her. She just picked flowers and smiled dutifully. Her family explained that the lobotomy had been performed to "calm her down." It felt like a horribly unfair punishment for some invisible sin that Annie had apparently committed. I don't recall anyone speaking about how unjust this treatment of my old friend really was. The silence was perhaps more horrifying than my sister and I witnessing her dad beating her, or the disappearance of our old friend into this bland and subservient version of who she'd once been.

It was a learning moment, but the lessons weren't the ones I wished someone had taught me. I learned that it was usually a bad idea to speak up because it could lead to dire consequences. I also learned that men seemed to get away with anything, especially when it came to harming women—even if those women were their daughters. And as brave and capable and intelligent as my mom was, as much as she attempted to shelter my sister and me from the harsh realities of the world, I learned that when it came down to it, women weren't safe.

CHAPTER 3

THE GIFTS OF TRAVELING ALONE

By the time I graduated high school, my oldest brother, Steve, had attended Yale and was now off to Stanford Medical School. I myself was academically inclined, and I also had dreams of studying abroad in Spain my junior year in college. I had studied Spanish since seventh grade. Steve went to Thailand his junior year to teach English, and I thought perhaps I could do the same thing in Spain, since I already knew Spanish and would probably find it easy to acclimate to the culture. At the same time, I was extremely practical. I knew I would have to pay for college and Spain with my own money, added to the money Mom saved for me in my college fund. If I attended school in Lincoln, I could live at home and would have plenty of money for college, without the extra burden of student loans. My ACT and SAT test scores were high and qualified me for an Alternate Regents scholarship to the University of Nebraska–Lincoln. All four of the Regent scholarship recipients chose UNL, so I didn't get to use my Alternate scholarship; however, I had a small home-economics scholarship from an interior-design competition I won during my senior year of high school.

When I got to UNL, I decided to join a sorority, which felt to me like a good way to acclimate myself to the social life of the campus. I had invitations for 14 of 15 houses my first day, but I could only choose eight. The second day, I had eight invitations and could choose five houses.

The third day, I had three invitations and could go to all three houses. I had a good friend at the Pi Beta Phi house who wanted me to join. There was also a girl at the Theta house I'd known since grade school. I wanted to be in her house. The final house was Delta

Gamma. The next day I was informed that I'd been accepted to the Pi Beta Phi house. I loved being a Pi Phi, and once in a sorority, you're an alum for life.

My freshman year I was shown the pledge room where we had meetings and ceremonies. On the bulletin board was a large tree with branches and the names of college boys who had assaulted college girls. We called it the Bastard Board. We were to check it before we went out on a date with anyone.

I suspect that this trend of women looking out for each other goes way back. After all, for so long, women on college campuses had little to no recourse when it came to sexual assault. Thankfully, I was not raped or assaulted on the UNL campus, but I heard stories from other women. It didn't occur to me (or anyone else, it seemed) that we could call the police. There was a tacit understanding that we were on our own. If anything did happen to us, we knew the burden of shame and blame rested squarely on a woman's shoulders. Boys would be boys, and as such, they were not held accountable for their actions. I heard a story about a woman who was secretly filmed having sex with a boy at the Sigma Chi house. Another woman was branded as a slut for having sex with several boys at a fraternity house. The euphemism was that someone had "pulled a train." Today, it would be called gang rape.

Aside from learning the ins and outs of the complex social world of sororities and fraternities, I was plunged into the world of academic and career choices. My plan was to major in interior design and minor in business finance. During my freshman year, I switched completely to business finance and minored in Spanish. Business was easier and more enjoyable, and the classes weren't as early in the morning. The business college was on the main campus, so I could walk to my part-time job at a specialty clothing store, whereas the home-economics college was on the east campus, meaning I had to drive there.

During my freshman year, I went on lots of dates but none of them were serious. I met Roger through a friend at the Delta Upsilon fraternity house. Roger was two grades above me. I asked him to a Pi Phi party and he said yes. I always had fun with him and liked him very much. He was tall, dark, and handsome and, while he had lots of friends, I appreciated that he didn't need to be the center of attention. He was attentive and open to new adventures; besides this, I felt safe and comfortable with him, which wasn't my experience with all boys. Just like my dad, he was studying to be a CPA. Overall, if anyone were to observe us, it would look like we belonged together.

Still, it was clear that I had plenty of options at my fingertips. Soon after Roger and I went out together, the president of the retail store I worked for asked me to dinner. Peter was 25 years old, and he was larger than life. He would waltz into the store and greet everyone by name, and he seemed to know something about everyone with whom he connected. I decided to go out with him because I was curious. At dinner, he spent a good amount of time asking me questions about myself and learning about me. When he mentioned he had been married at one point, I reacted with total candor: "If I had known, I never would have come to dinner." At that time, divorce was still taboo, and given the gap in age and experience, it felt like we were worlds apart. Still, I liked Peter well enough, so we went on a few more dates together and even attended some business networking events and service-club events. At the time, I was dating both Peter and Roger and, in my mind, neither relationship was serious enough to warrant a commitment. Peter knew about Roger, but I had not mentioned Peter to Roger...although I would come to learn that Roger had known about my other flame the whole time and had chosen not to mention it.

One evening, Peter and I were kissing and he mentioned something about sex. I said, "Oh, I've never had sex."

Peter was incredulous. How could I be a sophomore in college and never have had sex? He went on to tell me it was very important for me to not have sex until I was ready and to make sure it was with someone very special. I appreciated his words, as well as his sincerity.

After several more months, I decided I would finally like to experience sex. I felt that Peter was the right person for my first time. Roger felt too "important" for him to be my first. Although Peter had said that losing my virginity was an important decision, a part of me simply wanted to see what sex with no strings would be like. I went to my family doctor and asked him if he would prescribe birth-control pills for me. His jaw dropped but he wrote out the prescription.

A few weeks later, I announced to Peter that I was ready for sex. He was delighted but, much to his chagrin, he couldn't get an erection. It was very awkward. I told him not to worry about it. He informed me that it was up to me. I had no idea what I was doing and, by this time, I'd lost all interest. But before long, he was ready and we did it with him on top. It lasted just a few minutes, and I felt zero fireworks. I drove home disappointed, thinking, *All this hoopla about sex and this is all it is?*

Honestly, I wished I hadn't even bothered.

One evening, Peter told me I had to choose between him and Roger. Sex hadn't magically brought me any closer to Peter, and I wasn't ready to give Roger up, so I told him I chose both of them. Peter threatened to dump me if I didn't choose him, and this was enough to help me make my reluctant choice. I chose Peter.

I was preparing for my junior year abroad to Spain when Peter told me if I went to Spain to study, he would break up with me. I did (after all, I'd been planning for Spain since high school and wasn't going to let a possessive boyfriend hold me back), and he did. When he told me, we were sitting in his car. I let out a gasp, doubled over, and with my face practically to the floor and hidden from Peter, I realized I was smiling. Finally, a way to get out of this confining relationship!

I quickly called Roger, who was happy to take me back and even wrote me letters when I was abroad. I appreciated how solid and reliable he was, and it helped me to retrospectively recognize that a boyfriend who asks you to choose or gives you an ultimatum isn't one worth keeping around.

The fall semester of my junior year, I studied at the University of Seville as part of a study-abroad program through the University of Colorado. My Spanish name was Catalina, and I kept a diary in Spanish. I was fluent then, but now I can't understand much of what I wrote!

It was a wonderful and eye-opening experience. I lived in a third-floor walkup with a woman who owned the building, along with four Spanish students. At first, I had trouble understanding their Spanish accents and words, and they couldn't understand me, either. On one occasion, I was frustrated about getting interrupted so often, as I couldn't speak quickly enough, so I raised my voice and spoke in English. That quieted the entire dinner table. Thankfully, in a couple months, I was fluent.

We walked to the University of Seville every day. Classes were in the morning, then we'd walk home for siesta and lunch before heading back to school from 3 to 7 p.m., and finally, back home for a huge dinner. My host mom was a great cook, as she had studied at the Culinary Academy in Paris. The servings were enormous.

As we walked to and from school, the fat married men would hiss in my ear, "Te gusta ir a cama conmigo? (Do you want to go to bed with me?)" Sometimes, they would stick their tongues out and slobber on my ear. It was disgusting. I learned to trade my usual smile for a scowl when I walked in public.

**

My friends and I traveled during our school breaks, usually by train. During one trip, my friend Kathy and I rented a car to drive to the U.S. Navy base in Rota, Spain, to visit a couple of my brother's Navy friends. We went to dinner, and on the way back to the base,

I was pulled over by the U.S. military police. My Spanish was so good, they thought I was a Spaniard. The officer said, "I'll have to get an interpreter."

The next officer asked me for my driver's license in broken Spanish. I pulled out my Nebraska driver's license. He looked confused. "Are you an American?" Soon enough, they let us go. Shortly after that, however, my car was blocked by Spanish police cars. The officers jumped out and pointed at us what looked to me like machine guns. I was terrified, but they quickly let us go. We drove on to the base, and the U.S. military police stopped me again and smirked at me. "That's what you get for fooling us." I was glad to get out of Rota and back to Seville.

A group of us also hitchhiked to Valencia for an Independence Day parade. The scene was chaotic and, at some point, police started shooting and my friends and I ran for cover and got separated. When Sheila and I hitchhiked back to Seville, we found ourselves on a desolate country road. Two men picked us up. They were hunters and took us to dinner at a remote hunting lodge. Then the hunters drove us to a small hotel and told us we had to have sex with them. It was a disconcerting twist in what had already been a traumatizing day.

Behind the reception counter were a male clerk and his young son. Sheila and I desperately told the clerk we needed a room for "sola ellas (only us girls)." To our relief, the clerk helped us. He told the hunters he only had one room—and it was for Sheila and me. He had his son get our luggage out of the hunters' car. The hunters were furious and yelling, but the hotel clerk protected us. The next day, we hitchhiked back to Seville with no incident. That was the last time I hitchhiked in Spain.

Despite the challenging encounters during my time in Spain, I didn't want those experiences to deter me from having the time of my life. During Christmas vacation, we had a month off, so six of us rented a car and drove from Seville to the southern coast, known as the Costa del Sol (Coast of the Sun) and up the east coast, stopping at small towns along the way. On Christmas Day, we were overlooking the ocean of the Costa Del Sol. It was stunningly beautiful, but it was also my first Christmas away from my family, whom I dearly missed.

My classmate Kathy and I had planned to travel throughout Europe for several months after Christmas vacation. She had gone back to Chicago for Christmas to go skiing. She called me and told me she had broken her leg skiing and couldn't come back to Spain to travel, after all. I was devastated. I called my mom and told her, then asked her to sign me up for classes at UNL for spring semester, as it was clear that my previous plans were foiled. She refused and said, "You're already there, so why don't you just travel by yourself?"

I was shocked. I responded, "I would be afraid to travel all by myself." After everything I'd already been through, the notion of traveling alone was daunting. I had no idea where I'd stay, how I'd get money, or how I'd manage to keep myself safe. After all, this was back in the day when there were no mobile phones or Internet, and phone service was already quite poor.

Mom said, "Well, I'm not signing you up for classes. If you're afraid, you can always join a tour."

Never one to back down from fear, I decided to stay in Spain. I had money in my bank account, and the plan was for me to check in every once in a while on my travels—and if I needed more money, Mom would wire it to me.

As it turned out, traveling alone was one of the greatest gifts of my life.

I started out from Seville to Rome via train. Two other female students I had met during the study-abroad program went with me for the first three weeks. They departed from Rome to return to Seville for a second semester, while I headed south via train to Brindisi, Italy, to catch the ferry to Greece.

On the train to Brindisi, an Italian student my age asked me if she could practice her English on me. Of course, I said yes. When we got to Brindisi, she asked me if I would come to her hometown of Lecce for a week, and then her family would take me to Brindisi to catch the ferry. I was delighted and said yes—after all, I had no preordained schedule.

My new friend and her family toured me all over their town, introducing me as "our American." I met relatives, enjoyed feasts, and felt like one of the family. When it was time to return to Brindisi, they put me on a steam train with individual wooden doors to the outside and waved farewell.

In Brindisi, I went to the ferry ticket office. The ticket agent gestured to the gorgeous man behind me and said, "You're going to Greece and he's going to Greece, so why don't you go together?"

We looked at each other and he sealed the deal when he offered, "I have a car."

We slept in his car during the ride, and he later joked, "We slept together the first night we met." He was an architect working in Denmark, but he'd been raised in Athens and was on holiday to visit his family. He installed me at a small two-story hotel his friend owned for a reasonable price, and every day for two weeks, he came every morning and accompanied me throughout Athens and other parts of Greece. He also introduced me to his friends, who promptly adopted me.

My travels alone introduced me to many people I would not have met had I been traveling with others. I was lucky in that I was approachable and friendly, so I also had the opportunity to meet other friendly and approachable people who quickly warmed to me. One person would leave and another would show up. I was rarely alone.

I had a pair of gorgeous custom leather boots made for me in Greece. The boot maker traced my foot and hand-stitched the boots. My traveling uniform was a plaid wrap skirt, socks and boots to my knees, a nylon turtleneck, and a bomber jacket. I had a spare skirt, turtleneck, pair of jeans, and underwear, all in a small blue cotton backpack the size of a satchel.

When I left Greece, I flew to Italy and sat by a man who gave me a music tape with the title written in Farsi, which read right to left and contained lots of circles. I skied in Modena, Italy, and then in the Swiss Alps at Innsbruck with a young woman from Chicago. I gradually made my way to Germany, where I met a man who asked me if I'd like a ride through Yugoslavia and back to Athens. I called the Greek friend I'd met on the ferry; he said he was available to show me around in Athens, so I took the German man up on his offer.

In Yugoslavia, he was pulled over by the police and they took all of his money and his identification. They gave the ID back and off we went to Greece. When we arrived in Athens, the German demanded I pay him $450, half of what he'd lost.

"I don't have that kind of money," I insisted. "I'm a student!"

He replied, "But you're American!" He then took me to his friend's apartment and told me I was trapped there until I came up with the money. It was another terrifying situation, and I had no idea how it would end.

I sat on the floor in the corner and cried quietly. His friend, who was clearly put off by the entire situation, said, "You can't keep her. She's an American."

He reluctantly relented when I promised to pay them if they would take me to the YWCA. They did and, as soon as the door opened, I slipped inside and the guard slammed the door shut with a snarl. "No men allowed!"

The German was furious, but it didn't matter. I was safe for the moment. I never saw him again, thankfully. I ended my trip to Athens by meeting up with my handsome friend and enjoying more of the city.

As the weather warmed, I slowly traveled north by train—to Italy, the French Riviera, Paris, Germany, Switzerland, Austria, England, then back to Seville. Then I went back north to Switzerland and on to Dachau, where I learned things they didn't teach us in history class...such as how the U.S. supported Hitler at first, as well as how Americans profited from the war and were slow to help. It was extremely disappointing, as well as eye-opening. I wondered how much of my education had been filtered through the bias of history books that are designed to make the "winner" look good.

In May, I flew north to Luxembourg to ultimately travel back home. I sat in a train car with two other college-age American girls. We were all seated on one side, with an empty bench seat opposite us. I sat closest to the glass sliding door to our compartment. A rowdy group of Spanish boys were in the hallway outside our compartment, peering at us through the glass windows. One slid the door to our compartment open, stood facing me, unzipped his pants, exposed his flaccid penis, and commanded in Spanish, "Suck my dick."

While I may have wilted in horror and consternation just months ago, I gave him a withering look and responded, "Es demasiado pequeño (it's too small)." His friends laughed outside our compartment, taking pleasure in their friend's shame. His face turned red and he tried to charge me. I reacted quickly—my Greek boots were square on his stomach and I shoved as hard as possible, sending him off balance into the empty bench seat.

He seemed to slither down the wall; he was clearly dazed. One of the women squeezed past, saying, "I'm getting the conductor." I thought, *Little good that will do*. I was well aware that despite the occasional good Samaritan, Europe was a lot like the U.S. in that women who were accosted or assaulted by men were typically left to fend for themselves. But to my surprise, she soon returned with the conductor, who reprimanded the boys, told them to leave our compartment, and forbade them from entering.

Later, I had to go to the bathroom. As I was locked inside, the penis exposer snarled at me from the other side of the thin door. He threatened to throw me off the train when I came out of the bathroom. I waited him out; he finally left and I high-tailed it back to my compartment.

I continued my train trip through France. The two women exited the train and another got on. I asked her how she liked Paris. "Not at all," she said. She was going home after a few days. She went on to tell me that she had come to visit her boyfriend, who was studying in France. At the Paris train station, she had been waiting for her boyfriend. He was late. Three young French men picked her up and drove her to a remote area, where they raped her for hours. They snatched her passport and dumped her back at the train station. When her boyfriend found out what happened to her, he dumped her on the spot. In his eyes, she was sullied. She went to the police to report her passport being stolen and told them about being raped. The police took it seriously and in short order apprehended the boys. She ID'd them and they were promptly put in jail. I was impressed with the speedy arrest but disheartened at the pain and trauma this poor woman had been put through.

I realized how lucky I had been, traveling all over Europe since January without much incident, and how angry I was that I or other women had to even worry about being safe.

When I arrived in Luxemburg, I stayed at a youth hostel and flew to Chicago via Iceland en route to Lincoln. I was sad to see my travels end. The most rewarding part was learning from each of the people I was blessed to share time with. I loved hearing about their life experiences and passions, and watching as their eyes lit up as they spoke. I loved their passion, and it inspired me to seek out the very best life had to offer.

Kathy picked me up in Chicago; her broken leg had finally healed. I stayed with her and her family, then flew to Lincoln the next day, where I reunited with my mom and sister, as well as Roger and other friends.

During my time in Europe, I'd indulged in some amazing food

and, as a result, I gained ten pounds. I was still thin by all standards. Still, I was fat-shamed by a close friend, who commented, "It looks like you ate through Europe." In addition, Roger told me I should weigh 110 lbs. I was about 135 lbs., and my ideal weight was 125, so I'm not sure how he decided on 110. I eventually got down to 115, but being at this weight made me feel weak, so I quickly got back to 125. I always thought of Roger as a supportive boyfriend but, as I think about his reaction to my weight gain today, I wish I'd told him to go fly a kite.

I reunited with my sorority sisters but, after traveling for months alone and meeting so many interesting people, college parties and typical conversations seemed trivial and vapid. My sorority sisters were mostly concerned with what they would wear, whom they were dating, and gossip about others. I'd always been a worldly person and by this time I was more concerned with the state of the nation and the entire globe, as well as the role each individual could play in addressing such issues as poverty, homelessness, and human rights. It felt like I was ready to move on.

At this point, I was entering my senior year and learned I had enough credits to graduate midyear. What a relief! When I enrolled in one of my classes, I met several adult students all studying for their real-estate test. They told me it was extremely difficult to pass on the first try. Always up for a challenge, I signed up and went to the test, which was several hours long. I'd always enjoyed going to open houses, so it made sense to pursue my license. My mom and I would go out together on Sundays and admire the pristine new houses. They usually cost twice as much as ours and seemed quite opulent to me.

Unsurprisingly, I passed the test, received my license, and found a real-estate company that allowed me to hang it part time. I mostly used my license to scour open houses, although I did sell a few houses to friends and family as a favor.

I was still going to university at this time. I was taking a full load of classes, and I was very socially active with my sorority (although I'd received alumni status fall semester of my senior year, I could still attend all sorority functions).

Despite Roger's faux pas in asking me to lose weight, we were still dating. He was working as a CPA in Lincoln, and I was interviewing at the UNL job-placement center during my last semester, where companies wishing to recruit college graduates came directly to our campus. Students signed up for interview slots. Business majors were eligible to sign up for nearly all job openings. I interviewed at least 60 companies while receiving permission from my professors to leave class each time.

One of the business networking groups was for women in business, and one of the speakers, Lynn, was a stockbroker at Merrill Lynch. She was hired as the result of a lawsuit to recruit more women and was their top producer in the Lincoln office—not to mention, the only woman. She invited the women in the group to call her, so I took her up on that offer.

In finance classes, we were learning about the stock market and how to read and interpret company K-1 reports to analyze whether a stock might be a beneficial investment. I was naive as to all the ways one could earn a living, and when Lynn arrived and spoke about her work, I noticed she was confident and wore a suit, and I thought it would be wonderful to be just like her.

I told her I wanted to be a stockbroker, too. She advised me to go work for IBM and learn how to sell, because IBM had the best sales training program in the world. "Once you learn the skills of selling professionally, you can accomplish anything you want to," she said. "And if you still want to be a stockbroker at that point? Well, you'll be even more successful, as brokers are essentially salespeople."

I took her advice and interviewed with IBM at the job-placement center. By November, I had six solid job offers, including the one I had been hoping for: the one from IBM.

CHAPTER 4

THE PURSUIT OF EXCELLENCE

As I sit awaiting treatment for Stage 4 liver cancer, I marvel at how far I've traveled from my Nebraska roots, forging ahead through the male-dominated territory of IBM in the late 70s and early 80s. Little did I know I would make history. Indeed, before Ginny Rometty became IBM's first female CEO in 2012, I was one of the first to sue them in a significant discrimination case. Here's my story. Learn. Live. Soar.

**

When Roger asked me to marry him at around the same time I accepted my offer at IBM I was only 21 years old. I said yes without hesitating. I adored Roger, but now that I am older and wiser, I know I wasn't "in love" with him enough to make a commitment as strong as marriage. He was more of a companion to me than anything else, and I appreciated the sense of fun, ease, and security I had with him. Aside from that, he was loyal and kind. In my mind, there wasn't much more a girl could ask for.

We went to Kansas City to look for rings...and sadly, we were scammed. We found a ring we liked at a price in our budget of $500. The salesman looked at the price and said it was mismarked. It should have been $1,200, according to him, but if we bought it that day, we could get it for $500. Roger didn't have his checkbook. I did, so I paid $500 for my own engagement ring. In Lincoln, we had it assessed at a local jewelry store, where the clerk informed us that it was only worth $500 to begin with. It was an underwhelming experience, but I tried to maintain a positive attitude and make the best of it.

I told my IBM manager, Brian, that I was engaged when he took me to lunch to celebrate my acceptance of the job offer. He sputtered, "Of course, we won't cancel your job offer, but I have to admit I'm surprised to hear this."

The fact that he was making an issue out of my impending nuptials rather than congratulating me was a sign of the times. In 1978, it was illegal for a company to ask a woman questions about her plans around marriage or children, but during nearly every interview I had, the interviewer asked, anyway. I found it best to avoid discussing my personal life, so before I came out about my engagement, I imagine that Brian didn't even realize I was dating anyone. After all, IBM promotions usually involved relocation, and a married woman was assumed to be challenging to relocate. As ambitious as she might be, a married woman was expected to subordinate herself to her husband's career.

As I was navigating my new job at IBM, Roger and I made an offer on a house. If our loan application was accepted, the monthly payment would be over $900—a sizable chunk of money at the time. Roger coolly informed me that I would have to make the entire house payment and that I would not be able to buy a new car. I told him I would pay half, not all. He responded that he had to spend his money entertaining clients and wouldn't have any left over for the house payment. This set off a huge argument, in which I refused to make the entire payment. He didn't budge. While my career was quickly skyrocketing, as far as Roger was concerned, this was the beginning of the end.

**

I had just turned 22 when I embarked upon my career with IBM on December 26, 1978, as a systems engineer for the General Systems Division. I was responsible for selling and installing computers for various businesses and acting as a technical consultant on business operations, offering clients cost-effective business solutions.

IBM had originally invited me to interview with the Data Processing Division (DPD), which sold large mainframe computers, but I asked to interview with the General Systems Division (GSD), which sold medium-size computers, as it seemed to offer more variety. After I was hired, I learned there was a hierarchy of divisions at IBM. DPD was the most prestigious, followed by GSD and trailed by Office Products (OPD)—which sold typewriters, word processors, and copiers.

The plan was that I'd be a systems engineer for my first three years before becoming a marketing representative. I would be selling and installing computers, with a specialization in banking, finance, distribution, and construction. I still nursed my old childhood dream of owning a bank. IBM assured me that if I came to work for them, I could have all the banks as my accounts and learn banking that way.

I chose a career with IBM for one main reason: They offered the best opportunity for me to utilize my skills. I excelled at seeing the big picture of a situation and determining the best solution, down to the details. I was outgoing, professional, intelligent, and eager to learn. I would be responsible for a variety of accounts. I would also plan my own schedule and benefit from extensive training and travel. At the time, there were few women in the fascinating and mysterious field of computers and business, and IBM was one of the most vaunted American corporations. They offered excellent pay, pension after ten years, medical and dental benefits, and a stock purchase program—and being a pragmatist, I knew that a role at IBM would be a launching pad for an illustrious career.

My first year involved extensive classroom and on-the-job training. In fact, for the first year, my official title was Trainee. The classes were held in Marietta, Georgia, the headquarters for my division and the location of most of the education centers for new employees. There were three five-week classes and a final two-week systems school. My training consisted of reading, working on projects, and shadowing marketing reps and systems engineers on customer visits from all divisions in my building.

IBM headquarters were in Armonk, New York, and most of the promotions, if not all, came from DPD, which was headquartered in White Plains, New York. The Lincoln, Nebraska, office had a hundred people, all of whom were housed in a two-story off-white concrete building located at 1111 J Street, whose name was later changed to Lincoln Mall.

I thrived in this new world of innovation. I loved the new products and the environment that swam in technical jargon. The office buzzed with excitement. People called out loudly to each other from clear across the room with technical questions or off-color jokes. Since every phone conversation was heard by everyone in the room, unsolicited advice abounded. There was a great deal of lightness and camaraderie, but at the end of the month, everyone was serious about making their goals, which were set by corporate. Managers stewed and barked orders, while sales reps made last-minute contracts and pushed customers to sign by the end of the month.

In the GSD areas, several offices with windows housed the sales and systems-engineering managers. A few offices across the back, where the administration managers were stationed, lacked windows. The remaining space was shaped by a large open space called the "bullpen," where salespeople and systems engineers filled desks lined up and down the aisles. The place had nondescript carpet that looked like felt cloth, acoustic tile ceiling, and garish fluorescent lights. Smokers were allowed to light up at their desks. I sat between two of them, in the row that faced the opening to our area. My desk, like all the others, had cream metal sides with faux wood tops. A matching cream metal two-drawer file cabinet to the left of my desk completed the vintage look. A mustard-colored acoustical panel doubled as a bulletin board.

To my right was a free-standing acoustical panel divider and the secretary for our area. Dave, an experienced systems engineer, sat to my left. In these cramped quarters, he was so close that his desk touched my file cabinet. I could roll backwards on my chair to converse with the sales and systems people, who sat in another row. There were two women marketing representatives, Stephanie and Joyce, and one woman systems engineer, Linda. The rest, about a dozen total, were white men, except Harold, who was the only black person in our division.

I was introduced to the other employees that first day. Everyone was welcoming and friendly. They all spoke in IBM acronyms and in short order I, too, was speaking in this new language. Another trainee, Dillon, started the same day as I. He was engaged to the branch manager's daughter. Dillon reported to the marketing manager, Henry. I reported to the systems-engineering manager, Brian. Our training was identical for most of our one-year training program. For the last two-week class in Marietta, Dillon would attend marketing school and I would attend systems-engineering school, but our jobs were ranked at equivalent levels.

The marketing manager, Henry, was outgoing and jovial. He delighted in holding court in the bullpen. Brian was more subdued and stayed in his office most of the time. It was obvious Brian deferred to Henry, and it quickly became clear to me that the marketing reps were the most important people in the division, and everyone else was there to support their efforts to sell products to clients.

My first task as a trainee was to read the IBM Sales Manual from cover to cover. It was a book as thick as *War and Peace* and written entirely in legalese. It contained the rules, regulations, and procedures we were to uphold as employees. We were not allowed to disparage our competition. We could only say what we had to offer and why it was superior. I was amazed we were getting paid to read. I threw myself into it with vigor.

I was quickly introduced to IBM's three principles: respect for the individual, superlative customer service, and the pursuit of excellence in all tasks. They explained the IBM open-door policy: If we had a grievance, we were purportedly allowed and encouraged to go above our manager to the next level and continue up the chain to the very top of IBM.

Despite IBM's ostensible commitment to its employees, we were told that IBM had the highest divorce and alcoholism rates in corporate America. I wasn't surprised as I came to understand the organizational culture better. The job was high pressure, and employees, who constantly worked overtime, were stressed to the max. While the quotas were raised annually, sales reps' territories were also reduced, so they had to scramble to make their quotas. IBM had designed it so a certain percentage of sales reps never made their quota, and there was the constant threat of being fired.

There was no alcohol allowed at IBM-sponsored events due to a past function where an employee jumped to his death from a hotel balcony, but nearly everyone in my office regularly drank—and some bragged about how drunk they became before driving home, or about women whom they'd picked up and had sex with. Many of the married IBMers had regular affairs. Even my mousey manager had one and was caught by another employee in the office.

Almost every day that first year, Dillon and I walked two blocks to Sunny Side Cafe, a local diner, and devoured a bowl of chicken-noodle soup for $1.09. Our office hours were 8 a.m. to 4:45 p.m., with a 45-minute lunch. At 4:45, most people left for home, while others headed to the bars.

I had embraced learning my entire life, so I volunteered to take on any project offered. I was working on seven projects during my first year as a trainee and loved every second. I volunteered to learn the Series/1 computer, which had to be programmed down to the machine language code, made up of all zeroes and ones. Each zero or one was a bit, and eight bits equaled a character also called a byte.

To learn what the machine was doing internally, we had to print out what was called a "core dump": hundreds of pages of all zeroes and ones. Over time, I was able to learn and read this new language just as fluently as if I'd been born speaking it.

I had such focus that I was able to easily complete all my projects during office hours, so I had plenty of time to go to the bars with IBMers and other friends, work out at my gym, sew complete outfits, and visit sales reps' homes on weekends at the lake.

I was also asked to be the IBM loaned executive for United Way, which meant that IBM paid my salary and let me volunteer one day a month for United Way. I visited and learned about all the various charities and nonprofit organizations United Way funded. It was the perfect bonus for a job I was already falling in love with, as I was still very much attached to my humanitarian mission of making the world a better place.

**

The first three five-week classes that trainees took were called AMod, BMod and CMod. All the classes were comparable to taking finals every day. The teachers and advisors at the school were mostly promoted systems engineers and marketing reps on the next rung in the ladder to becoming managers in an IBM branch office. Every day, trainees received a grade, which determined whether they would remain working for IBM. The seasoned systems engineers from my office warned me about the constant homework and daily pressure. My eyes sparkled as I exclaimed in delight, "I thrive under pressure!"

I was excited to go to AMod, which was in Marietta, Georgia. My Lincoln coworkers told me to call ahead and request to be the designated driver for my apartment. I did, and they said yes. There were four people to an apartment, and the driver dictated where and when anyone in the apartment could go. Together, we partied to the hilt on the weekends, and the designated driver was responsible for ensuring everyone got home safely. During the week, most students studied, went to dinner together, danced or played pool at the local bars, swam at the apartment complex in nice weather, and barbecued as a group. It was great fun, and best of all, we were getting paid to do all of it.

At AMod, there were 48 people in my class: 36 men and 12 women, due to the 25% new-hires quota. I wondered why IBM didn't exceed their goal and hire 50/50.

I flew to Atlanta, picked up my Ford Fairlane four-door rental car, and drove to guest quarters in Marietta, where I met my roommates, Nancy and Susan. I was 22 at the time, and they were seasoned 25-year-olds, considered "professional hires" since they had post-college job experience under their belts. I learned many things from them for which I am forever grateful—including the importance of women standing up for each other. At the time, I was engaged to Roger, and my long conversations with Nancy and Susan helped me to understand that I probably wasn't ready to get married.

At school, we all sat at long tables, classroom-style. My classmates hailed from all across the U.S. and Canada. Most had never met a Nebraskan before. The caliber of students and instructors was impressive.

IBM sales training was considered one of the best, if not *the* best, in the world. The process was systematic, complete, and time-consuming. We learned how to sell in person and on the phone, and how to make winning presentations. We did numerous role-playing calls, after which we received thorough critiques. And our teachers were brutal. They were constantly putting us on the spot and attempting to trip us up.

One famous exercise was the "irate customer call." The teachers and advisors played the part of the irate customer. They yelled at us, called us names, and personally attacked us, sometimes even throwing things at us. We were taught not to take it personally. We were to calmly, patiently, and politely sit and listen to their complaints and wait until they became quiet. At that point, we were told to thank them for telling us how they felt, then ask, "Is there anything else you choose to share?" and keep listening if they had more to say. When all was quiet, we were to paraphrase what we thought we'd heard in order to confirm we were on the same page. Then we could calmly offer possible solutions.

AMod taught us the basics of how a business operates (contrasting manual operations with the advantages of using computers), how to make effective sales calls and presentations, and how to justify the cost of business computers. Computers were expensive and new, so we understood that companies approached their purchases with caution. IBM had many examples and formulas we would go through with clients, depending on their industry, to see if they could save enough money with the benefits of a computer to justify the computer's price. For example, with more accurate inventory tracking and control, a company could save money by stocking less product and use a "just in time" ordering strategy. They could also utilize sophisticated sales-analysis reports to pinpoint trends and see which clients were purchasing and which were not. Also, accounts-receivable tracking helped pinpoint clients who were slow to pay and therefore costing the company precious dollars.

We also learned IBM's "logical sales process." First, we were taught all the steps and told to practice them in order. When we became more experienced, we were encouraged to put our own personality into our sales presentations and create our own system and style. As long as we covered each of the steps, it didn't matter what order we used. We were free to make it our own.

The training served us well. Asserting one's worth was a cultivated skill, one that I learned to hone in a male-dominated field.

We learned life lessons, too. The "liquor, sex, and drugs" lecture taught us not to indulge in any of the aforementioned with clients and coworkers. The women teachers had a separate lecture for women only. The main message was that we were not to sleep with prospects/customers if they pressured us or made the sale contingent on sex. As I reflect back, I am struck by the tacit message we were given: As women, we would definitely be sexually harassed, and it was our responsibility to protect ourselves. There was no mention of reporting any offenses to our managers. While the women were subjected to this sexist lecture, the men were not given any equivalent lessons on their own behavior. In fact, I imagine they were largely unaware of the challenges their female colleagues faced. Silence is the unspoken accomplice when it comes to unequal treatment. Had the men been included, perhaps they could have stood up with and for us.

**

It was clear when I returned to Lincoln that my relationship with Roger was over. I'd already been turned off by his unwillingness to split the financial responsibilities of our future new home. But in truth, we'd never had serious conversations about our future together the way a genuinely committed couple might. We'd never spoken about having children or even cultivated a shared vision of our life together.

Despite the lack of a cogent plan, after our engagement, I'd walk home from my classes, thinking happily to myself, *My life is planned out now*—only to feel my body seize in panic as I recognized this was probably a death knell as far as excitement was concerned: *Oh, no, my life is planned out, and there won't be any more adventures!*

After getting back from AMOD, I told Roger, "I met someone else."

He shot back, "I knew it! I could tell by the sound of your voice when I called you in Georgia."

And it was true. I had met Cam at AMod. I was instantly drawn to him. He was caring, kind, and generous, as well as a natural leader to whom others gravitated. I felt the same safety and comfort I'd felt with Roger upon first meeting him, but there was an electricity and chemistry that Roger and I had never enjoyed.

I told Roger we could still date if he wanted to, but I needed to call off the engagement because I wasn't ready to be married. There was still so much I had yet to experience. Roger and I stayed connected for a short while but, when he figured out that I would never marry him, it was the final straw. He was distraught and refused to speak to me ever again.

While I was sorry to hurt Roger, I was also relieved that I could be with Cam. We dated for a little over two years, but the relationship was long-distance. He was a marketing rep in Kalamazoo, Michigan. The first month after AMod, he ran up a telephone bill of $800 after calling me long-distance from his office. Henry, our marketing manager, let me use his office to take Cam's calls. When we became serious, both of our branch managers got involved. There were no jobs available for me in Michigan, but Cam could take a job in Nebraska if he chose to. Unfortunately for me, Cam was not interested in moving to Nebraska. He had grown up in Michigan, and in Michigan he would stay. Despite the distance, it felt like I had the best of both worlds: a job that excited me and a boyfriend whom I absolutely adored. I was smitten. I had never felt this way in my life. My past relationships had felt more like casual companionships, but with Cam, I had love, tenderness, and passion.

In the meantime, after AMod, some of the students transferred from OPD (Office Products Division-Typewriters, Word Processors and Copiers) to my division of GSD (General Systems Division-Medium sized computers). They were all older white men. Typewriters were becoming obsolete, and IBM wanted to retrain willing OPD employees. These transfers regaled us with their stories and knowledge of IBM and told us about older employees at IBM who had lost their passion but stayed on the job to earn their pension. They were known as "quit and stayed employees."

When my advisor gave me my final review for AMod, he gave me a 2 on a 1–5 scale, with 1 being "walks on water" and 5 being "fired." He complimented me on how well I was doing, especially since I had three handicaps: I was young, I was a woman, and I was straight out of college. He told me I would outgrow being young and inexperienced, but there was nothing I could do about being a woman in a male-dominated workplace—something I felt could be viewed as an advantage rather than a handicap, had the organization been able to see it that way.

At my six-month performance review, I was rated a 2. Dillon, the colleague who'd started working at IBM the same day as me, told me he was rated a 4—two points lower than me. He asked me if I had received my raise. I said, "No—did you?"

Taken aback, he stammered, "Yes." What was more—Dillon hadn't even asked for the raise.

I didn't miss a beat. I went straight to my manager, Brian, and asked him where my raise was. Brian looked surprised. "What do you mean?" he asked. I told him Dillon mentioned he got a raise, and I'd like my raise, too. Brian didn't respond to that request.

I called my new contacts from AMod, who all confirmed they had received raises in the same amount as Dillon's—also without asking. They said it was standard. Henry, the sales manager, asked me how I was doing, and I told him I loved my job but was frustrated that Dillon had been given a raise and I hadn't. Henry went to bat for me, and I was finally given a retroactive raise in the same amount as Dillon's and the other IBM employees from my school.

It was clear to me that despite my hard work and verve, the fact that I wasn't a man would be held against me. Many employees who were far less knowledgeable still appeared to climb up the hierarchy at IBM, purely because they were men.

We were all given keys to the IBM office. One beautiful summer Saturday, I was working on programming one of the IBM computers. My manager, Brian, happened by and saw me working on the computer.

"Someday I hope to learn how to operate a computer," he said.

"You don't know how?" I was incredulous. "How did you get to be a manager?"

He gave me an odd look and replied, "I don't need to know how to run a computer to be a manager."

I hadn't meant to offend Brian with my candor. I simply thought it was common sense for a manager to know how to run a computer so he could fully understand the work his team was doing!

Unfortunately, although I continued to excel in my job despite the odds, my relationship with Cam eventually petered out. I was head over heels in love with him and could even see myself having children with him—something I'd never imagined with another man. Had we both been ready for marriage, perhaps things might have worked out differently. Our romance faded, but we remained friends. When I called him a few years ago, I discovered that he was still married to his wife of many years and had three grown children. It's hard to know what might have happened between us had we stayed together, but I treasure the memories I have of him to this day and can honestly say that Cam was my first true love.

**

BMod was the second five-week class that trainees were required to take. Just as with AMod, we had assigned advisors and elected class officers. I served as a class officer. Our job was to meet with IBM management and advisors, and to let management know if any student was having a breakdown due to stress.

Unlike AMod, BMod was highly technical in nature. Students learned many details about our computers, including the product line, inside out, in addition to several programming languages, including RPG, IBM's proprietary language. We worked diligently into the night, writing code until we got it done, sometimes in teams. It was laborious and rewarding when we finally got our programs to run perfectly.

We also honed our sales skills with recorded and videotaped role-playing in telesales, one-on-one sales calls, and group presentations. Our instructors and advisors evaluated our sales calls and offered suggestions for improvement.

CMod was the third class—an overview of the many industry application software programs IBM offered, which encompassed manufacturing, retail, finance, distribution, construction, law, accounting, trucking, and hospitals and medical groups.

In between classes, I was responsible for special projects and was free to accompany others on sales calls to improve my skills. When I started, there were no higher-ranking women role models for me to follow. I learned to cope with people who questioned the ability of women to do a complete job.

When I volunteered for new projects, Brian would actually say, "I don't know if you can handle this, Karen." Of course, as an overachiever with a can-do attitude, I always could.

When I went on calls, especially with men in my office, the customers usually ignored me and directed comments to the men, not me, even though I was the one who would do the work. The solution for me was to pursue my work with as much energy as possible, proving I was more than capable. At one point, I was asked to program a new routine for a customer. I asked what they wanted, researched the current computer code and wrote a special routine, and then ran the program to see the new report. When I was finished, the customer shamefacedly said, "I didn't think you could do it." It turned out they hadn't needed a new routine at all. They were simply testing me.

At sales meetings, the men would flirt with me but not take me seriously if I made a suggestion—which would invariably be repeated by a man who took credit for my idea. Small digs were common, and I was accustomed to being made the butt of a joke. My quick wit usually put my colleagues in their place, but I certainly didn't enjoy bracing myself for the next rude remark or off-color joke.

Systems school was the final leg of my training before becoming a systems engineer. The curriculum covered sales-call techniques, more programming, and the importance of customer service. It was intense but rewarding. Again, I served as class officer, Vice President.

Upon my one-year anniversary, I was once again rated a 2. And once again, Dillon got a raise but I didn't. This was the second time I was denied a raise following superior performance reviews over my male counterparts. I persisted and received a retroactive raise for the same amount a few months later. I learned to set goals and ask for such things as well-deserved raises and promotions, as I was beginning to recognize that they would not simply be handed to me on the basis of merit.

I was promoted to Associate Systems Engineer. With this came the responsibility of managing an entire territory. Mine started with 22 business accounts and more than doubled to 45 in Lincoln, Beatrice, Nebraska City, Fairbury, Seward, and Hebron—all current users of IBM equipment. I had all six banks, as well as hospitals, distribution, construction, accountants, and manufacturing. I covered the geography of 16 counties.

My customers were very important to me. I concentrated my efforts on learning more about their particular needs and offering better business solutions. The computer industry was rapidly, and constantly, changing. There was more to learn in every area, and it was up to me to keep my customers abreast of all the new possibilities available to them. With gusto, I did just that.

IBM offered annual conferences in certain industry areas. I requested to attend the Construction Conference in Washington, D.C. My manager Brian told me that if I signed up five customers, I could attend with my other colleagues. I did, and on the day of the flight, I had my suitcase in my car, ready to go to the airport. Right before I was ready to leave, Brian came to me and told me I couldn't go. I asked why and he refused to give me a reason. Stony-faced, he replied, "You just can't."

I called my customer and told him that because my manager refused to let me go, I would be unable to meet him and his team in D.C. He was furious and said, "Hang on, I'm going to call your manager." He later told me he'd informed Brian that if I couldn't attend the conference, he was never going to buy from IBM again. After his phone call, Brian came out of his office and reluctantly permitted me to go. I raced to the airport just in time—delighted to be vindicated but also crestfallen that Brian had been so unsupportive.

As a systems engineer, I was called upon to meet with prospective clients to see if our IBM software applications met their needs and were a good fit. After they purchased, it was my job to implement an installation schedule and help them migrate all their operations to the new computer. Some installations took up to a year to complete.

One such time, I was helping with a large construction company presentation. There were 20 people around our IBM conference room, including me, my manager, the sales rep, and his manager. At one point, the prospect asked me if the IBM construction software handled EEOC requirements.

I responded, "I'm sorry, I don't know what EEOC means."

The sales rep blurted out, "It's the reason you were hired, Karen."

Dead silence enveloped the room. I slowly looked around the table at 19 white men and calmly asked, "Oh, do you mean the 95% white male quota?"

The dead silence was tinged with tension.

Suddenly, the prospect burst out laughing and said, "We're buying your computer, and we want Karen as our systems engineer." My manager laughed, too, and everyone was happy. Only later would I discover that EEOC stood for the U.S. Equal Employment Opportunity Commission.

Despite the hiccups along the way, I genuinely loved my job. I loved helping my customers and troubleshooting the technical issues during our installation process. In the spring of 1981, I was asked to write an article about my job-search experience and what it was like to work for IBM. It was published in the University of Nebraska Business College's *Probe* magazine. The managing editor asked me to write the article. I knew her from college.

In the piece, I stated I had been fascinated with business since I was a child and that my single mother had constantly supported me, telling me I could be anything I desired if I tried hard enough. I mentioned that the more assertive I was, the more job offers I received. I wrote about my community involvement and also mentioned I had an active real-estate license and planned to get my MBA and mentor other business-college students. My last paragraph: "My overall advice to anyone is to maintain a positive mental attitude, know what you want and how to get it, develop a detailed plan of action, and then go for it. I truly believe that you can be anything you want to be, if you believe it yourself."

I was proud of the article, and surprisingly, so was my manager, Brian. However, I was taken aback when Eddy, the manager of the Office Products Division, called me into his office to chastise me for writing my article. He told me I was not allowed to speak or to have opinions outside of IBM. I felt his reaction was totally inappropriate and ridiculous, so I wrote him off as an angry windbag. At IBM, they had a saying: "You'd better be nice to everyone you work with because you never know when they might become your boss." I never dreamed that Eddy might end up becoming my manager. Hindsight is 20/20. In retrospect, I realize I could have nursed his ego instead of speaking up.

**

In late fall of 1981, I became a marketing representative—and I was the only woman sales rep in GSD in the Lincoln office. One saleswoman, Joyce, had been promoted along with her husband, a systems engineer, and the other woman had quit. The woman who quit warned me not to take the job. She said, "They won't treat you right when you are an equal. As long as you remain a systems engineer, you are golden."

However, I was hired to be marketing rep in three years and wanted to keep my word. Moreover, the salespeople were treated better and got to go on a fancy trip if they made quota. They also seemed to have better promotional opportunities, as they became sales managers and branch managers, and were paid more than systems-engineering managers. As an extrovert, the sales path was better suited to my personality and skills, while the systems-engineering path felt more appropriate for introverted types.

The sales manager, Twila, was relatively new to Lincoln. She had been a top marketing rep in California and drove a green Mercedes. I was excited to finally be working for a woman. Dillon and I were assigned as the new accounts-prospecting sales representatives, and each of us took half of the available territory. Instead of splitting the geographical area herself, which is standard procedure, Twila let Dillon split the territory in half and then allowed Dillon to choose his half.

The three of us sat in her office and Dillon revealed his territorial split, which was clearly lopsided. He took two-thirds for himself and gave me one-third. Due to my IBM training, I was able to remain calm and asked, "Do you feel this is a fair division?"

Dillon said, "Yes."

I replied, "OK, then let's trade."

Astonished by the suggestion, Dillon stammered over his words; he was clearly unwilling to make any kind of trade.

Twila finally stepped in and said, "It's not fair, Dillon. Go split it again and choose again."

I tried to grapple with why Twila was letting a sales rep split and choose a territory when it was her job to create the territories and quotas. I chalked it up to the fact that Dillon was now the Omaha branch manager's son-in-law.

**

At the end of each month, our office was a flurry of activity. We had a monthly and annual quota that went up the line to the very top management of IBM. We were pressured to get contracts signed even if it meant driving through snow storms. Sometimes, at the end of the year, the quotas would be adjusted to allow for a certain percentage of sales reps to make it to the One Hundred Percent Club.

I had a large quota my partial year, and it was not adjusted at the end of the year, but I still managed to qualify for the One Hundred Percent Club in 1981, which was held in Miami. I barely missed in 1982, but qualified in 1983. When I resigned from IBM in August of 1984, I was the highest-ranking sales rep on the quota board.

Following the IBM sales-training guidelines, I made 50 to 100 phone calls daily to prospects and existing customers when I was in the office. In addition, I always visualized everyone I spoke to or met as a long-term satisfied customer.

The great thing about being a systems engineer before moving into sales was that I already knew the intricacies of how the computer software operated and I had no need to schedule a systems engineer to come with me on sales calls. I was able to cover more territory this way. Besides drumming up new business, I was able to keep my small banks and some of the other accounts I had worked with as a systems engineer.

My customers were always supportive of me, and I never spoke to them of what I was going through in my office. I focused on their needs, and I was greatly rewarded. My customers continued to purchase products from me, which helped me cope with the difficult office politics. I suspect that had I shared with them that my management was not giving me the same raises as my male counterparts, they would have written glowing letters to IBM management on my behalf.

Thankfully, I wasn't in the office 24/7. My sales territory was so spread out that I would drive two hours to my accounts and be out all day. One evening as I drove back to Lincoln, I stopped in a drugstore in the small town of Wilber, to ask if I could use their phone. I told the young female clerk that I was a marketing rep for IBM. She blurted out, "I've never seen a lady salesman before!" I assured her there were lots of them. I always felt like a diplomat wherever I went, showing people—especially young women—what was possible.

CHAPTER 5

THE NIGHTMARE BEHIND CLOSED DOORS

The confidence and success I displayed in my public life as an IBM sales rep was a beautiful smokescreen for the horrors of my private life. What nobody in my life knew was that behind closed doors, I was a victim of systematic abuse. It took years of professional counseling to deprogram the damage and regain my true inner sense of self and reality.

How does this happen to such an intelligent woman?

First, our society doesn't prepare girls and boys for the reality of predatory or sociopathic behavior, or teach us what a healthy relationship looks like. I was warned about not taking candy from strangers. I was also told not to have sex until I was married. But I was never told what to do if I said "no" and was ignored.

Second, our laws don't protect the victims—and predators know it.

Third, our society blames women and girls for being assaulted and raped. This had been cemented in my mind ever since I was a young girl.

Fourth, not enough people have brought this issue to light, due to the shame and stigma of victimization. Unfortunately, as we are learning, our collective silence makes us complicit in the cycle of violence.

In my experience, predators are a cowardly, insecure type, but they can be charming. By the time they inflict physical pain, they have already methodically and systematically gained the trust of their intended target. They then skillfully dismantle her sense of self before going in for the attack.

This is my story.

**

I had been dating Cam long-distance since early 1979. In the fall of 1980, a few of my older male coworkers suggested, "Why don't you date someone in Lincoln? It would be easier." At the time, I didn't question why exactly they felt so entitled to have a say in my personal matters.

They pulled out their customer files to find eligible bachelors for me. They came up with three names. One, they questioned, because they said he might be too immature.

Incidentally, that's the one I ended up marrying.

That very Friday, my high-school friend, Jamal, called me. He was in town visiting his parents on his way north. We went out to a bar and sat at a huge table with ten other people. John said, "Karen, trade places with me. This guy likes finance and so do you."

I was astonished to discover that the finance guy, Donald, was the same one my IBM colleagues had told me might be too immature. My first impression was: ICK. Donald simply rubbed me the wrong way. He asked me questions, then would judge my answer and offer his opinion. If I pushed back, he would not budge. His opinion was the *right* one and mine was wrong. It was more of an interrogation than a conversation.

He asked me if I had a boyfriend in Lincoln. I said no. He asked me what was wrong with me that I didn't have a boyfriend. I explained that I was seeing someone who lived in Michigan, although I didn't really think he deserved to know anything about my personal life. Although the conversation seemed to be going south, Donald didn't seem to think so. He asked me what I was doing Saturday. I told him I was helping my mom sell Thai ornaments, imported by my sister-in-law, at a flea market.

I honestly thought that would be the last I'd ever see of Donald. I even told Jamal on the ride home that I wasn't impressed. In my eyes, the man had been arrogant and rude, and not particularly interesting.

The next day, when my mom and I were unloading for the flea market, Donald showed up and offered to help. Mom was delighted. He lifted the boxes and came back at the end to load them back up. At that point, he asked me to dinner. Despite my first impressions, I figured this show of kindness deserved a second chance.

Shortly afterwards, Donald and I started dating. He asked me to come to a Young Republicans meeting, as he was chapter president. As I discovered, he and his friend had gone to an election meeting and bought drinks for everyone in return for a vote for Donald—and Donald won. The regulars were upset. At the meeting I attended, Donald spoke, but it was clear the members did not respect him. He was awkward in front of the group, and no one was paying attention. I felt sorry for him.

When the group voted for delegates for the upcoming conference in Grand Island, I was elected delegate, but Donald, the president, was not. Rather than being happy for me, Donald was incensed. He asked me to take some flyers to the conference. I didn't want to, but I felt sorry for him, so I assented. I left them on a chair in an envelope.

When I saw what the flyers said, I was angry with myself for bringing them. In retaliation, his flyers announced the Lincoln chapter had not paid their registration fee and their bank account had a zero balance; therefore, they should be disqualified and unseated at the convention. As it turned out, he was the one who had depleted the bank account, stopped payment on the conference registration fee, and mailed each member on the roster $3 cash. I thought, *Wow, all that because he didn't get his way?*

Despite Donald's vindictive and childish behavior, I still felt sorry for him. He often shared his insecurities with me, and it seemed to me that he had nobody in whom to confide. Although he knew a lot of people due to his wealthy family's connections, he had few real friends.

Despite my better instincts, I saw some redeeming qualities in

Donald. He seemed to be kind to his mother—although I later learned that his kindness was a calculated attempt to trick his mother out of the family company stock so he could take over the business. He was helpful to my mother—although he would later admit almost proudly, "I get to the daughter through the mother."

Donald also knew how to take advantage of my unspoken weaknesses...such as my fear of being alone at home after dark. Despite my independent career-woman persona, I harbored an underlying terror that someone would break into my house at night and hurt me. It was so pervasive that it lasted for years. At first, I called my friend, Abigail, and she came over with her umbrella as a weapon. There was never anyone around or any sign of attempted entry, but my fear persisted. When I told Donald, he offered to come over and sleep on the couch. It was a relief to have him there, and it made me feel safe.

It didn't occur to me that he would be the one I'd someday come to fear.

I was still dating Cam, although it was clear that the initial intensity was fading due to the long-distance nature of the relationship. I also met another man, Rick. He was friends with Abigail and her boyfriend, so we double-dated. His family owned a construction company and some banks. He lived in a house on a private lake. His family was wealthy but didn't flaunt it. At one point, he flew a group of us to his family home to go hot-air ballooning. Rick piloted the plane and then the balloon. He was hard to get to know due to his shyness, so I wasn't sure if he liked me all that much.

At this time, I had three men in my life, although none of the relationships were serious and I was not having sex with any of them. Cam and I were in contact by phone but hadn't seen each other in a while. Donald, on the other hand, was calling every night and we went somewhere three to four times a week.

In December 1980, IBM was having its annual Christmas party and I wanted to ask Rick to come with me. I called but he didn't call back that day, so in the evening, I asked Donald, who said yes. The next day, Rick called to say he'd be happy to accompany me, but I had to break the news that I'd already asked someone else. I wished I would have waited one day.

I kept dating Donald, and finally, we made love. Afterward, with me on top, he blurted out, "You're nothing but a whore." I sprang back in horror, tears of shock streaming down my face. "How could you say such a thing!" I shouted in disbelief.

He apologized profusely. "I'm sorry, I'm sorry, I'm sorry. I don't know what came over me!"

Although it was a humiliating moment for me, I chose to believe that Donald was sincere in his apology. I had no way of knowing it would get worse—and that he had merely been testing my boundaries to see how much of his abuse I was willing to take.

Unfortunately, I did not run away. I believed his apology and we kept dating.

As time passed, Donald's true colors began to shine through. His moods were erratic and he could fly off the handle without provocation. One evening, while he was at my house, one of my bank customers called me at home. He sounded inebriated. He said he was attending the banking convention in downtown Lincoln and wondered if I would like to come down and join him for a drink. I thanked him and politely declined. He became insistent. "Only for an hour?"

"No, I'm home for the night. Have a good night," I said.

He was about to hang up when Donald grabbed my phone from my hand and yelled, "This is her boyfriend. Don't ever call her again!" He slammed the phone down with such force that it scared me. Out of sheer mortification, I didn't bring this incident up to my customer, and neither did he.

Despite all the warning signs, by the time Donald asked me to marry him, it didn't feel I had any other choice but to say yes. By then, many of my friends were getting married and I felt the social pressure to tie the knot. Cam was drifting away, Rick hadn't called me in a while, and it seemed that Donald—although my last choice—was the only prospect left.

We told his parents and my mom at the same time. His parents shrieked in delight, while my mom's face fell. I had never seen such an expression, one of disappointment and disbelief, on her face before.

I knew I wasn't excited about marrying him, but I felt obligated. At this point, I told Donald I didn't want to have sex until our wedding and he agreed, which was a relief. (Another huge red flag!) At first, sex with Donald had been fine, albeit lackluster and certainly nothing like the magic I'd experienced with Cam. After about six months, the glow of a new relationship wore off and I started resenting the fact that I'd never had an orgasm with him. Donald was a selfish lover, and it was all about his pleasure. Despite the lack of sexual compatibility, I still enjoyed his company in that he read a lot about business and we had a shared vocabulary there, which meant a lot to me.

However, Donald didn't share one of my primary passions: music. He often complained that I didn't have a TV. I didn't feel I was missing much, as I got my news from the newspaper and had little interest in sitting around and watching TV in my spare time. My piano was in the living room and I played it for enjoyment. But just to placate Donald, I bought a TV—to which his eyes and attention were constantly glued whenever he visited. He was staying more and more, and pretty soon I hardly ever had space to play my piano.

Donald was clearly not the kind of person to encourage his significant other's passions and talents. Once, his family and my mom and I were having a lovely dinner in the private dining room at the country club. My future sister-in-law mentioned she would like a piano. She had been playing the one in Donald's parents' house, but it was old and out of tune.

Without a trace of humor to indicate he was joking, Donald piped up: "Karen has a piano. You can have it."

This clearly rubbed Mom the wrong way. She quipped, "If Karen is giving her piano away, she's giving it to me, because I'm the one who gave it to her."

I kept calm, as the entire conversation was absurd. "I'm keeping my piano. I love it and would never give it away." End of discussion.

Aside from assuming a false sense of ownership over my belongings, it seemed that Donald also felt entitled to other things.

We were at dinner at the Lincoln Country Club with my friend Jasmine and her boyfriend. Toward the end, Jasmine said, "You're not going to change your name when you get married, are you?"

I said emphatically, "Oh, no!"

Donald's face turned red with indignation and he said, "Of course she is!" It was almost as if I hadn't spoken. It was another awkward moment that created unnecessary conflict in what had been an otherwise delightful evening.

Unfortunately, we couldn't just leave it there. He continued to bring up the subject and beat a dead horse. "I will never call you by your last name. I will always introduce you as Karen," he snapped.

I was nonplussed. "Fine, I'll introduce you by your first name, too."

When he complained to my mom and attempted to gain her sympathy, she asked, "Would you change your name?"

He said, "No, but I don't have to. She does!"

My mom seemed amused. "Would you like to be called Mr. Karen Dunning?"

Donald made a sour face. "Of course not!"

"Well then, you can understand why she doesn't want to be called Mrs. your name, either!"

I agreed with Mom, of course. I had always found it strange and regressive that women had to change their names after getting married. Plus, I had a career and was known by my surname. I realized how women tended to lose the history of their accomplishments once they changed their names, and to simply become extensions of their husbands. I wasn't about to let that happen.

Still, Donald persisted. When we went to register for our marriage license, he got into an argument with the female clerk. He declared, "She *has* to change her name." The clerk explained I could use a variety of names as long as I wasn't defrauding anyone, and I was not required to change my name. True to form, he wouldn't accept her answer and kept pushing her until she got red in the face and abruptly ended the conversation. Again, they were talking about me in front of me as if I wasn't there.

Looking back on it so many decades later, I see we had no business getting married. I was much too young, even though social pressure was telling me otherwise. We were clearly incompatible on some key issues, and we didn't know each other well enough. We had only gone on dates or trips, with him doing the bulk of the talking and expressing little to no curiosity about my inner and outer world...that is, unless he was setting out to contradict me. Similar to my experience with Roger, we hadn't discussed the goals of our married life: such as money matters, how we'd split household duties, whether or not we wanted children, or anything else that would place us on the same page with respect to our dreams and essential values.

One thing we did discuss, however, was where we would live. We each had a two-bedroom house. Mine was bigger, with two bathrooms, in east Lincoln, and his was located near the Lincoln Country Club. He suggested that we both try to rent our houses. The first person who rented their house would move into the other house for a year, and then we'd buy a bigger house near the Lincoln Country Club. I agreed to this, as it seemed like a reasonable plan. Before I could even place an ad in the paper, he announced he'd rented his house. He would be moving his stuff into my house. As it turned out, his "stuff" would end up taking up most of the lower level and the extra bedroom space. I couldn't help but think, in retrospect, that he'd orchestrated this from the beginning.

Despite Donald's seeming eagerness to join our lives together, one evening he disclosed that he didn't feel ready to be married. I responded with as much empathy and thoughtfulness as I could, almost more like a counselor than his fiancé. "If that's how you feel, then you shouldn't get married," I affirmed.

I didn't take his hesitation personally. I think I was relieved we could break off the engagement and still be friends. However, instead of breaking things off, we continued to date. At the time, I didn't feel capable of asserting myself in my personal life. I did the thing that many Nebraskans do—go along to get along.

However, Donald quickly changed his mind. Another evening, he announced to me, "OK, I'm ready now." I didn't stop to think whether I was the one who wasn't ready. That was that, and we made a date for the late fall.

Donald had two brothers who were already married at this point. Before our wedding, my future sisters-in-law invited me to lunch. One of them, whom I'd once witnessed in shock as her husband pushed her off the couch and nobody batted an eye—informed me, "We invited you to lunch to tell you not to get married into this family. You'll never be blood. You won't be treated well."

They weren't specific about the mistreatment I might expect, and I didn't ask for specifics...although I wish I had. I completely blanked on the encounter where her husband had pushed her off the couch and acted like it was a big joke—while everyone else appeared entirely oblivious to this spectacle of power and dominance. It wasn't until years later that many of the details I'd ignored began to surface. Looking back, I recognize that I seemed to be unable to interrogate the nuances, especially when it came to men. To me, "abuse" needed to be overt in order for me to recognize it. I also imagine that I unconsciously internalized all the sexist gender roles

I'd learned, even as I questioned and pushed back on them.

I didn't ask my future sisters-in-law why they were still married if it was that bad, either. I simply chalked it up to the fact that perhaps they didn't like me and this was their attempt to talk me out of the marriage. Their focus seemed to be less on the actual details of their marriages and more on the possibility of inheriting wealth or being part of the family company. Some of their concerns also seemed petty. My future sisters-in-law told me never to call Donald's mother "Mom," because then they'd also be forced to do so. I learned that they hated her because she was always offering unsolicited advice on how they could be better wives.

Perhaps had they warned me immediately after getting engaged I might have acted on this information, or told my mom. I didn't fully understand their motives, as they were both still in the family and didn't seem to be interested in leaving or conceding their privileges. *If it's that bad, why don't they leave?* I wondered.

After we sent the invitations, I called Cam to tell him I was getting married. He was surprised but congratulated me. He asked, "Are you at least going to invite me to the wedding?"

I replied, "Sure, do you want to come?" Donald was hovering and listening to our conversation, which was very awkward for me. I felt like I was in a movie where the audience can see the wrong people are getting together, but the two who are meant to be can't seem to see this or communicate clearly.

"Yes, of course!" he said.

I wished he had said, "Marry me, instead." I might have even asked Cam to marry me if Donald wasn't around!

Of course, I sent him an invitation...but he didn't come.

Today, it seems ridiculous, and horribly sad, to think I felt so limited in my choices at the time.

**

Donald and I were married in January 1982. He'd suggested that we move our fall date to the new year so we could still file our taxes separately (another red flag!).

Our wedding was beautiful but on one of the coldest nights I'd experienced in years. We invited 350 guests. It was a veritable list of Who's Who of Lincoln, including the Lincoln Country Club types, as well as my friends and IBM coworkers. My mom said she knew some of the guests from her high-school days, but they didn't give her the time of day, as she was a "lowly" widowed teacher and they were "high" society. It infuriated me to hear this.

When I said "I do," it was barely audible. The walk down the aisle was also awkward. My grandfather gave me away. He had not been told in detail that after the minister asked, "Who gives this woman away in marriage?" he was to say, "Her mother and I do." So when the minister asked, Grandpa was silent. The minister asked again and Grandpa replied, "I can't understand you." Grandma had died the year before, and Grandpa was 89 and hard of hearing. Grandpa was eventually taken to his seat, and I was crying by this time. I could barely talk. I simply hid my face from the audience's view. I didn't feel good about the whole ordeal.

The reception itself was a festive occasion. I wanted to stay longer at the reception, but Donald insisted we leave immediately. He and his father had planned our honeymoon to St. Johns and other islands. We stayed at Bluebeard's Castle in the honeymoon suite, which contained a massive round bed. I felt as if I were being ravished. The months without sex had not increased my desire or created the possibility of greater tenderness and reciprocity. One day, Donald insisted on having sex on the public beach, which was not a nude beach. I said no, but as it would become the pattern in our relationship, he got his way. At that time, I had no real awareness of the concept of consent, but I felt guilted into it, shamed, and disrespected.

Back in Lincoln, I went back to work at IBM and Donald resumed his daily routine of getting his mail, playing basketball at the Y, having lunch with his best friend at the same restaurant (at the same table and always with the same waitress), then going back home. When I arrived home, Donald always had dinner ready. He also did the laundry and mowed the lawn. We had never discussed having children or if we even desired children, or what roles we would play in our marriage. I knew I would keep my IBM job, and although Donald had told me he worked as an independent investor, he did little else beyond his daily routine. Before getting married, I'd have to do everything to take care of my house plus work, but now all I had to do was work. It was tantalizingly easy! It seemed he had taken on the role of a traditional wife. I thought, *Everyone should have a wife! This is great.*

However, despite Donald's family's wealth, I continued to pay all the bills and it wasn't all easy sailing for me. The television was constantly on and Donald was always at home, so I rarely got to play my beloved piano. He had already stuffed his furniture into the spare bedroom and basement prior to our wedding, so I had no privacy or alone time. When we'd been dating, we went out three to four times a week, but now he refused to do anything unless it involved his family or an occasional function at the Lincoln Country Club. At the country club, people would ask him what he did and he'd say, "Nothing. I'm a house husband, but Karen works at IBM." They'd turn to me and say, "You must be very smart," and we'd have a conversation. But behind closed doors, Donald's seeming pride in my accomplishments gave way to resentment and animosity.

For example, Donald was still giving me trouble about my decision to keep my maiden name. Apparently, Donald wasn't alone in his belief that I should take his surname. IBM had already changed my name on their records without asking me and refused to change it back—ever. I was never given a reason. The secretary who ordered my new business cards with the wrong name was disgusted with me. (Years later, she started using her maiden name and apologized for her behavior.) My manager, Gloria, was fine with my name choice, but the administration manager was adamantly opposed to a married woman not taking her husband's name and he refused to change my name on IBM's records. Because he was the one who ultimately held the power in my office, my request was denied. (Ten years ago, IBM had a security breach and sent everyone a notice and one year of free identity-theft services. I was denied, because IBM still had the wrong name, and I was unable to "prove" who I was.)

I wonder now if Donald's attitude around my insistence to keep my maiden name had to do with his own insecurities about his place in the world. He didn't have any visible ambitions or projects he felt passionate about. It seemed his only goal was a hostile takeover of the family construction business by tricking his mother and aunt to hand over their stock to him. I learned after marriage that he had been fired from the family business and "worked" unsuccessfully at one of the family banks. He had repeatedly been offered other family business opportunities but refused them.

Donald's family owned a large business, Wizco. Wizco was a conglomerate of companies related to the construction industry. They supplied materials to construct buildings, streets, and highways. They owned land, private lakes, a limestone quarry, sand and gravel pits, and a railroad. They had over 1,000 employees and claimed to be the largest privately held employer in Nebraska. The company was founded by Donald's grandparents. After both the grandparents died, their children (one son and four daughters) each received 20 percent of the stock, but the son, Lyle, took over and ran everything with zero regard for his sisters. My mother-in-law was a sister. Another sister, Aunt Olivia never married and also lived in Lincoln. Today, only the third generation is alive and I was told Lyle's son (Donald's cousin, Lyle Jr.) bought out all the other stockholders who were not in his immediate family.

In May of our first year of marriage, Donald informed me that Wizco was having its annual meeting. I took off my IBM lunchtime and showed up for the meeting. Most family members were already seated around the large conference table in the boardroom. There wasn't a chair for me, so the in-house attorney brought me a chair. Financials were passed around, but I had to get back to work, so I grabbed all the papers and left for IBM. I received an irritated phone call from Donald informing me that nobody was allowed to take the financials out of the building.

At the stockholder dinner that evening, my two sisters-in-law who'd warned me not to get married were upset because I'd gone to the meeting and they had never been invited. I learned that in truth, I hadn't been invited, either! Donald had given me the details about the meeting and, being a newlywed, I assumed this was what married people did—and I showed up at the appointed time! Even the surprised looks and the lack of a chair for me didn't register. Marrying into the family hadn't guaranteed me a spot in the family business.

I had joined Donald's family Congregational church and served as chair of the finance committee, the women's ministries, and RCAR (Religious Coalition for Abortion Rights).

I was also co-chair of the YWCA Tribute to Women Awards Ceremony. We sponsored Sarah Weddington, who successfully argued for women's privacy rights before the US Supreme Court, to speak on women's leadership.

**

Although Donald's and my marriage was dismal on the surface, I still had plenty of things in my work life that kept me feeling optimistic and occupied. I didn't stop to ponder whether Donald was a good husband or not...until one evening about a year into our marriage.

I took a shower and was on my way to the bedroom to change into my nightgown and go to sleep. The kitchen phone rang, and Donald answered it. It was for me. It was my friend and former housemate, Charlotte, who had called to chat.

After the phone call, I was on my way to bed, but Donald blocked my way to the bedroom and started pawing at me. This was unusual, as our sex life was infrequent and quite unsatisfying—and he never typically initiated sex at night.

"I need to go to sleep—I have a big day tomorrow," I said.

Donald ignored me and started pushing me backwards toward the bedroom, laughing all the while. I stumbled from the kitchen, through the living room, past the stairs leading to the front door, through the hallway, and into the crowded spare bedroom. I fell onto his ugly plaid couch, which was crammed into the room and jutting out toward the front door.

At this point, everything was a blur. "No, I need to go to sleep!" I pleaded, over and over, as he shoved me. When I fell onto the couch, I saw he was nude from the waist down.

It was almost as if I were watching my own demise as I thought to myself in dread and horror, *He's going to rape me.* I put my hands up to protect myself as I screamed, "No!" but I was no match for him. He held me down with his left forearm with such a force it knocked the wind out of me. I couldn't get air. Then I saw he was winding up to punch me and was directing the punch at my face. Instinctively, I jerked to my right, but his blow landed hard on my upper arm. I let out a yelp of pain and shock. He had never displayed this kind of physical violence toward me before.

He was still holding me down, but by now, I was precariously hanging off the edge of the couch. Was he going to punch me again? Thankfully, he stood up and I thudded to the wooden floor with a moan. He looked at me in disgust, and then he turned and left, shutting me in the dark bedroom.

As a victim of this peculiar burst of rage, I was dumbfounded. It had seemed to come out of left field. We had not had an argument, and aside from his frequent negativity and offhand remarks, Donald had never been violent toward me. Much to my chagrin, he didn't apologize. He didn't ask how I was or try to help me up. He seemed to lack regret for his behavior altogether.

I was petrified...afraid to move or breathe. I sobbed as quietly as possible. I tried to get myself to think clearly. I had no shoes on, only a robe. It was late, probably 11 p.m. It was also severely cold outside. Could I sneak out to the phone and call my mom? Would the police help me? Could I get to the front door without Donald intercepting me? Could I run to my neighbors in my robe, barefooted, and pound on their door? Would they even answer? My car was in the garage, but the keys were in my purse in our bedroom, and I could hear Donald in there, perhaps getting ready for bed. Plus, was his car parked behind mine?

I couldn't come up with a feasible solution. I was in pain, emotionally and physically. I lay on the wood floor and tried to stay awake all night, in case Donald decided to come back. The next morning, I heard him leave. Thank God! I got ready for work as fast as possible and drove there in a daze. That day, I sat at my desk at IBM and didn't speak to anyone. No one seemed to notice I wasn't doing anything beyond sitting at my desk in a daze. I felt numb. Hollow. Empty.

My marriage was over.

I had to get divorced...but how? It didn't occur to me to tell anyone, not even my mom. I kept it to myself. Today, I understand that traumatized minds make traumatized choices. I know that shame and a sense of being incapacitated kept me from talking to others about my experience. Knowing what I know now, I wish I had told someone: police, family, trusted friend, counselor, attorney. It is critical to release the trauma from one's body or it will get stuck and negatively affect you in numerous ways.

By the end of the day, I still hadn't said anything to anyone. I didn't know how I would manage to do it, but I resolved to get divorced. I would go home and tell him.

When I got home, dread spread throughout my body. Donald had parked his car in the single driveway so I couldn't get into my garage. It was with trepidation that I unlocked and entered the front door. Donald cheerfully greeted me from the kitchen. Dinner was on the table. Through snippets of small talk, he acted as if last night had not occurred.

I felt like I was in an episode of *The Twilight Zone*. I was uncertain as to how to approach the matter, but after dinner, I summoned my courage and broached the subject, trying to keep my voice level. "Last night, you held me down and punched me. That is unacceptable. I'd like a divorce."

In a matter of moments, gone was the cheerful oblivious husband with his veneer of care and kindness. He was enraged. First, he tried to deny what had actually happened. He said, "You hit me first!"

I'd learned to stay calm from my sales training around dealing with irate customers. I calmly said, "No, that's not what happened," and continued to verbalize my experience.

At that point, the gloves were off. With a force that shook my soul, Donald said, "If you tell anyone, I will make you penniless and fix it so no one will ever believe you again. You made a vow. *What's yours is mine, what's mine is mine, and what's ours is mine.*"

I was rattled to my core. The truth was finally out. Behind Donald's strange and sometimes abhorrent behavior, I'd never dreamt that he actually wished to do me harm if I went "against" him. And based on his family's power and influence, I knew they could do practically whatever they desired with impunity.

At that point, I flashed back to the lunch with my sisters-in-law. I felt like slapping my forehead in a recognition that was coming all too late. No wonder they were still married even though they were clearly disgruntled and unhappy! *They were trapped.* How brave of them to even warn me. I wished I had heeded their advice then. I had no idea what the future held for me, but it didn't look good.

**

In the second year of my marriage, Donald and I made the

decision to sell my house. This had been Donald's plan all along: to rent one house (his, as it turned out, with him keeping all the rent money) and live in the other (mine, while I also paid for all our expenses) for the first year, and then buy a bigger house.

By this time, I knew my marriage was over, but I felt stuck with this person—who may as well have been a stranger to me, given the emotional chasm between us. I also thought things might be better if I got out of my house, where he'd punched me. I distinctly recall thinking, *If I'm going to be stuck with this asshole, then he's going to make good on the plan to buy a bigger house.*

At this point, I tried to avoid sex altogether but never said no again. It was just too risky in my mind. I didn't get punched again, but Donald did other things to undermine me from that point on...such as taking credit for the success of the business I built later in my marriage, even as he was seemingly sabotaging it most of the time.

My private life was in shambles by this point. When I turned 30, Donald asked me well in advance what I'd like, and I told him I wanted a party at the country club with a live band and dancing. He never organized it so, at the last second, I hosted my own birthday party in our home, and I also prepared the food and drinks. It was the first time many of my friends had even been to my house since I was married.

Being married was the loneliest time of my life.

Moreover, I had been grinding my teeth at night for a few years. When I went to my IBM customer dentist, he said, "You've ground down so much enamel, your teeth look like a 40-year-old's." At the time, I was 27. He gave me a tooth guard to wear at night and informed me, with a look of concern on his face, that stress causes grinding.

Beyond that, I endured nightmares and heart palpitations. I couldn't bear it when Donald touched me, and having sex with him always elicited tears from me. I felt trapped, and it didn't even occur to me that there might be a way out.

At some point, I decided that I wanted to go to law school. After working with the IBM attorneys, I found law fascinating. As a child, I admired what I knew of the law, especially upon that visit to my dad's childhood friend's law office. As I was learning more about the inequities that women and minority groups faced in the corporate world, it seemed to me that my knowledge of the law could make the kind of difference I'd always sought to make in the world. Perhaps this was how I would leave my mark. However, Donald quickly came in to wreck that dream. "If you go to law school, I'll divorce you," he threatened.

I believe that he was so insecure, anything oriented toward growth for me threatened him. At the time, my friend Barbara, who had also married unhappily into a wealthy Lincoln family, was getting her master's degree to be a marriage and family counselor. She told me many times that when one partner of a couple experiences personal growth, the other one experiences personal decline, almost as if they are on a teeter totter. She said I was on the way UP and he was on the way DOWN.

I liked the divorce idea, but as Donald was coming at me in a menacing way while waging the threat, I instinctively put my LSAT training guide in front of my face to protect myself from harm. I secretly studied and planned to go despite his wishes. I would pay for law school with my IBM stock. As afraid as I was of Donald, I was not the kind of woman to let a man trample her dreams.

Unfortunately, my plans to go to law school were ruined when, a few months later, Donald sold my IBM stock without my permission or knowledge: all $46,000 worth of it.

**

While I'd had my reservations about Donald from the very beginning, I had been raised to give everyone I met the benefit of the doubt. While I should have been meticulously assessing my life partner's character and allowing myself to clearly see the good and the bad, I had always been the kind of person who chose to see the best in the people around me. Yes, Donald's boorish behavior bothered me and tested my patience at times, but because I could see how much he struggled with insecurity and a lack of true friendship in his life, some part of me believed he could be redeemed and that his other qualities could finally get a chance to shine through.

Back then, I didn't understand that some people choose to do bad things because it actually gives them pleasure. Some people take a sadistic delight in the suffering of others, because it buoys their own sense of themselves. And yes, this kind of behavior likely stems from trauma, but not everyone who is traumatized chooses to act out in this way.

Not knowing all of this, it was very difficult to empower myself to leave. Most women feel this way when they are in an abusive situation. The question, "If it was so bad, why didn't she just leave?" still haunts me to this day, because it's something I used to ask when I heard stories about women who were victims of domestic violence. When you are actually in such a situation, you know it's not that easy—and your will and sense of power have likely been eroded by threats, manipulation, and emotional and physical violence...so even if you want to make such a decision, you simply can't. In addition, leaving is the most dangerous time for the woman.

I was held in a weird stasis where I knew I was unhappy and in a constant state of fear, as Donald's behavior was volatile and unpredictable, but I had no idea how to evaluate the situation or consider my options. And given the power that both Donald and his family wielded, as well as Donald's vow to make my life a living hell if I left him or did anything to displease him, it felt safer to bide my time.

As time passed, I also discovered that my initial impressions of Donald were an illusion. Donald had attended Princeton during his undergraduate years and, before we married, I accompanied him to his reunion, which was a lot of fun. The reunion after our marriage was the opposite. There was no dancing whatsoever, because he didn't want to. While his former classmates had been civil when I'd met them, it was clear to me that few of them respected him.

Donald's old roommate brought up how he remembered what Donald had done to girls in their dorm room. He looked disturbed as he said, "It wasn't good."

I turned to Donald and asked, "What does he mean?"

Donald was nonplussed when he admitted that he was always trying to get girls to kiss him back then, so he would hold them down until they did.

My stomach turned. So Donald had been predatory even before I dated him. His patterns of behavior were beginning to emerge. My eyes were beginning to open. And yet, I still felt helpless to do anything about it.

**

In 1984, my friend Jasmine won an award trip from Allstate Insurance to Hawaii. Because Allstate didn't allow award winners to invite boyfriends, only spouses, Jill asked if I would accompany her. When I informed Donald that I was going to Hawaii, he said, "You can't go. You can't go anywhere without me."

"What?" I said, incredulous. That was too much to bear. Of course I was going.

He then spat out, "If you go, I will hate you."

It already felt like he hated me, so what did I have to lose? I made plans to go. Like a child upping the ante on his tantrum, Donald blathered, "If you go, my parents will hate you."

I ignored him and packed my bags. As it turned out, my in-laws were in Maui at the same time and they were delighted I was there. One night, they took me and Jill out to dinner. It was a small moment of triumph for me. Despite Donald's desire to keep a tight leash on me, there were certain things he could not and would never be able to do to hurt me.

Jasmine's awards trip included hundreds of Allstate reps, and Norman Vincent Peale, the beloved author of *The Power of Positive Thinking*, spoke. It was an uplifting experience for me that helped me to remember there was a world much larger than the one in which Donald seemed to want to imprison me.

Although I still felt more or less trapped in my marriage, the trip also provided an outlet for the loneliness and lack of passion that were such a big part of my marriage. One evening, while I was walking on the beach path with an especially attentive Allstate rep we socialized with, he leaned over and kissed me, then promptly apologized. The kiss felt natural. I liked it, so I told him he had nothing to be sorry about. After talking for a while, we decided we would have sex. I was sure I was broken and would never enjoy sex again due to the abuse and degradation I'd endured from Donald...and for me, this was the only way to find out if my fears were warranted.

They weren't. The evening was a delicious experience. I wasn't broken in any way.

It didn't fully occur to me that my experience of feeling sexually shut down with Donald had less to do with me and more to do with him. When I got home, I decided I should have sex with Donald to see if I was permanently "fixed" or if sex was still awful with him. I put on a porn flick and initiated sex for the first time in my married life.

As I had dreaded, it was horrible, still. The tears flowed and my insides turned and knotted in fear.

So now, I knew: Sex was good with a near stranger I felt safe with, but not with Donald...but I was stuck with Donald.

**

In January 1985, I knew I no longer had a choice. I had to divorce Donald.

My doctor brother, Steve, as well as his wife and seven-year-old daughter, were living in Thailand for the school year. My niece was attending international school, and my brother was doing medical research and helping at refugee camps. They owned a beautiful home with Western-style bathrooms and a kitchen and had three live-in helpers. They invited me to visit, and Donald insisted on coming along. We flew to Bangkok and my brother picked us up and drove us to his home in Chiang Mai, which was several hours north.

It was embarrassing to be accompanied by Donald, who was the proverbial ugly American: constantly making fun of and criticizing the customs, people, house, and helpers. One evening, as Donald and I were in our guest bedroom preparing for bed, Steve and his wife, Duang, knocked on our door to ask us about our plans for the following day. As I answered the door, their expressions transformed into disbelief and horror. Donald was behind me, wearing my orthodontic headgear and jumping up and down, yelling, "This is what Karen looks like in bed!"

I was completely mortified, but the look on their faces helped me realize what an immature asshole I had married.

One of our day trips was a visit to the Golden Triangle where the borders of Thailand, Laos, and Burma (now Myanmar) meet at the confluence of the Ruak and Mekong rivers. American citizens were not allowed to walk across the bridge to Burma, but Duang could, since she was a Thai citizen. Duang walked across and came back. She had already warned both me and Donald not to attempt to take pictures or walk near the guards.

True to form, Donald had no interest in heeding the rules of a foreign country. He was upset that Duang had gotten to walk across the bridge, while he couldn't. So after she returned, he raised his camera and walked straight at the armed guards who were stationed at the bridge entrance. The guards furiously waved him away and yelled in Thai for him to stay back, but he laughed and kept going, yelling, "I only want a picture," as if to appease them. Duang was yelling for him to stop and put the camera down, as his behavior was provoking the guards to shoot him. I looked on and thought, *Go ahead—shoot him.* At this point, I had absolutely no love for Donald...not even the early pity that had softened my heart and encouraged me to seek out the best in him. All that was left was a cold revulsion.

I felt relatively safe while staying at my brother's home, but the last few nights, Donald and I were on our own in Bangkok at a fancy hotel called the Royal Orchid before our international flight back to the U.S. The hotel was beautiful and had a highly rated restaurant.

At this point, we had not had sex since March 1984, after I returned from Hawaii. I hadn't even considered packing my diaphragm for birth control. That first night at the hotel, as I sat on the edge of the bed watching TV in my nightgown, Donald started pawing at me. Fear overcame me as he pushed me over and got on top. I had no chance to say no—and thank goodness, it was over almost immediately. No sooner had he penetrated me than he was finished. I felt humiliated and helpless.

The next day, however, I experienced something that was a strong source of confusion. My body was so sensitive that if I touched myself, I felt a ripple of orgasmic energy. It felt so good, and so unaccustomed, that I wondered what was happening. Mysteriously, I also felt a deep love inside me. I wondered if I *could* have feelings for Donald again. In retrospect, it's almost unimaginable that I would have felt this way after he had essentially raped me.

I reached out for his hand, and he batted it away. I tried one more time and got the same result. He went from constantly pawing at me to physically rejecting me.

**

On the flight home, I felt a tugging sensation in my body and wondered, "Am I pregnant?" Back in Lincoln, I called my

OB/GYN, and she told me I could get a blood serum test at the hospital and find out immediately if I was pregnant. The test came out positive.

Oh, no! My heart immediately sank, and I felt as if someone had turned a blade inside my guts.

Donald and I had never spoken of having children. I certainly had not planned to have any with him. My doctor told me where to call in case I wanted an abortion. The clinic was in Omaha, one hour away from Lincoln. They told me I had to wait for about six weeks for the abortion to be effective, so I made an appointment for February 14. The irony of scheduling my abortion on Valentine's Day after my abusive husband had raped me was not lost on me.

I was distraught. I thought about presenting Donald with papers and arranging for a quick divorce, then moving away and secretly giving birth to my child. But as my thoughts flitted to and fro and I attempted to weigh the pros and cons of my decision, I could feel my resolve crumbling. Donald and his family would find me, I was sure. Even if I got divorced and had the baby, I feared they would fix it so I would never be able to see my baby.

The thought of subjecting my child to a father like Donald made me want to vomit. I didn't want my baby to have a father who pushed and held down women. And what if he also hurt my baby? Plus, there was the poster I'd read at a local nonprofit organization with questions to answer for clues that someone might be a pedophile. As I went through the questions, it occurred to me that based on Donald's behavior, the answer was yes.

So that settled it for me. As God was my witness, I would never bring a child into the world if it meant that Donald was in my life.

The day before I was scheduled for an abortion, I decided I would tell Donald, at the very least to alleviate my guilt around keeping a secret...but I was afraid because I had no idea how he'd react. I prayed for guidance and a clear sign. When I got home, Donald wasn't there. How odd. I sat on the side of the bed.

Donald came in, fuming. He had gone to see his brother(the same one who'd unceremoniously pushed his wife off the couch). His wife was newly pregnant and was having terrible morning sickness, and Donald's brother was tired of hearing about it. Talk about empathy!

As Donald told me about the whole situation, he snarled at me, "If *you* ever get pregnant, I never want to hear about it."

He was standing in the bedroom, and my back was to him as I sat on the edge of the bed. Was he going to hit me due to his anger? There was a tense silence. He didn't end up acting on his clear agitation, but his violent response to something that should have been cause for joy was all I needed to know.

The next day, on February 14, I put on my black suit, drove to Omaha, received a necessary blood-type test, and checked in for my abortion appointment. I paid $300 cash. No anesthesia. The doctor inserted a tube and suctioned the sides of my vagina. The cramping was terrible. The doctor accused me during my procedure, "I bet you didn't tell your husband." I didn't answer.

After the procedure, I put my suit back on and sat through a required lecture on birth control. No one asked if my husband had been abusive toward me and if that might have influenced my decision—and I didn't volunteer any information, either. I was afraid they might have to report it and I would be in danger. I dutifully listened to their lecture, then was free to leave.

I went to Mutual of Omaha for a short work appointment; in fact, this had been my alibi for going to Omaha. Donald seemed to always need to know where I was. When I drove back to Lincoln, I felt completely disoriented. I was bleeding from the medical procedure, which was normal and would last up to a few weeks. I also had such continual severe cramping, I called my OB/GYN at home to report my symptoms and see if I needed to go to the ER.

I had been told that I needed to refrain from sex for a time, and while I managed to make excuses that kept Donald at bay, he assumed that my reluctance to sleep with him was yet another sign of my brokenness. It never once occurred to him that his selfishness and abuse were the culprit. When we finally had sex again, the cascade of tears reemerged. Donald snapped at me and turned away in disgust. "You need to get over this!"

Since my friend Barbara was getting a master's in counseling, I asked her for advice. She referred me to a counselor in Omaha, as Lincoln was too small and someone might discover that I had been seeking mental-health advice. In those years, there was a major stigma regarding counseling, as it was believed that people who sought it were "crazy."

I told Donald I wanted to see a counselor to determine whether I was frigid, and if I could do anything about it. Given that this decision directly impacted him, he said OK to my going. I made an appointment and met with my counselor, Ellie, in Omaha. At the first meeting, I told her I couldn't have sex with my husband without tears flowing down my face. Not a sob, or a sound, or a change in my expression—simply a steady stream of tears. I also admitted to her how Donald had held me down and punched me when I said no to sex. As the sordid details came out, I was more and more effusive. I told her about my short-lived affair in Hawaii and burst into tears of shame and sorrow. "I know it was wrong! I just needed to know if I was broken."

Ellie gave me a Kleenex. She listened patiently, without an iota of judgment, and asked more questions. She said matter-of-factly, "You are reacting like a rape victim."

I didn't know what that meant and she didn't explain. Our time was up. My assignment for the next week was to divide a piece of paper into two columns and write out two separate lists. On the left side, I'd include the cons about my relationship with Donald, and on the right side the pros.

When I drove into the garage after that first counseling session, Donald was waiting for me. "Well, are you fixed?" he impatiently demanded, not a trace of kindness or compassion in his voice.

I sighed. "No. She said I need to go back next week. She said...that I was reacting like a rape victim."

He looked perturbed and was clearly caught off guard by this admission. He replied acidly, "I'm sorry I hit you, but I did not rape you." It was the only apology I'd ever received from Donald, and it was still tainted by a lie.

I repeated, "She said I'm reacting like a rape victim," and quickly escaped inside to avoid any further wrath.

The next week, I took out the piece of paper with the two lists I had created. The left side was filled with cons. The right side had only two entries: my mother-in-law, Ava, and my father-in-law.

I appreciated Ava's enthusiastic attitude and zest for life. She was markedly different from her sour-tempered son. She always invited me to go shopping for clothes with her, or to lunch, or some other kind of outing. Like me, she loved flowers, birds, and travel. She was also the only one who ever said anything at the annual stockholder meetings about her disapproval of their business tactics. I don't recall her ever losing her temper or saying a negative thing about others. Contrary to what my sisters-in-law had expressed to me, Ava was always warm and inviting.

My father-in-law, Daniel, was a good host at family dinners in their home. He was much quieter and more reserved than Ava, but he was witty. I also enjoyed talking to him about business. Early in my marriage, one of my IBM accounts was a high-end specialty retail store owned in part by my married family. I told Daniel I felt it was being run into the ground by their president. He was offended by this and gently told me to mind my own business, but soon after, the store closed and all the stockholders lost their investments. After that, he seemed to listen to what I had to say.

Still, this wasn't enough to save a marriage. And Ellie agreed. After one look at my lists, she said, "You don't have a relationship." She directed me to get a divorce, as she was concerned for my safety.

Back at home, I told Donald what Ellie had recommended. He was not happy and immediately put a moratorium on further counseling for me, while repeating the same threats I'd already heard so many times before. As he continued to harangue me, I felt exhausted. At the same time, I knew Ellie was right.

I made an appointment with a divorce attorney. He listened to me before asking if there was anyone else. I didn't understand. "Is there another man in the picture?" he asked.

I quickly said, "Oh, no."

He looked surprised and informed me that at least 80 percent of people who came to him for divorce already had a new lover. (He also advised me to get divorced sooner rather than later, as my growing business would become more valuable—and that could be a problem...which it would absolutely prove to be, as I will share in a later chapter.)

At the time, I was doing a great job never being home, always working, avoiding Donald as best I could. I now used the second-floor bathroom and not the main bathroom adjoined to our bedroom, so I wouldn't be pawed and grabbed. I locked the bathroom door and changed my clothes in there, too. I worked until midnight, hoping that Donald would be asleep when I got home. I woke up before him and left for work before he was up. We didn't eat together. We lived like roommates.

I couldn't imagine that this tacit agreement was acceptable to Donald, so I continued to ask for a divorce. He was impervious to my attempts to reason with him. "We have to stay married...otherwise I'll be seen as a failure!" he insisted.

I was stunned by his response, but not surprised. For Donald, everything was about keeping up appearances. He made no mention of staying married because he loved me. So we discussed staying married but never seeing each other again. Amazingly, he seemed to be fine with that. In fact, his grandparents reportedly had a marriage not unlike this. She lived in San Diego, and he lived in Lincoln. Their excuse to strangers and friends was that she'd gone to California to care for her daughter, who had asthma and preferred the West Coast air. The one thing that few people in Donald's family admitted to was that his grandmother had spent time in California because of alleged abuse.

As tempting as it was to have an arrangement like his grandparents, I knew that was not a genuine marriage. And despite the fact that I didn't love Donald, I liked him enough to stay. We made a conscious decision to stay together as friends but, in retrospect, I believe that was a ploy to keep me off my guard.

Sometimes, I think back on it and contemplate how much easier it could have been to live in a house with a beautiful ocean view purchased for me in San Diego, to never have to work again, and to never have to see him again, all the while benefiting from his family's connections. But today, I recognize that I made the best choice for myself. Throughout the heartache, I learned numerous lessons and learned to stand on my own—and to stand up for myself and learn to create a life on my own terms.

CHAPTER 6

MAKING MY VOICE HEARD

Amid the chaos of my married life, there were major changes I was weathering at IBM. John Opel went from being the president of IBM to its CEO in 1981. My work was greatly impacted by the reorganization, as all employees in Lincoln now fell under the same umbrella instead of being separated into three different divisions. IBM reorganized from three divisions to two divisions. They were called NMD (National Marketing Division) and NAD (National Accounts Division). The Lincoln office was small, so we were all combined into the NMD and considered our own branch office.

The up side: I now had an opportunity to work with the four largest banks and savings & loans in Lincoln, as I was the banking specialist. The down side: I had to sell copiers in addition to computers. And now, Eddy—the former Office Products Division manager and someone I'd never have imagined would end up with authority over me—had become my manager.

I'd missed the kickoff meeting that went into some of these changes in detail, as it was held in January 1982, when I was on my honeymoon. To my surprise, my manager, Twila, was bypassed as the new branch manager. Instead, Eddy, the manager who had lectured me on my *Probe* article, was now the new branch manager and Twila reported to him. Eddy did not like me (or women, it turns out) and helped his former OPD reps at my expense by giving them my accounts that planned to purchase equipment. This reduced my ability to earn commissions and achieve my annual quota. And although I was the banking specialist, I was now no longer allowed to attend banking classes...which led Eddy to deny me the four big banks due to my lack of training. To add insult to injury, the former

OPD(Office Products Division) rep who was given my banks had zero training.

Eddy seemed to be blatantly and purposely damaging my career, simply because he didn't like me. I knew he made disparaging remarks to other employees about me behind my back. If he had done this about our competition, according to our sales manual, he could have been fired. But as far as I knew, Eddy's reprehensible behavior was not called into question, and nobody stood up for me.

**

We had our first joint sales meeting after IBM's reorganization. I had cut out an article from the morning paper about an upcoming school bid. Most, if not all, public entities were required to solicit bids for their products to ensure a fair process. My colleague Oliver was the marketing rep for all the schools. As such, he needed to be aware of all the schools and when they were soliciting for bids. I read the paper each morning looking for leads, and when I saw the article, I immediately cut it out and took it to work, naively giving it to Oliver (who thanked me profusely, as he had not seen the article) instead of presenting it at the meeting.

At the meeting, Oliver waved the article I had given him and said, "Look what I cut out of the paper this morning!"

Eddy praised him effusively. "See, this is what we need, more initiative like Oliver's." Oliver beamed as I sat in stunned silence waiting for him to say, "Karen gave it to me," but he never did.

I could have said "Thanks, Eddy, I brought that to Oliver just before the meeting," but I chose not to. At that moment, I felt sorry for Oliver. I was 26 and he had to be 50. He was not one of Eddy's favorite employees, and many of my colleagues made fun of him. In addition, I didn't know how to call out Oliver's faux pas without appearing aggressive. Our training hadn't taught us what to do when colleagues or managers appropriated our ideas or screwed us over.

My colleague Emma was a former OPD rep, and we were now

both in the same division—so for the first time, I had another female coworker in sales. We became friends and I enjoyed coming to work. It made such a huge difference to have another woman in the same position! When Emma's husband was promoted to a job in Phoenix, much to my sadness, she quit and moved away. She tried to transfer with IBM but was told by Eddy they didn't have a job for her in Phoenix.

As it was, it felt that no matter what my accomplishments may have been, Eddy was continuing to sabotage my opportunities. At the beginning of each year, sales reps were assigned a new annual sales quota and asked to submit a forecast on which customers were planning to purchase new or upgraded computers. I still had my six smaller banks, all in small towns in Nebraska, and two of them were planning to purchase a computer in 1982. I turned in my forecast, and soon after, Eddy went over Twila's head and gave my two best banks to one of his former OPD reps, Adam. I was shocked. Adam didn't have any bank or computer training. I, on the other hand, had been working with these banks since 1979. Adam had not even bothered to visit the banks.

Beatrix, the IBM customer engineer for the banks, asked me to configure the correct computer for one of the banks to purchase. I did the configuration, and she drove the contract out to the bank and brought back the signed contract. But who ended up receiving credit for the sale? Oliver. It was a large sale and put him over 100 percent of the quota, while I received nothing.

One of the former OPD reps came over to talk to me and asked if I was upset that Oliver had received credit for my former account when I had done all the work. I told him I was happy for Oliver, which I was. After all, it wasn't Oliver's fault Eddy had been working against me.

The former OPD rep studied me closely and commented in astonishment, "You really *are* happy."

I said, "Yes, aren't you?"

He shook his head and made a sour face. "No, it means the rest of us have to work harder."

I was taken aback by his candor, as well as the total lack of camaraderie. I had always assumed we were all on the same team, cooperating with each other for the good of IBM. I am still struck by how none of my coworkers stood up for me when they saw injustices, and how easily Oliver took credit at my expense.

Even so, although I didn't feel very appreciated at work, I was continuing to make strides out in the world. One of my favorite experiences occurred with a medical-supply distributor. Harvey, the data-processing manager, was trying to convince the company to purchase a new IBM System/38 from me. The first time I visited the president, he told me flat out, "I don't like IBM, and I don't like working with women."

I wasn't deterred. I simply smiled and kept coming back, and eventually, they bought the computer. I asked him if I could bring my manager over to meet him and he said yes. When I told him her name was Twila, he exclaimed, "Another woman!"

Over the years, he purchased from me, gave me business advice, and even invited me to fly with him and his employee in their private plane to a customer call in South Dakota when he rented projection equipment from me. I eventually met his wife at a networking event, and she told me I was the first woman in business he respected, and that my role and attitude had opened his eyes. Before he met me, he wouldn't even let his wife get a job, and he thought women were only good as secretaries or clerical workers. After meeting me, however, he was apparently so impressed that he let his wife go to work. She was a bank officer when I met her. She said, "You are the only reason I have a job." It was one of the proudest moments I can recall.

**

In time, my manager Twila was promoted, and a man named

Spencer was hired to replace her. Eddy told me he was a banking expert from New York and was going to help me. During my first meeting with Spencer, he said, "I hear you are a troublemaker. I'm not going to let you ruin my career."

I was surprised by the hostility and force of his statement. "I'm not sure what you're talking about," I said, remaining calm. "Who told you this?"

Spencer informed me that Eddy had filled him in. This was the first time I learned about my reputation as a so-called troublemaker, but Spencer couldn't give me any details beyond the hearsay.

Because Spencer was purportedly there to help me, he told me to take him to one of my small banks. I drove with him an hour and a half to a small bank customer who already had an IBM computer. Spencer asked for a tour, and the bank president took us to the operations area where a check sorter was sorting checks. The checks were fed in automatically, read, and deposited to the proper pockets for further processing.

Unbelievably, Spencer asked, "What is that machine?" I thought he must be kidding. He wasn't.

The bank president replied, "It's a check sorter."

Spencer looked impressed and asked, "What does it do?"

The bank president looked at him like he was an idiot and replied, "It sorts checks."

The president would later call me and say, "Don't ever bring him back here. If you do, I will never buy from IBM again."

Clearly, Spencer was not viewed favorably by this client, as he was a self-described "banking expert" who didn't know the first thing about banks. He'd also been arrogant during the client visit, interrogating the president about his bank and what they were willing to purchase from us. He clearly didn't care about him as a person, and he made it clear that his sole purpose was to land a purchase.

Despite the fact that I knew I was an asset to IBM when it came to establishing rapport with clients, Eddy attempted to block my success.

One of my clients was a trucking firm I had worked with for years. They were about to purchase a very large computer from me, the System\38. Days before they signed the contract, Eddy called me into his office to inform me that my client didn't want to work with me anymore, so he was giving my account to another former OPD rep.

"Frank doesn't think you understand lease versus purchase," Eddy said, as if to explain the matter was no longer in his hands.

I raised an eyebrow. "Did you tell him I managed the lease/purchase program for IBM keypunch machines in 1979?" I asked.

"No."

"Did you tell him I have a degree in finance?"

"No."

"Is it OK if I go out and talk to Frank to find out why he doesn't want to work with me?" I asked.

Casually dismissive, Eddy laced his fingers behind his head. "Go ahead," he responded.

I went to see Frank. "I understand you have a problem working with me," I said.

"*What*? What are you talking about? I love working with you. Where would you get an idea like that?" asked a bewildered Frank.

"My manager just told me he was taking your account from me because you don't like working with me," I explained. I was happy that Frank felt the way he did, but livid at Eddy for attempting to steal one of my accounts on the basis of a blatant, underhanded lie.

I returned to Eddy and told him Frank wanted to work with me.

"OK," said Eddy.

End of discussion. No apology. Eddy looked up at the ceiling, not at me.

**

By this time, we had a new Omaha branch manager, Robert, to whom Eddy reported. I was so miserable at work due to Eddy's efforts to undermine me that I thought if I used the IBM open-door policy and told the upper management about my experiences, they would fix what was broken in the Lincoln office.

I had been talking to IBM employees throughout the U.S. and some in my office who told me they were not getting raises but were afraid to ask out of fear of retaliation. Some women told me they were hired as "professional hires," only to find out they were paid the lower college-grad starting salary, while the men in their office who were also "professional hires" were being paid the correct higher salary. I went up the ladder for myself as well as them. When I got to the regional manager, he asked me if there were any sexual jokes being told at our sales meetings. I said yes. He asked me to repeat some, which I did. He asked me what my managers were doing about it. I told him they were either telling the jokes or laughing along. He acted concerned, but nothing was done.

I lodged my wage complaints at every level up to Frank Cary, who was Chairman of the Board. At every level, the manager was a white man who came back and said I was the problem. They had no rationale and, when I asked for specifics, one held up a glass of water and said, "I bet you would say this class of water is half empty." Not once did they address my legitimate complaints about the wage disparities between female and male employees. It seemed to me that they had chosen to take Eddy's side on principle. They even had the gall to tell me that since Twila, a woman, had been my manager, it was impossible for me to be discriminated against. In retrospect, it reminds me a great deal of the struggles that women and people of color experience when lodging similar complaints; they are told that their mere presence in their organization invalidates any claims of discrimination—something many of us know, through documentation and common sense, is simply not true.

I knew that I could not simply take this treatment. I felt a grave sense of responsibility for other people in the same shoes as me who might be under duress but felt there was no avenue to recourse. So I contacted an attorney. I told her about my IBM experience and asked if she thought it was discrimination. She said yes and recommended I speak to the Nebraska Human Rights Commission.

I visited them in person in their Lincoln office on my lunch hour. Their representative listened to my experience and confirmed it was discrimination but, before I could sue IBM, I was required to undergo an Equal Employment Opportunity Commission (EEOC) investigation; if warranted, the EEOC had authority to grant me permission to sue IBM. I filed a complaint and went through an EEOC investigation while I was still employed at IBM. I was 26 years old. My investigation started with the Lincoln office of the Nebraska Human Rights Commission, but soon I received a call from them telling me my case was a very important case—too important to be handled by the Lincoln office. My case was elevated from Lincoln to the larger EEOC office in Denver, Colorado.

After the EEOC investigation was launched, my manager, Spencer, made me meet him in his office every morning at 8 a.m., tell him my itinerary for the day, and come back at 5 p.m. and review everything I did all day. I was never given a reason but it was clear this was IBM's attempt to punish me for taking my qualms to a higher authority. This clearly violated the "non-retaliation" clause of the EEOC regulations.

I was the only sales rep required to report to Spencer like this, even though I had seniority compared to others. Spencer would sit on his desk, his head above mine, about two feet from me. It was unpleasant and intimidating. Sometimes he would stand up, walk to the side wall, and punch it, eyes flashing. Spencer's temper was highly unprofessional but, again, despite the complaints I had lodged about his abusive behavior, nothing had been done to address it. In fact, it seemed the EEOC investigation had only fanned the flames of Spencer's anger and disdain.

I was also shut out by my formerly friendly coworkers. No one would speak to me if a manager was around. None of them gave me an explanation, but it was as if my EEOC investigation had turned me into a pariah overnight. Instead of offering me support and solace, everyone kept their heads down. They seemed to want to avoid guilt by association.

One evening after Spencer had grilled me during our 5 p.m. debrief, one of the systems engineers I had worked with for years whispered conspiratorially in my ear before scurrying off: "Don't let them get to you. They're doing it on purpose." I was more chagrined than comforted; all the while, as he was talking to me, he was scoping out the scene as if to ensure that nobody would see him. I couldn't help but wonder: *What might be possible if we all stood up for each other?*

**

The EEOC investigation of IBM that was launched in 1983 included my complaints of sexual harassment, sexual discrimination, and wage discrimination. Before the EEOC Denver office assigned an investigator to my case, I had planned to quit IBM and do something else altogether, as I knew the situation was not sustainable. Aside from the stress of dealing with Donald at home, the workplace that had once been a refuge for me was quickly transforming into yet another den of abuse. However, my investigator burst my bubble. According to her, I needed to stay employed, as the EEOC could do nothing for me if I quit.

I had to travel to Denver at my own expense and take vacation time to participate in a hearing. I was not allowed to bring an attorney. The EEOC investigator told me that when Ronald Reagan became president, he'd stripped all the authority the EEOC had previously enjoyed. The EEOC could listen and make suggestions, but they could not coerce a settlement. The employee bringing the investigation was not allowed legal counsel, but the employer was.

The employee was required to go through an EEOC investigation before being allowed to sue a company, and the employee needed permission from the EEOC in order to be able to sue a company.

The EEOC investigator met me and brought me to a conference room with a large oval-shaped table. I sat alone at one end of the table. At the other end of the table were the Lincoln branch manager, Eddy; my manager, Spencer; and three white male IBM attorneys. The investigator sat at the side of the table between both parties. She asked me to share my experience of working at IBM in detail, so I did. I talked about how I was denied raises for doing the same job as my male colleagues and receiving higher ratings than them, denied bank training, and then denied the banks due to "lack of training"—although the men with no training at all were given my accounts shortly before the customer was ready to purchase, thereby negatively affecting my performance.

I shared that my desire was to be treated fairly and respectfully, to be granted permission to attend bank training classes, and to be given the four large banks and all the other banks. I also wanted to receive fair compensation. No more, and no less.

The investigator then told me to leave the room and wait while she talked to IBM alone.

I sat in the hall. It all seemed very unfair. IBM got to hear everything I had to say, but I was not allowed to sit in on their response. I already knew that the EEOC process favored employers. Most employees would never be able to pay their way to Denver, take time off from work, and risk their job to stand up for their rights. The system was stacked in favor of employers who discriminated against their workers. As I sat there, I felt defeated. How could IBM's wrongs ever be righted? How could we have a "fair" society when the rules were so stacked against some but not others?

She called me back in and told me the EEOC was recommending that IBM assign me all four of the large banks and send me to the bank training my managers had canceled for me. I was relieved, and I could see that the managers at the table were chagrined at the recommendations, although they kept their mouths shut about it.

When I got home to Lincoln, my IBM managers gave me only one of the big banks and no training. I was disappointed, but I couldn't say that I was surprised. I knew from their cavalier dismissal of my concerns that I was not a priority, and that my audacity in complaining had further incensed them. It felt like they were giving me a giant middle finger and affirming that, at the end of the day, there really was a glass ceiling at IBM that I would not ultimately be able to break. It was clear that they didn't care. Moreover, I continued to be iced out by my coworkers. But while I remained an outcast in my workplace, the quota board in the bullpen still had me as the top sales rep at our branch. The disparity between my accomplishments and IBM's treatment of me was glaring.

The EEOC investigator called me while I was still at IBM. "I'm so sorry, Karen, but your management is never going to treat you well. If you stay at IBM, I have a feeling that you'll continue to face discrimination. I think your only remedy is court. It's time to sue."

Her pronouncement made my heart sink. Although I'd received permission from the EEOC to sue, I was not a litigious person and didn't want to do this. I simply wanted them to pay women equally, promote women, and confirm that all women were being paid within the proper salary grids—period. I also wanted IBM to prohibit sexual harassment in the offices. Based on our lofty ideals, I didn't understand why they were violating civil-rights laws and why they didn't agree to abide by their own stated policies.

However, I knew in my heart that I had to sue. Women who worked at IBM throughout the country were too afraid to speak up. I was already planning my next adventure of owning a computer-supply company, so I would be quitting anyway, and I was finally in a position to sue IBM. Plus, my attorneys were so excited to take on IBM, they told me they would take my case on a contingency.

According to them, my managers' violations were so blatant, it was a cut-and-dried legal case.

I walked into Spencer's office and gave him my resignation letter on August 20, 1984. He was silent and barely even acknowledged my presence. I told him I was quitting and that I would be suing IBM. Brian, the systems-engineering manager, told me I could leave immediately and would receive a two-week severance check. I told him I would stay for two weeks and call all my customers to say thank you and goodbye—and if he knew which sales rep would replace me, I would introduce them.

Every day for two weeks, I phoned my customers, thanked them, and told them I was leaving. The first question they asked was, "Where are you going?" The second question was, "Who is replacing you?" IBM never did figure out who would replace me during my last two weeks. Even up to a year later, many of my former customers hadn't heard from IBM.

After the two weeks were over, I walked out of IBM and sued them on October 2, 1984. I was 27 years old. It didn't feel like an especially triumphant moment for me. I was incredibly sad—sad for IBM that they had lost a great employee and limited their own greatness, and sad that the men who discriminated against women were free to continue their illegal behavior, unchecked.

My attorney, Susan, recommended we team up with Thom Cope, a labor lawyer also located in Lincoln. They subpoenaed the employee evaluations in the IBM Lincoln and Omaha offices, as well as other documents. I read through the evaluations and marveled at how all the female evaluations were negative, whereas all the male evaluations were glowing.

Finally, on May 7, 1985, the IBM attorneys came to Lincoln to take my deposition. They scheduled it over three days. IBM would be evaluating how credible a witness I would be on the stand at trial. I was told by my attorneys to answer questions but not to elaborate.

Back in 1985, the laws didn't allow for any damages, only what a person would be paid had they not been discriminated against. But what I was demanding could not have been settled in court. If I wanted to change a system for the better, I needed to acquire it in a settlement. I was intent on changing a system and creating equal pay at IBM across the United States. If I went to court, all I would get was whatever the court decided I would have been paid had I not been discriminated against. But if IBM would agree to my demands, more people would benefit and IBM would be a better company.

On the day of my deposition, I wore a black suit, white blouse, and red scarf around my neck—the perfect IBM uniform. I was calm, credible, professional, sincere, and articulate. I was 28 years old.

Susan and Thom sat beside me. Across the table were two attorneys from IBM—a man and a woman. As I spoke, the man asked questions, and the woman sat silently. We broke for lunch. I saw IBM's woman lawyer in the bathroom. I asked her if she liked her job and attempted to make small talk by asking her a series of questions about herself. She was not receptive.

All afternoon, the male IBM attorney questioned me. After one break, I walked in on my attorneys telling IBM they had a tee time for all of them to golf together. I immediately asked where and when, as I wanted to be there, too. My attorneys explained that I wasn't invited. I have since learned it's very important for your attorney to get along with the opposite side's attorney, because then they can come up with a workable solution. If they butt heads, they come to an impasse and everyone loses as the case drags on and on and costs the client more and more money.

After the first day of depositions, Thom called me into his office; he was clearly ecstatic. He showed me a settlement in disbelief. "This is incredible!" he said.

I looked it over, laughed out loud, signed it, and practically floated out of his office to my car.

I have since learned that the IBM lawsuit is considered a

significant case to this day. Coincidentally, my divorce attorney shared with me that his first job after law school was with IBM's legal department at IBM Headquarters in Armonk, New York. He told me their job was to settle all lawsuits and not go to trial, in order to avoid public awareness of their problem with discrimination. "The entire legal community knows IBM has a problem with discrimination," he told me.

To this day, I don't know if IBM fulfilled the promises it made me around making the workplace a fair and equitable one. When I visited IBM Lincoln after my settlement, I was happy to see a woman branch manager, so it made me think they were following through. Apparently, Eddy got sidelined and was demoted to being a marketing rep in Omaha but was not fired. Later, he complained to one of my clients, "Karen ruined my career." I smiled in amusement, "He ruined his own career," and my client agreed wholeheartedly.

Years later I met a woman who had been a marketing rep at IBM Lincoln for 16 years. I didn't tell her I had sued IBM, but I did ask if she would share her experiences. She informed me that she'd had many managers who'd climbed the ladder. They were all white men. She also shared a few other disturbing things, which made me realize IBM likely had not made good on their promises to do better.

Sadly, despite close to five decades of increased awareness when it comes to race, gender, and sexual orientation, it's clear that companies like IBM require pressure from the outside in order to truly change.

CHAPTER 7

MOVING ON TO A NEW ENDEAVOR

Throughout the ordeal with IBM, I was already in the process of growing my computer-supply company, Data Source Media.

Data Source Media was my first company of several. It was my baby, and my employees were like my children. I knew from experience that I had a God-given talent to see the big picture, and to develop and execute a plan for success. Many times, I was the only one around me who could see the bird's-eye view, but I forged ahead, anyway. My company grew and afforded me many awards and great happiness. I so dearly loved Data Source Media that when I lost it to a messy divorce, the grief I felt was overwhelming. This is my story.

**

In August 1984 when I was 27 and still reluctantly married to Donald, I resigned from IBM to become president and majority stockholder of a fledgling computer-supply company, Data Source Media (DSM), originally founded by Evan Moffit in his basement in 1973. Unfortunately, because Donald became involved in the transition of DSM from Ev to me, nothing about my leadership was as straightforward as it could have been.

While I was still working at IBM, I met Ev at a time when he was offering to sell his one-third interest in a company called Regal Ribbon, located in Omaha. I met the other owners and toured their operation. They were "re-inking" ribbons, a practice frowned upon by IBM. Open vats of printer ink littered the tiny industrial warehouse space. The concrete floors were stained with black ink. Workers took apart the plastic cases of used ribbons, unspooled and hand-dipped the already-used ones, sent nylon into the vats of ink, and replaced the dripping nylon in the original plastic cases so the ribbons could be used again. The smell of ink was overpowering.

I enjoyed seeing their operation and listening to their tales of how they could sell these used ribbons and make more money than they had on a brand-new ribbon, but I had no interest in buying into this business. I was open to better possibilities. As I got to know Ev more, I learned about the computer-supply company he'd started in his basement.

At this time, the IBM personal computer was announced, and independent computer stores were popping up all over the country. One of my customers had asked me if I might consider being the store manager of a Valcom he was planning to open. There were 27 computer stores in Lincoln and no one specializing in computer supplies. I told Ev I was interested in buying his computer supply company. I was ready to quit IBM immediately but, when the EEOC told me I had to stay at IBM to complete the investigation, I stayed—and Ev held DSM for me.

Donald, my husband, offered to work with Ev until I could quit IBM, as I didn't want IBM to say I had a conflict of interest since DSM sold computer supplies and IBM did, too. The plan was for Donald to quit DSM after I got there, and then go do something else. He incorporated DSM (Ev only had DSM as a sole proprietor) with Ev owning a third and Donald two-thirds. As the plan went, when I arrived, I would own 100 percent, Ev would retire, and Donald would be gone.

When I quit IBM and came to DSM in September 1984, Ev left. Given Donald's deceptive nature, he only wanted to sell me 51 percent stock and keep 49 percent for himself. He also wanted to remain the president of the company.

I was angry at myself for not realizing that Donald would pull something like this. Since I didn't have an agreement with him in writing beforehand, I felt I didn't have a choice but to succumb to at least some of his wishes. He already owned 100 percent and didn't have to sell anything. He didn't even have to resign as president. I had quit my job at IBM and stupidly taken Donald at his word, which I should have known wasn't any good, but I would fall for it many times over before my time with him was kaput. It didn't occur to me that I wouldn't be able to afford to buy the other 49 percent or even need to if I got divorced. At this point, I was still resigned to staying married. (This entire experience preceded my traumatic trip to Thailand. It was only then, a few months later, that I would determine I could not stay married.)

"What's the big deal?" Donald asked when I balked at his request to be president of DSM. "It's just a title." I told him I would quit and open my own company, at which point he relented to being the vice president.

Despite the fact that Donald had not kept his word and insisted on being a co-owner of the company, I focused on my ultimate goal: creating a computer-supply company with the best customer service and highest-quality products, and having the largest market share in the Midwest.

I went from selling $200,000 computers to $3 ribbons, but I had grit and a plan—and I had full confidence in my abilities.

**

When I walked into the DSM office after finally quitting IBM, Ev was waiting for me. My sister, Linda, was already working there as the office manager. Ev was in the only office, which had a window overlooking the front parking lot. The office space was 1,000 square feet and was part of a long one-story building that housed several other businesses.

I took a look around as Ev put on his hat, gave me a hug, and said, "It's all yours now, kid," as he wished me the best and left for home. He had no idea that Donald had lied to both of us and schemed his way into co-owning the company Ev had held for me.

My first task was to assess the situation at hand in the workplace. Donald didn't do much of anything but read the paper and talk on the phone. He had a phobia about calling people, so he made no phone calls and didn't like to answer the phone, either. In frustration, I asked Donald, "What do you actually do?" He snapped back at me, "I think." He was inept and seemingly clueless as to how to run, grow, and manage a business.

My sister was extremely helpful, though. Linda was answering multiple phone lines, taking and filling orders, researching products, running inventory, and doing all the bookkeeping and office management. She had already mastered the Great Plains accounting software. We had about two invoices a day from present customers. We used an IBM PC, which I had purchased while still at IBM. It cost $5,000 and had a 10-Megabyte hard drive—impressive at the time.

We were selling enough to cover rent and Linda's salary. I paid myself $200 a month to start, thinking I would increase my own salary as I grew the business. When I started on September 4, 1984, we were not profitable—but by year end, 1984 sales were $271,000.

I knew that if I took care of my customers, success would follow. My goal was to purchase enough product directly from manufacturers so I could get the best prices possible in the U.S. to enable me to compete with any computer-supply company from larger market areas, such as New York City or Los Angeles. We were buying direct from Verbatim, the largest diskette supplier; if we purchased enough, we would get a better price and could in turn pass that price on to our customers. Since our market in Lincoln was very small compared to another dealer in a larger city, it was important for DSM to be the largest computer-supply company in our area. Thus, I went to every computer store in Lincoln and asked them if they were willing to purchase supplies from me. They were. They would then sell those products directly to their customers, who were also called end users.

I could sell a box of Verbatim diskettes to one of my customers for $70, and the computer store could also sell the same product to their customer for $70. They could buy from a wholesale company that carried Verbatim, or they could buy the same product from me at a 10% markup and take advantage of immediate local delivery.

Overall, I became very good at judging my business dealings. I didn't learn until years later to apply this same kind of judgment to my personal relationships. My vision was to work with my customers for the long term and build lasting relationships. In all my years at DSM, I only recall writing off $1,200 in bad accounts receivable.

My first month was spent calling all the people and companies I knew, telling them about my business, and asking if they would consider buying ribbons from me. I had an unlimited territory and could call on anyone and everyone. I kept a daily log of my phone calls and visits. I averaged 50 to 100 phone calls a day in the office, and 10 to 15 calls a day when I went visiting customers. At night, I wrote custom price quotes and stayed at work until I completed all customer and prospect paperwork. My typical day started at 8 a.m. and went until 10 p.m. I sometimes went to networking events and returned to my office afterwards.

Many of my customers gave me a chance, and my company steadily grew. One of my contacts at a large bank told me she was already happy with her computer-supply company, but that she would buy any new supplies from me. As most companies already had a supplier, I asked them if they would consider me as a backup source. Many times, their original supplier would mess up an order and DSM would cheerfully help them out.

My former IBM customers were especially supportive, and since I knew what printers they had, it was easy for them to order ribbons. Julie a plumbing-supply company, would call and say, "Karen, I need a ribbon for my big printer." Linda would get everything ready for delivery. It was fun to see how excited everyone was to get their ribbons.

Joseph was the Verbatim manufacturer representative for our area. He lived in Minneapolis and traveled to Lincoln on occasion. Verbatim manufactured high-quality products and specialized in diskettes and other computer-data tapes used for storage of computer information. Joseph needed to be sure we were taking care of our own customers and fairly representing Verbatim, so we went on many joint sales calls to visit potential clients. My IBM sales training was invaluable, but Joseph helped me understand that I needed to show why anyone should work with me and DSM versus another supply company. IBM needed no introduction, but DSM did.

We were the only Verbatim dealer in Nebraska, which meant we had to sell enough of their products to justify remaining the only Verbatim dealer in Nebraska. The goal of the manufacturers was to have a trusted relationship with a dealer who would provide service and sales for their products. The manufacturers had a suggested retail price, but dealers were free to deviate. Because of the service needed, most dealers focused on their own local markets and did not encroach on or poach in another dealer's area.

There was another Verbatim dealer who covered Iowa. Unfortunately, before I started at DSM, the Iowa Verbatim dealer lodged a complaint against DSM due to an extremely low bid we made on diskettes to the Iowa public schools. DSM had bid only 2 cents over cost and won the bid from the Iowa dealer—who had cultivated, cared for, and serviced this account in the past. He was understandably upset. A dealer must make enough profit in order to sustain their business over time.

Verbatim had a co-op advertising program to help DSM get our name and services known. A small percentage of what we purchased from Verbatim was set aside for us to spend on approved advertising. In short order, I created a catalog to give to customers and prospects, signed up to display at computer trade shows in Lincoln and Omaha, created direct-mail flyers, and purchased radio and billboard ads and even some TV spots. I also joined the Lincoln Independent Business Association and the Lincoln Chamber of Commerce, and I became a founding member of the National Association of Women Business Owners (NAWBO).

At some point, I turned my attention to IBM brand computer supplies. Many of my customers had IBM printers. They had a choice to purchase IBM supplies directly from the IBM Supplies Division, or they could purchase IBM supplies from me. Unfortunately, IBM did not sell supplies to dealers like me. My only choice was to buy from an authorized IBM wholesaler at a marked-up price. It was hard for me to compete for large contracts due to the extra markup. The other choice was for customers to purchase non-IBM ribbons, known as compatible ribbons. The compatible ribbons were less expensive and usually of inferior quality. Some customers were trying to save even more money by buying the "re-inked" ribbons from places like Regal Ribbon in Omaha. We could also purchase wholesale from Regal Ribbon, but it was difficult to compete due to the markup.

Then, a wonderful thing happened for computer-supply dealers across the United States. IBM announced it was discontinuing selling supplies directly to business consumers, and was instead setting up authorized IBM supplies dealers across the country. I called IBM, and the IBM Supplies sales rep came to visit me in my office. When he saw how well we were doing and learned I had worked at IBM and gone through IBM's sales training, he helped me become an IBM Authorized Supplies Dealer for Nebraska and Iowa. The sales rep provided me with a list of all the large data centers that purchased IBM supplies in the two states, and that list included the products they purchased. Very quickly, all of that business was converted to DSM.

All this happened in the first year I was at DSM and transformed it from a fledgling company to a profitable one. Sales in 1984 were $270,000, with three employees. Sales in 1985 were $751,000, with three employees and one part-time employee. I was honored to be listed in the *Lincoln Sun* newspaper as a "person to watch." Without a doubt, DSM's star was on the rise.

**

In May of 1986, using what I learned from my IBM training, DSM bought Anderson Data of Omaha in June and added more salespeople to our staff. We sent announcement letters to all of our customers. Anderson Data made about $20,000 to $30,000 a month in sales, and by this time, had zero employees and an old Digital Electronics Corporation (DEC) computer. DEC was one of IBM's brand competitors and had a completely different operating system and programs that didn't seem to work well and that also produced inaccurate reports.

Before DSM bought Anderson Data, Donald had invested $75,000 of our money in partnership. Unbeknownst to me, he neglected to name me as a stockholder. While I made $72,000 in profit at DSM, he lost $60,000 at Anderson Data. I was upset and experienced it as yet another betrayal of my trust. I was resentful that I had worked my tail off to earn $72,000, and his incompetence was costing us $60,000. The female President of Anderson Data was making a large salary despite her lack of sales and profits, while I was making $200 a month to ensure that DSM could stay afloat. My rationalization for Donald's stupidity was that at least DSM was my company—I never dreamed I might someday lose it.

My goal was to retain at least $10,000 a month of sales out of Anderson Data's current $20,000 to $30,000. From my experience, whenever a salesperson leaves, for whatever reason, about half the customers go elsewhere for supplies. The key is to reach out to every customer within two weeks and gain their trust. If this is done immediately and sincerely, the percentage of customer retention increases.

I continued to network with other businesses to do what I did best: make my company shine. In May of 1986, two representatives from 3M, Doug, the manager and Craig, the sales rep, invited me to their dealer council weekend at 3M's exclusive rustic resort, Wonewok. This event was for the top 30 U.S. dealers. There was another woman business owner from Dallas. The rest were all men.

Wonewok had a main lodge and smaller cabins. The woman from Dallas and I stayed in the main lodge. We enjoyed great dinners, meetings by day, poker by night, cigars, skeet shooting, fishing, golfing, and ping pong.

At dinner one day, one of the dealers blurted out in front of everyone, "You're really smart for how pretty you are." The other dealers sat in stunned silence.

I shot back acerbically, "You're as dumb as you look." Everyone laughed.

At the final dinner, which was also an awards night, 3M gave me a humorous plaque labeled *Worst Cards*, in honor of winning the most at poker during the week. It was a memorable trip, and one in which my characteristic humor transformed what might have been an awkward occasion into one where I knew without a doubt I belonged.

**

Throughout my journey with DSM, I was eager to continue to learn how I could improve my leadership skills. In the Fall of 1985, I applied for and was accepted to the first class of Leadership Lincoln, which is part of a similar network of programs throughout the nation that are focused on developing community leaders.

The purpose was for future leaders to learn from current leaders. There were about 30 students selected from business, government, and nonprofits. We met for one entire business day each month. We toured various businesses and learned many aspects of business, government, and nonprofits. The first big event was a weekend retreat. We were required to stay overnight and were assigned to a roommate in a different field. Mine was an experienced government worker. She taught me invaluable information about the inefficiencies of government agencies. She told me that most agencies operated on a fiscal year from October 1 through September 30, and each department had a budget for the year. If they hadn't spent the money by the end of the fiscal year, they lost the excess money and their budget was slashed for the upcoming year. These practices caused the departments to spend everything they could at year end (many times, on items they didn't need or couldn't use) so they could get the same amount the next year. I was shocked at how inefficient these processes were, and so different from my own, as I always spent within a budget and was elated to spend less and get the same results. According to this government worker, there was no incentive to improve departments or save money, as rocking the boat could get one fired (something I was well aware of in the private sector).

At one meeting held at a bank with current business leaders, one of my classmates spoke about the need for reliable childcare for employees to excel in their careers. One current business leader leaned toward his friend and quipped, loudly enough for all to hear, "Isn't that what wives are for?"

Another man I was speaking to seemed genuinely shocked I went to work each day. He asked in disbelief, "You go into the office?"

I responded, "Yes, I go in every single day to run my company." He was bewildered and had nothing else to say.

Although it was a relatively diverse place for somewhere like Lincoln, I was accustomed to idiotic and ignorant remarks like these. At the first meeting, one young man was overheard as he said, "I don't like how many skirts are in our class."

That shocking comment gave us all an opportunity to discuss gender issues with perspective and grace. The facilitator repeated the man's comments for the class to hear and said they were hurtful, unacceptable, and inappropriate—and moreover, women and men needed to work together with mutual respect.

I don't think the young man ever got it, but at least it was openly addressed. His comments put a chill on the whole premise of being community leaders and working for the good of the community, but it also made many of us more determined than ever to battle against stereotypes and prejudice—and to prove our opponents wrong.

**

As DSM grew, we doubled our space to 2,000 square feet, and we added more office staff in Lincoln and Omaha. Meanwhile, the original Omaha company I had looked at buying from Ev, Regal Ribbon, was quickly going out of business and their Omaha sales rep, Herbert, asked if he could work for me. Another employee of Regal Ribbon, approached me to purchase his Regal Ribbon customer list. I said no, as I already called on most of the same companies in Lincoln and Omaha.

Herbert, the Omaha rep, wanted to be paid a salary for three months, then go on straight commission. He was sued by Regal Ribbon over a non-compete clause, but the judge threw it out due to "no consideration." DSM did not have non-compete clauses. I thought people should be free to work where they desired rather than getting locked into non-competes. My most important priority was for DSM employees to take good care of customers and never disparage competition.

I was still selling by day and doing paperwork by night. Every month, I scoured all the computer reports to get a feel for what was happening in the business. I read through the customer sales-analysis reports to make sure we were retaining current customers and adding new ones. I made sure our accounts receivable were collected on a timely basis, our accounts payable paid on time, and our inventory balanced so we didn't waste money on old inventory.

At some point, my 3M rep, Craig, was promoted and replaced by another rep, Sam. No rep could measure up to Craig. The contrast between Craig and Sam was significant. Craig was well-groomed, respectful, courteous, and professional. Sam reminded me of a leprechaun in his looks. He had a crooked smile and wore a constantly rumpled suit. He was friendly but seemed to be the type to do the least possible to get the job done. He was clearly misplaced in his role.

Sam asked me to open an office in Des Moines, Iowa, in mid-1986. At the time, 3M did not have a strong presence or 3M dealer in that market, and Sam needed to make his quota with the company. It was a good opportunity, especially with him telling his clients to work with us and taking time to personally introduce me to the buyers of large Des Moines companies. Sam seemed to be well liked by the buyers he introduced me to. For my market research, I started with the Des Moines Chamber of Commerce and looked at existing competition and potential office space. I visited 50 potential customers in Des Moines, such as Greyhound Lines, Inc., and asked them if they were satisfied with their computer-supply dealer. I told them I'd like to open a Des Moines office, and if I did, asked if they'd consider purchasing from me. Almost all of them said yes. When I opened, I already had nearly 50 clients who had already committed to working with me.

I did the same in Davenport, Iowa. I was stretched very thin, driving to Davenport, Des Moines, and Omaha, and basing myself out of Lincoln.

I filled out a company survey for 3M, where I had to note who was doing the different jobs at DSM. I filled my name in for President, CEO, CFO, Sales Manager, Salesperson, and Operations. It was obvious I was doing too much.

I was also president of the Lincoln Data Processing Managers Association chapter. Every month, we had a board meeting and a general meeting. The general meetings stipulated that no soliciting of business was allowed. It was OK to meet people and later work with them, but not at these meetings. I took one of my employees to one of the meetings after instructing him in the art of proper networking, and I told him that soliciting was not allowed. He ignored my instructions and immediately started soliciting business. He was not invited back.

The insubordination displayed would have been grounds for firing, but unfortunately, this person was my husband. He seemed to enjoy purposely breaking socially acceptable norms and loved being the thorn in my side rather than offering help. He told me he would find something else to do, but he never did. He'd already been fired by his uncle Lyle from one of the family companies and was still very bitter when his mom refused to call Uncle Lyle to get his job back. It seemed that Donald was perpetually attempting to take DSM down, and by now, I knew that something had to give.

**

My partnership with 3M had become challenging, in that it was clear that Sam was not a person to be trusted.

The first time I met him, he took me and Donald out to dinner. It was customary in those days for vendors to take their customers to lunch or dinner; as a result, he and I had dinner several times. After I got to know him better, he confided in me that he routinely had affairs. I asked him if his wife knew, and he said yes. She had told him years ago that she was OK with him having affairs as long as they happened out of town. He painted her as a real nag. In the counseling I would undergo years later, I learned that when men tell you things like Sam was sharing, they are fishing for your reaction to see if you might be open to similar activity. I hadn't met anyone who openly admitted to having affairs, so I was curious and asked a lot of questions. I couldn't imagine anyone wanting to have sex with him on the basis of his looks alone. Over time, he asked me why I worked all the time and was rarely home. I grew comfortable with him, so I shared with him that my husband had held me down and punched me and I was afraid of him. That's all the ammunition he needed to target me and start the predator's proverbial grooming process.

We made many joint sales calls to increase 3M business, and Sam was very helpful. One day in Omaha, we had drinks together. I drove us to the bar, and he left his car in the hotel parking lot where he was staying. In those years, I usually limited myself to one drink, maybe two when I was driving. Later, that changed to no drinks when driving. When I stood to leave, I didn't feel well. I was surprised to see I had left my car door open in the parking lot. I still drove him the short distance to his hotel in Omaha but suddenly felt too tired to start driving home. I told him I was going to close my eyes and rest, and then drive home. He invited me in for coffee, and I recall starting to get out of the car, but the next memory I had was someone buttoning my blouse and telling me, "You make love nice." Much to my horror, it was Sam.

"I've been wanting to do this ever since the first time I met you," he said, as if it were the most natural thing.

I was confused and in disbelief. I had my hose on but no skirt. I didn't feel like I'd had sex. I drove the hour home with a barrage of questions. Did I actually have sex with my 3M rep, or was he playing some kind of strange trick on me? Did I simply take a nap? I had no idea. Whatever the case, I didn't think twice about it: I blamed myself. I didn't mention what happened to anyone else. It didn't occur to me that I might have been drugged until I listened to survivors' stories about Bill Cosby decades later.

The next time I saw Sam was in Lincoln after DSM purchased a commercial building. Sam asked to see the empty building. I drove him and gave him a tour of the space. In one office, without provocation, he suddenly said, "Let's make love."

I was dumbfounded. I awkwardly but forcefully said, "Oh no, that other time was a mistake, an accident."

At that point, any pretenses of kindness and care that he may have put up as a front fell away. With predatory nonchalance, he informed me that if I didn't have sex with him, he wouldn't help our business anymore or give me business reports. That didn't bother me in the least, and I told him so. I was actually annoyed by this. How dare he try to intimidate me into doing something against my will!

Then, he told me he would tell my husband about the time in Omaha. I went cold, and then I panicked. By this point, Sam was in my personal space and pushing on me with his body. I had already told him my husband had held me down and punched me, and now I was more afraid of my husband than having sex with my 3M rep to whom I had no physical attraction.

I couldn't think. I felt I had no choice but to succumb. It never occurred to me to report this assault to the authorities. I was simply petrified that Sam would tell my husband about our affair, even though I had zero recollection of it. I later learned that I hadn't simply just "given in"—I was in a freeze state, where it felt that I didn't have control over my faculties and the only proper survival response was to disassociate from my body as Sam had sex with me. Looking back, I feel I was in a state of frozen numbness most of the time.

After this, it felt that the wisest thing to do was compartmentalize the assault and continue with my life as if nothing had happened. A few months later, Sam asked me to meet his friend, Harold, who he said had been laid off from Deluxe Check. It turned out he had been fired for cheating on his expense report, but I didn't learn this until too late. Sa, wanted me to hire him as sales manager to work out of Des Moines. I met him with Sam for lunch in Des Moines sometime in 1986, and my instincts immediately said no. The experience was uncannily similar to the first time I met Donald, when my entire body recoiled in revulsion. Harold was similarly arrogant and continued to relay stories in which he was the winner or star. He seemed to be putting himself on display rather than having a conversation. And just like Sam, he was disrespectful and dismissive of his wife when he talked about her. Luckily, Harold got a job for a different company in Omaha—ACI, one of my clients.

I didn't see Harold again until my 30th birthday in 1986, when I met my friend Jasmine to celebrate in Omaha. Sam showed up with Harold without telling me in advance. Harold disclosed that he had a lover in Kansas City for the past two years, even though he had been married to his second wife for several years. I was upset with him and told him he should be honest with his wife. He informed me he was going to divorce his wife and move to Florida with his lover, Bertha.

My friend Jasmine went home early and, despite the uncomfortable topic of conversation, I stayed out to celebrate—to my detriment. I don't know what happened, but I ended up becoming very sick. I was still with Sam and Harold, throwing up out of the car window on the interstate, and lost one of my earrings. Instead of taking me to the ER, they took me to a hotel and another woman showed up. She put me in bed with my clothes still on and placed a washcloth on my forehead. The room seemed like an extended stay suite, with a big bed and a living room on the other end of the room.

They turned off the lights. As I was coming in and out of consciousness, I heard the woman and Harold having noisy, sloppy sex somewhere in the hotel room. When I woke the next morning, she was gone, but Sam and Harold were still there. I felt well enough to drive home. I asked Harold who the woman who had been so kind to me was. He said she was a friend he called whenever he wanted to have sex. He was now off to Des Moines for the weekend to see his wife. Sam was off to Des Moines to see his wife, too. I was off to Lincoln and happy to be away from them.

I wondered to myself: *If I'd gotten divorced when I first asked Donald, would I be in this horrible situation?* As confident as I was to the external world, my inner sense of self-worth had gradually eroded. I was ashamed that I'd been abused by Donald but, on top of this, I felt an extra layer of disgust with myself for having stayed with him. In spiritual terms, I believe I was in a downward spiral that served to lower my vibration, thus attracting predatory and low-vibration beings.

Both Sam and Harold had started out pretending they were my friends and confiding in me, and I had done the same. They were sympathetic listeners who had earned my trust, and then they turned around and drugged me and most likely had sex with me. I was in a state of denial for a long time, because it was difficult to admit I had been raped by people I trusted. Although I didn't consciously name what was happening, my trust in myself and my judgment of other people was rapidly deteriorating. It felt like I was the pinata being swung from a rope and getting whacked on all sides.

I had hit rock bottom, and I saw no way out.

**

My denial continued to grow, to the extent that I didn't think twice about seeing Harold again. On one occasion, Harold asked me to meet him in Omaha to dance when I was driving from Des Moines to Lincoln. I told him it would be too late. I couldn't get there until 10 p.m. and could only stay for one hour, as I'd be tired from working all day. He convinced me, however, and I went against my instincts.

We danced a few dances. Before I left, I went to the ladies' room and came back to say goodbye. He asked, "Aren't you going to finish your water?" I noticed I had a full glass of water. I stood by the table and guzzled it down and left for Lincoln...or so I thought.

The next memory I have is hearing a constant thud, thud, thud...but I couldn't feel anything. I opened my eyes to see Harold on top of me, having sex with me. Raping me. But still...I could feel nothing. I was in a state of paralysis and couldn't move. I quickly realized the thudding sound was my own head hitting the headboard with each thrust, even though I couldn't feel the sensation.

Harold continued raping me and ejaculated inside my body; he then rolled off and sat on the side of the bed. I got my voice, and my bearings, and asked quietly, "Where am I?"

He responded, "My corporate apartment."

"How did I get here?"

He coolly replied, "Oh, I brought you."

I was completely nude but had no sensation of either heat or cold. He proceeded to tell me he'd had a vasectomy, so I didn't need to worry about getting pregnant with him. I was aghast as I listened to him speak so matter-of-factly about what had just occurred. I wondered if he was holding me hostage or if I would be able to get away safely.

Years later, I ruminated on what had happened. Harold had most likely drugged my water and me, brought me to an apartment, stripped me nude, raped me, and then acted as if nothing unusual or out of the ordinary had happened. It was eerily similar to what had occurred with Sam. I simply didn't have the bandwidth to consider the enormity of the problem at hand. In evaluating my discombobulated state, I assumed that I must have a drinking problem. I had blamed myself for this horrific abuse.

After a while, I was able to move. Harold helped me out of bed and led me to the bathroom. He turned on the water for me to take a shower, washing off all evidence that I had been raped. He helped me put my suit on and drove me to my car. I then drove home, utterly baffled as to how any of this happened. I resolved to drink less and tried to put it all out of my mind.

**

Unfortunately, the disconcerting encounter with Harold was not my last one. In late 1987, Harold was out of work again, and Sam once again asked me to hire him to be our sales manager. He interviewed with me and Donald in my Lincoln office and was hired.

I have often wondered what might have happened had I simply

been rid of Harold altogether and broke off all ties after that horrible experience of finding myself in bed with him, impervious to any sensation whatsoever. But the truth of the matter was, I was frightened. I was afraid that if I didn't hire Sam's friend, Sam would retaliate against me and tell my husband he'd had sex with me. I thought if I had my husband interview Harold, he would object to hiring him, so I secretly hoped Donald would make the final decision for me. Instead, Donald was fine with Harold, much to my surprise. I reasoned that maybe I could make the best of a sticky situation. I was doing almost all the work but, if Harold worked in Des Moines, where he lived, he could manage Iowa and save me from driving to my Iowa clients in the future.

Sales in 1986 were $1.2 million, with five employees in Lincoln and two in Omaha. Sales in 1987 rose to $2.5 million after we decided to move into a 9,000-square-foot building, which we purchased for about $200,000. In 1987, there were seven Lincoln employees, three Omaha employees, two Des Moines employees, and one Davenport employee.

In November 1987, *Inc.* magazine announced DSM as one of the Inc. 500 companies, and we were ranked #250 in their 500 fastest-growing, privately held U.S. companies. It was a big honor, and DSM received a great deal of press coverage. In addition to the *Lincoln Journal Star,* we were written up by several regional newspapers, including the *Midlands Business Journal*, the *Omaha World Herald,* and the *Des Moines Register* in Iowa. We appeared on the evening news on November 25, 1987. Lincoln's mayor and countless others sent notes of congratulations.

In one of the articles, I was quoted as saying: "My goal is that everyone in this office can handle everything that comes up without me, so the company can go forward." Little did I know that after all I'd done to build DSM and ensure the success of my business and my employees, my statement would be an unwitting premonition of the days to come.

CHAPTER 8

THE END OF THE ROAD

I was married on January 9, 1982, at age 26 and I filed for divorce and moved out of our home on February 4, 1988 at age 32.

By the time I filed, I had seen the Omaha counselor who advised me to get divorced—for my safety. Moreover, my friend Barbara had gotten divorced and moved to San Diego, where she was so much happier. Donald's cousin's wife also got divorced, and she and I became friends, so I asked her how she'd gone about getting a divorce, as I figured that I could surreptitiously collect details that might help me in making the same decision—which I now had my heart set on, given the horrific experience I'd gone through in Thailand in January of 1985. After that incident, Donald didn't exactly rape me again...but I discovered he had been molesting me in my sleep. I found wet spots in my bed and wondered about them, and to my dismay, I woke up one night to find him thrusting himself between my buttocks. I pretended to be asleep, and I was deeply disturbed and disgusted when I realized how many times he must have done this.

It was clear to me that Donald had to go.

I didn't really consider how divorce might affect my existing business relationship with Donald, who'd named himself the vice president of DSM. Given that there was no way he'd be able to run the business without me, the person who was single-handedly doing the bulk of the work, it didn't seem feasible that a divorce would negatively impact my professional life.

I also recall taking my mother out to lunch and admitting to her, "Mom, I don't think I want to be married anymore." I was afraid she would be disappointed because she was always concerned as to what the neighbors might think. She was even concerned that my postal carrier would think I was living in sin because I had a different last name from my husband. But this time around, she simply looked me in my eye and said, "If you have any doubts whatsoever, you should get divorced right away. I've had too many friends stay too long in a bad marriage and be miserable."

I remember, as well, being at a hotel and seeing a Gideon Bible in the nightstand drawer. When I flipped the book open, I landed on a verse stating that if a husband hit his wife, the wife could leave the marriage. I had never seen this before (and I haven't since), but I recall very clearly the sense of relief that coursed through my body as I recognized that the universe was, in its own way, giving me the permission I never had before to get divorced.

To my delight, in December of 1987, Donald said he would grant me a divorce but I'd have to move out. We agreed to remain friends...and I thought we really *would* be friends. We even went to a Christmas party and told people we were getting divorced but that the decision was an amicable one. I was severely naive.

After filing for divorce, I gave myself a raise from $200 a month to $4,000 a month and moved out of my house to a rented townhouse at an undisclosed address. My mother-in-law, Ava, whom I called Mom, invited me to come to her house and talk to her. She reassured me that whatever happened, I would always be her daughter, she would always love me, and I could always call her "Mom." She told me what a good job I had done with DSM and assured me that I could walk away with full ownership of my business. Ava, with her husband Daniel nodding along said that they would find something else for their son to do in one of their many companies.

In March of 1988, Ava suddenly died of cancer, and while in the hospital, she called me to visit her. I cried when I saw the look of fear in her eyes. She communicated to me to please promise to go to a Christian counselor she knew. Ava was a born-again Christian, and I assumed that she believed I might change my mind and stay married to her son if I spoke with a counselor. I assured her that I would go. At the funeral, I was asked to sit with the family and attend the festive dinner party at the Lincoln Country Club afterwards with the extended family. I wept my eyes out at the funeral. I had loved Ava so much.

Later in the bathroom, Aunt Olivia took me aside and told me she knew I had been abused by Donald. I asked her how she could have possibly known and she admitted, "I could see it in your face."

"Did Ava know?" I asked.

She nodded. "Yes, we all knew. We were proud of you. You took it like a lady." She then attempted to convince me to remain married and offered a half-hearted, "Remember the vacations!"

I responded stiffly, "There were no vacations."

She hung her head dolefully and gave me a resigned "I know."

Donald's other aunt, Lilly, informed me that I was fortunate to have a career so I could leave, and how much harder it had been for her generation. She told me to keep the golf clubs she had let me borrow as a gift.

These lackluster assurances did nothing to lift my spirits. I felt betrayed by the cowardice and resignation I'd heard in these women's voices. As I recalled the cautionary tales I'd heard from my sisters-in-law, anger blazed through me. I finally realized what this family had done: They had purposely let me suffer in silence, alone, while knowing the truth about my marriage the whole time. I wished that I'd read between the lines and heeded the red flags long ago.

**

Back at DSM, besides my usual work, I revamped and streamlined the operations, updated the basic sales strategy of the company, and implemented the current computer systems throughout our offices.

I also told Donald I could not work with him anymore, and he resigned in January 1988, a month before I filed for divorced. Without him interfering with my employees' ability to get their work done and arguing with me at company meetings, the entire office thrived. I hired a woman to take over his job of ordering inventory. She was appalled by all the loose ends and the lack of a streamlined system, and she worked diligently to get everything on track as it should have been the entire time.

Although Donald was no longer an employee, after his mother died, he began harassing DSM employees by calling them at home and sneaking in through the back warehouse door of our building. He'd even driven to our Omaha office to pump employees for information about me and what was going on in my life.

One employee told me he'd threatened her by saying, "You'd better be nice to me. I may end up with the company." Some employees quit, including my bookkeeper, so I hired a new one. Evette was told before she was hired that I may or may not have the company after my divorce. Evette adamantly said, "Well, I won't work for Donald."

Donald didn't have any allies at DSM. The main complaints were that he was incompetent and interfered with their ability to do their work. He would say he'd do something, such as purchase products to fill a customer order, and not follow through. He refused to input standardized prices in the computer, so employees had to ask him what they should charge for a certain product. Prices were all over the board. This made it impossible for employees to help customers unless he would tell them what to charge. We had custom quotes for almost every customer. When I would determine standard pricing, he actually went into the computer and wiped them out. When inventory came in, he would put it on the shelves in the warehouse but not label it or input the location codes into the computer, so no one could find the items but him. He created a control-freak bottleneck. He was also condescending and arrogant. He loved disagreeing for the sake of it. Evette hadn't even worked with him, but what she heard from other employees made her despise him.

I was coming to despise him myself. Donald told me he could be as vindictive as he wanted now that his mother was dead. I'd already filed a restraining order when I filed for divorce, but Donald's obscene phone calls to my home didn't register as threats to the authorities.

His agreement to keep things civil and courteous was another lie.

At this point, I started to realize I might not get to keep my own company, as Ava and Daniel had promised. Even my vendors reported that he was calling them, which added an extra layer of stress and uncertainty. Still, I was determined to stay on top of making DSM the most successful company it could be, regardless of what my divorce settlement might bring. Starting in January 1988, I improved training for employees by having the vendors do special seminars on their products and benefits, and on how to best meet the needs of our customers. This improved employee sales skills and product knowledge.

I also developed job descriptions and was motivated by the satisfaction of seeing my employees and company grow. In addition, I streamlined the product line. All paperwork was entered in the computer on a timely basis, and the company became organized so we could be on the offense instead of in constant reaction mode. DSM went into being in the best financial shape it had ever been in, even with my larger salary and company car. The cash position went from $5,000 in January to over $100,000 in November 1988.

By June, my divorce was dragging on and on, and it was clear that Donald and his lawyer were intentionally delaying the settlement. My Lincoln attorney was slow in getting back to me, so I called a retired judge and told him my situation. He advised me by saying I needed a new attorney and recommended Warren, an attorney based in Omaha. So I called Warren and hired him. Thankfully, he was able to get the process moving along.

Amid the havoc Donald was wreaking, I was invited to my

second Wonewok trip by 3M, where I met executives from a new office-supply company called Staples. 3M executives were excited about the prospect of having their products in a huge retail store dedicated to computer supplies, so 3M was offering Staples their own special packaging of diskettes. There was an outcry from dealers like me—after all, this would make it very difficult for us to compete. I could see the writing on the wall. Staples would put a lot of my dealer friends out of business...that is, unless they adapted. Somehow, I knew I would be one of the dealers who'd manage to stay afloat. Adaptability was practically my middle name! It was easy for me to see the big picture, as well as develop a moment-by-moment strategy for achieving success. My profit margins were 30 percent at that time, while most other dealers were only 12 percent, which is barely enough to survive long-term.

I knew how to provide service worthy of paying more to work with me—and everyone else knew it, too. That's why it came as no surprise when DSM was named #185 on the Inc. 500 list, which we'd made the second year in a row. As far as I was concerned, Donald or no Donald, I had carved out a niche for DSM that I would always be proud of.

**

As my divorce kept dragging on, I was unable to get a bank loan to purchase the remaining DSM stock. The original business evaluator suddenly called to tell me I was unable to use his evaluation of DSM. I learned later that the entire legal community in Lincoln was warned not to "help" Karen or they would never work in Lincoln again. My ex's family was powerful by virtue of their wealth, and like many other wealthy families, they exercised their power by being bullies.

I realized that if I was to get my company back, I might need to go to court and my employees would have to testify. I went to most of them to see how they felt, and I was fully expecting some pushback. But I was so grateful and relieved to hear their support. "Of course, we'll testify on your behalf!" most of them said. I wasn't the only person horrified by the prospect of having a loose cannon like Donald take charge of the company I'd built up so painstakingly.

As my attorney, Warren, got to know me and my business sense, he told me about his friend and client, Gary, of West Telemarketing, in Omaha, and he introduced us. By then, despite my employees' commitment to backing me in court, it was becoming clearer that I would not get to keep my company. Gary was opening up a brand-new 900 service and was looking for a manager. It was the beginning of the paid 1-900 telephone number era; in contrast to toll-free 1-800 numbers, people paid by the minute when they called 1-900 numbers. Gary told me it would be used mostly for weather information (although, over the years, I noticed it was also used for things like phone sex and dial-a-psychic hotlines). Gary's business ended up being so profitable that he wanted me to come on board. He asked me if I was interested. I definitely was. I'd never been the kind of person to put all my eggs in one basket, and I was doubly excited by the prospect of moving into a new industry and applying my skills there. Gary said he could connect me to Omaha business leaders and get me a membership at the Omaha Country Clubs. It was an incredible opportunity. He told me he had learned through experience to have potential employees take the SRI (Selection Research, now called Gallup) assessment to help determine if they were a good fit for employment. I did a four-hour phone interview with SRI while I was still at DSM. Gary called back and said I tested as "Super Sales." Ultimately, it meant that although I was suited to management, my highest gifts were in sales. But he still wanted to hire me. I was planning to move to Omaha after my divorce was final and work for Gary. I had a plan in place, and although the prospect of losing DSM saddened me greatly, I knew that by dint of my resilience and capability, I would bounce back.

At this time, my vendors got wind that I might not get to keep my company, and they started calling me to say they would like to help me build my own business if that was what ended up happening. The 3M regional manager told me he needed help building the Kansas City market, and if I set up an office there, they would ensure I had more than enough work to start over again. I called the president of that 3M division, Bill, and the national manager, Ron, and talked to them, as well. Ron said I could go anywhere in the country and 3M would set me up as a dealer and help me build my business.

As I pondered my two good options—working with Gary or with 3M—I was torn. Both would be fun. I knew I could build another company, but I wasn't sure if I would like either the telecommunications industry or working for someone else. I had no idea where my future would take me, but after everything I'd been through—first with IBM and now the drama with Donald and DSM—I knew that I wanted to make the right choice...the best choice...for me.

Finally, it looked like the sun was beginning to shine through the clouds onto a dismal situation. Donald and I were close to finalizing our settlement details, but then his attorney sent over a cryptic non-compete clause and a new paragraph stating I would receive $400,000 for my share of DSM. I frowned immediately when I saw it and had a bad feeling in my stomach. The numbers just didn't add up. I quickly calculated that I'd actually be getting about $26,000 for my company—the one for which I had worked practically for free three out of four of the years I'd spent building it up and valued at about $1,000,000.00.

In October, when Donald was back from a trip abroad, he and his attorney came to Warren's office to discuss this new non-compete clause. I was told that it only applied to ribbons and diskettes, and only accounts I currently worked with, even though it clearly noted "computer supplies."

Donald and his attorney sat across from me and my attorney,

Warren, and assured us that the paragraph referring to the $400,000 was not describing what I would be paid for my half of DSM. It was in the settlement solely for Donald's tax purposes. This paragraph allowed Donald to use $400,000 as DSM's "goodwill" amount to reduce his taxes in case he ever decided to sell the business. I asked what consideration I would receive for having a non-compete, and I was told I would be getting nothing-there was no consideration.

I had a bad feeling about this and told Warren I didn't agree with having this bogus paragraph stating $400,000 when I wasn't getting anything. It made it sound like I was being paid when I wasn't. I explained to him that it seemed like the type of thing I'd seen at Wizco stockholder meetings to screw people over later. He assured me it was fine. At this point, Warren seemed to be sick and tired of dealing with my divorce. It was clear that he wanted me to move on and settle with what little I was being given, but I learned from that experience that it was a bad idea to sell myself out merely to placate others or alleviate conflict.

I told Warren I felt our marital personal property and business property should be dealt with separately. In retrospect, I wish we'd had a list of personal property on one page, and then a separate page with only business items and their assigned values. The business I'd built was valued at about $1 million but, since I was married, Donald received $500,000 worth. The business also owned a building valued at $200,000. The marital personal property was about $400,000, and my personal property was about $150,000. In an even split, I would get $800,000 for our joint property; instead, I received $475,000 less than I deserved and next to nothing for my business share.

I went back to my office and called a retired judge I knew. He told me to settle for whatever was offered and that I was lucky to get out alive. "The wealthy own judges. There might not be a paper trail, but they own them," he pronounced. The judge's cautionary note was especially chilling, considering I'd been told I had a hit on my head ordered by Donald's close friend soon after I moved into my rented townhouse, and that I needed to be careful.

I felt sick when I heard the judge's words. I recalled Wizco legal counsel talking about how they were assigned a judge "favorable to us" when Wizco got caught in a federal bid-rigging scheme. Uncle Lyle gloated at the annual meeting about how they'd made an extra $10 million and only had to pay a fine of $1.5 million; the fine was paid in community service so the public only saw their good deeds, plus none of the "blood" went to jail-someone else went.

At this point, I imagined that Warren, too, had resigned himself to the fact that Donald would take what Donald would take. I felt I had no choice but to sign away my company and get almost nothing in return. Financially and emotionally, I would have benefited from never having met Donald in the first place.

**

On November 21, 1988, when I had lunch with most of my employees to tell them I wouldn't get to keep my company after all and would be signing papers later that day, I broke down crying. They all tried to comfort me, but I could tell they were just as shocked and despairing as I had been when I finally realized what may have always been inevitable.

After that lunch, I drove to Lincoln and met Warren at the Lincoln Lancaster Court House. I had an overwhelming feeling of remorse out in the hallway when I told him, "Warren, I can't sign this."

Warren spoke to me as if I were a child, explaining that if I refused to sign, we'd have to start all over at the beginning and this was the best I was ever going to get. In his eyes, I needed to buck up, sign the settlement, and get on with my life.

We went into the courtroom, where I was asked to take the stand. The judge asked me if I was agreeing to this of my free will. I almost said, "No!" For a moment, I was tempted to sob out my entire story to him and to appeal to his sympathy. His eyes were cold and empty.

He was all business. I looked at Warren, and he said, barely audibly, "Yes."

Back in the hallway, Warren told me I had until midnight to get anything out of my office. After that, it would become Donald's property. This took me by surprise. My employee Evette's husband had a truck, so they helped me move as much as I could from my office to my townhouse. I couldn't get everything, however, and Donald never let me come back for some of my own personal belongings, which even included a family table that was my mother's, made for her by her father. She had only been loaning it to our company, and it broke my heart to lose it. And even after my mom wrote a letter to Donald beseeching him to give the table back, he sent her a scathing letter about how worried he was about me because I was crazy and needed psychological help—and no, he would not give her table back. In fact, he told her that I'd sold it to DSM for $50 and sent her a copy of a check for a different warehouse table of mine that I'd sold to the company. He refused to sell it back to her in the amount of $50. As Mom showed me the letter, her hands shook. Both of us cried.

Overall, I lost almost everything I owned: my company, my job, my house, and my car. Moreover, my non-compete clause was in effect for two full years.

I was then forced to endure two weeks of consulting for DSM— during which Donald dished out even more emotional abuse. I was sobbing daily while he ranted, threatened, and ordered me around. When I got to work, Donald stood in my office as I sat at my desk, and he ordered me to call all my customers and tell them I was leaving—and then, to physically take the new sales rep to meet them. All of this was impossible to do in two weeks.

I was so upset over losing my company that whenever I explained to customers that Donald had gotten the company after our divorce, I burst into tears and could barely get my words out. You might imagine the reaction on the other end of the phone: a mixture of sympathy, shock, and disbelief. I spent most of the first few days making the sobbing calls. When I told Donald I couldn't bear to do it anymore, he yelled, "You have to! It's part of the agreement!"

I called my counselor Ellie in Omaha, and she was livid. She told me that losing my business to Donald was equivalent to losing a child, and this two-week consulting clause should never have been included, as it was adding to my trauma.

As Donald had always told me, "If you divorce me, what's yours is mine, what's mine is mine, what's ours is mine. I will make you penniless and fix it so no one will believe you." It seemed as if he'd carried through with this threat, and his victory had not lessened his spite and hatred.

CHAPTER 9

A NEW BEGINNING AND A BITTER END

Throughout much of the ordeal of my divorce, I hadn't necessarily felt supported...but I hadn't been alone, either. Perhaps sensing my vulnerability, Harold had shown up on my doorstep in June 1988, when I was in the midst of my turbulent divorce settlement with Donald. Harold was working for me in Des Moines but, much to my surprise, and without any warning, he landed on my doorstep with a moving van full of furniture.

By this time, Ava had already died and Donald was desperately attempting to find out where I lived. In many ways, Harold showing up felt like it could offer some protection from my ex's threats and the oppressive specter of his presence that loomed over us. Moreover, Harold had a convenient sob story. According to him, his wife had divorced him and moved to Arizona, and he had nowhere else to go. He said he was still planning to move to Florida with his lover.

Many Nebraskans, especially my family, are unknowing enablers to people who say they need help. I felt obligated to help Harold even though it was clearly ridiculous to let him stay at my townhouse. I had no desire for anyone else to live with me, let alone a man, but I didn't know what to do about this dejected, crying employee on my doorstep. Some part of me knew it was entirely inappropriate to let him stay with me, but he swore that it would be only for a few days, until he got his bearings.

Long story short: That was a lie. Harold turned out to be a parasite, never paying a dime in rent or contributing in any way.

A few days after he showed up on my doorstep, my phone rang. It was Harold's ex-wife. She said, "I want you to know you didn't ruin my marriage." Before I could even respond, she hung up. I had no idea what she was talking about. The last I knew their marriage had been on the rocks long before I came into the picture. Harold had told me back in 1986 that he'd been planning to divorce his wife and move to Florida with his lover, Bertha. Had I not been so traumatized by everything I was going through with Donald, I would have likely followed my first instincts and never had anything to do with this manipulator.

It was awkward to have Harold in Lincoln when he was hired to work in Des Moines. He didn't know anyone, so I introduced him to everyone I knew. On the weekends, he tagged along with me to work. One Saturday while at work, he suddenly got angry at me and said, "Just because you're working all the time doesn't mean I have to."

I worked every day, while everyone else worked Monday through Friday. I told Harold he certainly didn't have to work on weekends or evenings, as I did, but I imagine that his outburst came from a place of shame and defensiveness, as I was clearly working extremely hard to maintain DSM's profit margins.

Harold was little more than an unwelcome distraction in my home, and since I was mostly busy working and dealing with my impending divorce, I didn't pay too much attention to him. I simply waited for news that would let me know he was ready to move out, so I could get him out of my hair. Although Harold might have believed differently, at this stage, we were not even a couple. I was simply his employer, doing a favor to help him through a bad situation.

After my divorce in November of that year, I was still grappling with whether or not to move to Omaha to work for Gary West or Kansas City to start a company with 3M's support. I assumed Harold would be moving to Florida with his lover Bertha, as planned. But when the time came, he cried even more and said that Bertha didn't want him after all and had decided to stay with her husband and was moving to Florida with him.

It was almost unbearable to see this grown man crying. I felt sorry for him, even though he blamed me for him not having a job (Donald had ultimately fired him after he took over DSM completely) or being able to pay rent. On one occasion, he flew to Arizona to try to patch things up with his ex-wife. When he returned, he was visibly irritated; he got angry and accused me of moving a picture of his from my bedroom dresser, then accused me of being dramatic while I calmly stood there as he worked his way into a frenzy. He seemed to be egging me on to fight back, but my "irate customer call" training from IBM had taught me to stay quiet and let him rant. It was unnerving, though, and a foreshadowing of things to come.

This is how manipulators brainwash their targets: like the drip, drip, drip of water, which over time creates a crevasse, and entirely changes their targets' reality.

**

After my divorce, I was grieving the loss of my first company, but I had complete faith in myself. When one door closes, another opens—which is what happened for me. I decided to go with the option of working with 3M in the Kansas City area...and I also became a pioneer in a new industry: electronic presentation equipment. I grew my electronic presentation and computer-supplies business single-handedly for the next two years, becoming one of the largest dealers of Proxima LCD projectors in the U.S. and the largest 3M dealer in the Kansas City area. My first year, my sales were $500,000. Growth continued my second year, and I added one employee to help me. Overall, I had several hundred clients.

In December 1988, Joseph, my Verbatim rep, called me at home after I lost DSM. He had a revolutionary new product called a liquid crystal display (LCD) panel that attached to a computer and projected the image of the computer screen. It had no light source and required being placed on top of an overhead projector in order to project the computer screen to the large white classroom screen. He offered to mail me one to show potential clients to see if they liked it. I immediately said yes! This was the beginning of an exciting new industry, and I was poised to be on the ground floor.

Later that month, my new business attorney, Mike, filed papers to incorporate Computer Products, NE corporation, with locations in Kansas City and Lincoln. For my Nebraska office, I worked out of my rented townhouse in Lincoln, but eventually moved to office space in downtown Lincoln. In addition to LCD panels, I sold paper products to consumers in Nebraska and Iowa. I also lived in Overland Park, Kansas, and opened my Kansas City office and rented separate warehouse space in early 1989. My Computer Products Kansas City office operated as DBA Business Media, Inc. because the business name Computer Products was not available for use in Kansas. I spent three to four work days in Kansas City building my business and the rest in Lincoln and Omaha showing off LCD panels. My mom lived in Lincoln, and it was important to me to see her regularly.

I had been devastated over the loss of DSM, but just as with the loss of my IBM job, it turned out to be a blessing—as I could devote my efforts to a new industry in Lincoln and Omaha, where I knew clients, and sell 3M supplies and Proxima LCD panels in a new market, Kansas City.

I was most excited about LCD panels. Joseph sent me his Chisholm LCD panel, and I called ten of my former IBM customers in Lincoln to ask if they would please look at my new LCD panel and tell me what they thought. They agreed, and I demonstrated the equipment at each of their offices. Within a short time, nine out of ten called me back and said, "You know that thing you brought out and showed us? We want one!"

Even better, after they bought one and started using it for training, they would call me and say how great it was because they could train twice as many people in half the time. Their management was very impressed with their innovation. I also bought a small computer, known as the Brick, that Proxima (the brand I'd decided to go with because their products were superior to other brands) recommended to attach to my LCD panel to display the computer image on the screen. The laptop was not invented yet, and this was the latest and greatest at the time.

Baxter, the Proxima sales rep who originally set me up as a Proxima dealer, helped me immensely as I built my business. He came to Kansas City often and went on customer calls with me, as well as helped me put on trade shows and presentation training seminars. He assisted me with large shows where I would rent an auditorium and put on presentations on such topics as "How best to make a persuasive presentation." These events easily garnered over a thousand attendees from all sizes of companies in the Kansas City area.

Proxima also sent me any leads from companies looking to purchase LCD panels, and I would follow up. I learned half of all dealers never followed up on these invaluable leads, so I was way ahead of the game. They were such new products that there weren't many dealers. The Internet wasn't around, so most customers purchased from the dealer who took the time to show them the products. The products were also quite profitable compared to computer supplies. As it had been made clear to me at the IBM school I had attended, computer supplies had become a price war commodity and some supplies dealers were at risk of going out of business.

In early March of 1989, Gary of West Telemarketing called me at home with a second business opportunity. He informed me that the 900 service had taken off even better than he'd anticipated and inquired as to whether I might reconsider working for him. It was so tempting but, by then, I already had my Kansas City operation established and I had purchased $30,000 worth of inventory warehoused in Kansas City. Moreover, I loved the entrepreneurial nature of what I was doing, and I simply didn't know if I could work for another person, given all I'd accomplished in the past few years on my own.

In Spring of 1989, I went to Infocomm, the large annual trade show for the audiovisual industry, held in Anaheim, California. My Proxima sales rep had encouraged me to go. I arranged to meet the owners of Data Image (another projection-equipment dealer in my industry). They had sold me Proxima equipment when I first got started and before Proxima set me up directly. All the major manufacturers were there. The attendees were mostly A/V dealers who carried expensive projectors and other equipment as well as overhead projectors, and many of the dealers were impressed that I specialized in LCD panels only. The traditional A/V dealers thought of the LCD panels as more of a "toy" than a serious product and didn't seem to spend much time showing off LCD panels. They were more concerned with larger projectors of higher quality, basic overhead projectors, white screens, and overhead transparencies. Their dismissive attitude toward LCD panels opened the door for LCD panel specialists like me to break into their industry. Had they paid more attention, my business and many like it would never have taken off! It reminded me of the IBM days when we thought of the personal computer as a "toy" and not a serious business computer.

At one Omaha product show I participated in, another vendor, a traditional Audio Visual (A/V) dealer headquartered in Iowa, was also displaying their product. They carried Sharp brand LCD panels, but not Proxima. A man came over and introduced himself as their Omaha sales manager. He told me, half-jokingly and half-earnestly, that he was going to put me out of business. I smiled and said, "If you ever need anything, such as a cable or Proxima LCD panel, please let me know."

I was being entirely serious. I always felt there was room for everyone to be successful. I still adhere to the abundance theory, not the scarcity theory, of business. I knew I had competition, but I always sent positive thoughts their way.

I also did onsite presentations and seminars in large corporations with many departments. Many presenters put too many words on one screen to be effective, and they were hungry for all the tips I had to make effective presentations, such as the importance of easy-to-read color combinations (yellow and navy blue being the best) and how to determine the best amount of readable information to present on each slide (three main points per slide, to be exact—you could test out the proper length by writing out each slide on a 3x5 card, tossing it to the floor, and recognizing that if you could still read it, so could your audience).

I continued attending Infocomm every year and learning more about the industry, equipment, and dealers, and winning award trips. Proxima continued to support me and send me leads, and I remained their only dealer in Nebraska, Kansas City, and Iowa.

**

Just as things were falling into place and going so well, I received notice that Donald was suing me for violating my non-compete, which was part of my divorce settlement. I was shocked and had no idea what I could have possibly done. I was being deposed immediately in Lincoln. Donald had been threatening me even after our divorce, going so far as to say he would depose my mom, and harass her and me to death for the two years of my non-compete clause. I documented the calls to my attorney and to the police. I was sincerely frightened. Despite the fact that he got everything after our divorce, it seemed he was still intent on making my life a living hell.

I learned in court that my ex had sued me after Harold had co-founded a computer supply company with another woman called Business Media (BMI) in Lincoln. I sold 3M products to BMI on my attorney's advice and also followed my attorney Warren's advice to tell the purchasing agent at Mutual of Omaha that he could not buy toner from me but he could buy toner from Harold's company.

But in no way could any of this be deemed a violation of my non-compete clause. My non-compete only applied to existing customers I called on in Nebraska and Iowa, and Donald told me it excluded all products except ribbons and diskettes. It was such a blatant violation of our agreement that, according to Warren, Donald's divorce attorney refused to take the case. But Donald wasn't deterred. Donald was employing a strategy rich people often use to screw over average people in the legal system. That is, rich people can afford to sue and last longer financially until the poorer people they are suing are forced to settle or give in. This is the nature of the despicably litigious behavior that operates in courtrooms across the nation.

Some of my former DSM employees had quit, and they told me Donald was obsessed with what I was doing. He was also obsessed with what Harold was doing, and he seemed to be especially bitter over the fact that Harold had moved into my townhouse...which gave me every reason to believe his lawsuit was being fueled by a personal vendetta. However, I was perfectly justified in selling to Harold's company; since they were a new company, selling to them didn't violate my non-compete.

Still, I knew it would be tough to stand up and receive justice due to Donald's family's extreme wealth and influence, but I had settled so many times with him in the past, I knew I must stand up and defend myself no matter the consequences. I had settled when I stayed married to him, settled when I let him work for me, and settled when I lost my company—and I was dead tired of settling and giving in to bullies. I sensed that if I settled now, he would simply come up with yet another grievance.

It was a long-drawn-out and relentless legal sideshow, with stalling techniques and witness after witness.

At this time, I had already found a house to purchase in Overland Park, Kansas, on a private lake, but I called the realtor and didn't bid on it after all. As long as I was in the midst of this lawsuit, I had to put my house hunting on hold in Kansas City. I also spent more time in Lincoln than I would have liked due to this new intrusion (meaning I saw Harold more frequently). When I was forced to come to Lincoln for a hearing or deposition, I'd call on Nebraska companies and show them my Proxima LCD panels. At this time in my budding business, I was my only employee, as I found that anyone associated with me was targeted by the attorney for DSM. I was forced to turn over my calendars. Customers and prospects listed on my calendars reported receiving calls from an angry lawyer who threatened that if they worked with me, they would get caught up in a lawsuit.

Even my Kansas City warehouse got a call. They gave me 24 hours to remove all my inventory from their premises. Luckily, I found a new warehouse that was even better than my first warehouse. I had to divulge my business secrets and methods in court, and DSM copied my methods and set up a competing office in the Kansas City area within a mile of my office. I had to stomach seeing them at my Kansas City trade shows. They also started carrying LCD panels and tried to get signed up directly with Proxima.

Then and there, I resolved to build my business alone, so none of my employees would have to be dragged through court. It was a lonely time. My resilience shone through, and I was able to juggle the lawsuit while building my business in Kansas City and Nebraska.

I am amazed at what I was able to accomplish with all these obstacles thrown at me. I attribute my resilience to my mother. She stepped up to the plate when my father died—and hit a home run. I knew I was destined to do the same.

The judge presiding over the lawsuit refused to allow into evidence the letter I had written in early 1989 for Warren to present—describing the abuse I experienced during my marriage and asking for clarification on the non-compete I'd acquired as part of the divorce. This judge had no idea I had not been paid $400,000 for my 51 percent of DSM, but instead, the $400,000 was only put into our settlement to allow Donald a tax advantage so he could claim $400,000 of goodwill. Of course, it was a clause I had vehemently opposed, but I'd been overruled by my attorney. The judge for this lawsuit didn't understand what had actually happened. Had the judge bothered to do the math on my settlement, as I had, he would see I received less than $30,000 for DSM, the company I built to profitability. But Donald's attorney tried to claim I actually got paid $400,000 in addition to half of the marital property and my personal assets and painted Donald as a victim.

Through the lawsuit, things became even more complicated when I learned that the Lincoln office of Harold's company, BMI, had been taking my sales in Kansas City as theirs. When I was out and about making calls, I would forward my calls to BMI's Lincoln office so they could take orders from customers for me, as Harold had offered to act as a type of answering service for my business. BMI was supposed to pass my clients' orders on to me, but instead they kept the business, invoiced them with their address, shipped the product, and kept the money. I only found this out due to my former employee Evette's testimony. She now worked for Harold, and Harold was the one who'd told her to pretend my sales were theirs instead of simply taking orders for me from my clients. In fact, Evette seemed entirely confused that my company was completely separate from the one she worked for. After I learned about this, I didn't forward my calls to BMI Lincoln anymore, and instead forwarded them to my own answering service—who couldn't answer specific questions but could take messages.

My attorney, Warren, insisted that BMI pay me what they owed me for the 3M supplies I sold them—in case Donald tried to construe their non-payment as a loan from me. Before Warren, I had tried numerous times to get paid on a timely basis from BMI Lincoln, to no avail. Harold's company paid up, which was one benefit of the lawsuit. Unfortunately, I still couldn't see that Harold acted like a con artist. Even when Warren would say things to help me see, I remained blind. However, it did make me realize I had to watch my back in business, but I hadn't translated that to watching my back in personal relationships with men.

At the time of the lawsuit, I swore I had never seen Donald happier in my entire life than when I was on the stand and he was sitting with his lawyer, prodding him to ask me certain questions. I wanted Donald to take the stand, but Warren said, "No, he's a loose cannon and doesn't have a case. You did nothing to violate your non-compete, and under the law you can't be liable for something your attorney tells you to do."

Boy, was he wrong! Not only did the judge find me guilty—he fined me and extended the non-compete clause for another year. After losing my case, Warren told me he was shocked the judge would rule against me. I paid $35,000 in fines on November 21, 1990. I was 33 years old. The addition of a year to my non-compete was later overturned by the Nebraska Supreme Court (but only in 1993), and I was refunded my money. Still, the lawsuit had taken most of the two years of my non-compete period, and it cost me as much as $12,000 a month, so the damage had been done.

Donald was attempting to make good on his threat from late 1982 to render me penniless, and fix it so no one would believe me—but I was absolutely determined: He could not break my spirit.

CHAPTER 10

THE MONSTER BEHIND CLOSED DOORS

While the lawsuit was dragging on, much to my distress, so was the drama with my new roommate, Harold. "You don't care about me!" he'd whine to me as I came to him month after month to ask for his share of the rent. "I have to pay child support, and alimony to my ex-wife. You don't care about my son!" He would rant on and on until he was in tears by the end. Despite his hostile attitude toward me, I truly felt bad for him. Although he was ten years older than me, I clearly had more money and resources. His constant shaming of me on the basis of this fact wore me down.

My attorney, Warren, had tried to warn me about Harold shortly after he showed up on my doorstep. Warren said, "You are so successful, and you are ten years younger than this loser! Don't get involved with this man."

I realize now that I was so brainwashed I was falling for all the lies, to the extent that I felt responsible for all of Harold's problems. I'd even give him money when we went out so it would look like he was paying for me, when in reality I was paying for him. What made it more complicated is that our relationship had grown closer, and I gradually came to consider him my boyfriend.

After my lawsuit, the landlord at my townhouse visited me and asked if I might like to buy his townhouse for $160,000. It was a wonderful space, but I wasn't sure of my future plans and I appreciated the flexibility of renting, especially as I still had my apartment in Kansas City (which I later gave up when I hired a Kansas City sales rep). My sister's mother-in-law's husband had died, and she wanted to downsize, so she ended up buying it. Harold was angry at me over this. It meant both of us now had to move. He didn't have a good credit score, so he couldn't qualify for a lease. I knew I didn't want to live with him, but my guilt kept me from setting this boundary. I told him I'd only consider it if we found a two-bedroom, two-bathroom apartment and he paid a separate check for his half of the rent. He readily agreed.

So, I made the mistake of letting Harold move in with me, despite my reservations.

It felt that the new sharing of personal space was bringing out aspects of Harold's behavior and personality that had only been in the shadows in the past. The things that had always made me intuitively uncomfortable came to a head in 1989, after a camping trip we went on together. I knew he was angry at me because I'd been on a six-week trip to Thailand without him, during which I didn't call him at all...but I had no idea it would culminate in what I can only describe as rape. At one point in the camping trip, he sodomized me. I attempted to move my body, but it was all in vain. I was taken back to the time in the hotel, when he was moving above me but I was absolutely paralyzed and couldn't do anything. I felt a searing pain...and my next memory was that it was now morning. I awoke on my belly, and I couldn't move. Finally, I was on all fours, and much to my horror, I discovered that I was bleeding from my rectum. Flickers of the night before...me saying no but him proceeding, anyway...and the sense of being utterly immobile...all came over me.

"What have you done to me? I need you to take me to the hospital now!" I screamed.

He simply laughed and said, "What are you talking about? It was the best sex we've ever had!"

And then, the cycle I was so accustomed to was set in place with Harold. Shame. Denial. Self-blame.

The violence ensued, and there were more examples than I can possibly count. One time, we stayed in Lexington, Nebraska, to have dinner with Harold's friend Barry and his wife Paula. We stayed at their cabin on the lake, while they remained at their house in Lexington. After dinner, Harold became angry at me for some inexplicable reason. He pushed me down on the concrete patio and I hit my head. As I fell, I could see him running away—in my mind, I thought he was going for help. I passed out and awoke at 3 a.m., outside and alone. He was gone. I was furious, scared, and confused, so I drove home for three hours. He called the next day to say, "I'm so worried about you. Come back for dinner!" I was appalled at his inability to admit to what had happened...and the fact that he had left me outside and unconscious for hours. I refused. Although I didn't break up with him, I rarely went anywhere with him alone ever again.

At this point, Harold's behavior abruptly changed. He made all sorts of excuses for losing his temper, but he attempted to be kinder and more attentive, and he made all sorts of promises to me. I later learned that this is what is called the cycle of violence: It begins with the violent event, continues with the groveling apology (in which the abuser seems genuinely repentant), then the abuser's kindness (during which the victim thinks everything is better and lets her guard fall). This is called the honeymoon period, and it can last days or years. It's a matter of time until the next violent act—and each subsequent violent act escalates in seriousness.

In the summer of 1989, as I recall, Harold's college-age son, Jack, stayed with us for the summer. When I was in Lincoln, I worked out of my downtown office and Jack worked for his dad at BMI, a fledgling computer supply company, which was located in the same building. One morning, I drove Jack downtown and he turned to me and said, "You'll never be my mother. My dad goes through so many women."

I replied, "Thanks for letting me know how you feel. I have no desire to ever replace your mother. Let's just try to be friends and leave it at that."

Jack came to my office whenever he needed to vent about what was happening in his dad's office. I taught Jack about my presentation equipment, and he helped me do demonstrations by carrying and setting up equipment. Jack and I quickly became friends. He was sweet and thoughtful, a strange contrast to his father. Jack also had a girlfriend out of state to whom he was fiercely loyal and faithful. Harold routinely chastised him for not cheating on her and spending his spare time working out instead of bar hopping. As I listened to Harold tear apart his loyal son, I noticed that the fight was quickly escalating into yelling and insults. Not wanting to get in between them, I requested that they fight out of my sight and when I wasn't around. It was so stressful to watch Jack being verbally abused. I noticed that when Jack reacted to Harold, Harold became smug and satisfied. I realized that was what he always did with me—he wanted to get a rise out of me in order to see me distressed. But because I didn't allow myself to get flummoxed, I saw that he was redirecting his attention to Jack. It was a painful situation, but one I didn't feel I had the agency to change.

**

What complicated the experience with Harold is the fact that I decided to merge my presentation company with his after December 1990, when my non-compete clause with DSM was finally over.

The decision to merge my company with BMI was one of the toughest decisions I'd made in my life. Harold, whose company sold only computer supplies at this point, was eager for us to join our businesses together. He said I could serve as CEO and train his employees on everything about the presentation-equipment industry. It was clear the presentation-equipment industry was an exciting and ever-growing goldmine, and the computer-supply industry was a low-price, commodity-driven, low-profit industry, getting worse every year.

If I kept my own company separate, I would be independent and stay financially ahead. I could *see* my industry was the future. I owned the contracts with the best manufacturers. On the other hand, I was afraid BMI could easily go under due to eroding price margins. I felt I was BMI's only hope for sustainability. I still felt guilty about Harold losing his job when I lost DSM in my divorce. I went with the guilt instead of being true to myself.

The other factor weighing heavily on me was how best to take care of my current customers and my former DSM customers, who were now free to purchase products from me. I was confident they would support me, and I needed to make sure they could get both computer supplies and presentation equipment. I called 3M and asked them whether, if I merged my company with BMI, they would be willing to transfer my 3M distributorship to the new company. They said yes. Previously, 3M had refused to set up BMI directly, but if the two companies merged, 3M was fine with the entire company buying directly from them in all geographic areas.

I had been so attached to my first company, DSM, and I had grieved losing it. It was horrible. With my presentation-equipment company, I was not so attached. My long-term goal was to build my business for five years, sell it, and start a new adventure. Now, I would serve as CEO of the merged companies and keep running and building the presentation-equipment side of the business. I would teach the BMI Lincoln personnel about presentation equipment, and they would keep handling computer supplies. I would do most, if not all, of the demonstrations until all employees were sufficiently trained.

In December 1990, I merged my company with Harold's. We sent letters to our clients notifying them that the companies had merged, with me serving as CEO. Of course, this new situation was not without its difficulties. Harold had a Jekyll and Hyde persona: He was pleasant in front of vendors, but then he'd turn on a dime and be unpleasant with me and our colleagues. He was also a good salesperson, as he could charm anyone into buying from him, but he often overpromised and underdelivered, leaving other people to fix his messes. He seemed to have no remorse about creating problems by misleading customers.

It was definitely a transition to merge the companies together and get everyone excited about presentation equipment. It was easy for me to see the long-term potential, but not for everyone else. It was like pulling teeth. I even got calls from some of my vendors that their invoices were not being paid on time, so I became involved in the accounting and oversight of the office procedures and cash flow, in addition to running the presentation side of the business. Operations smoothed out in the ensuing years. In October 1994, *Inc.* magazine named BMI #384 on its Top 500 list. By this time, we had six employees and $2 million in sales. This was the third time that companies I owned were named to the Inc. 500 list.

It seemed as if I were repeating the situation I'd been in with Donald, all over again...the good and the bad.

After we went public about the merger, I received several phone calls from friends who were worried about what I had done. One of them, Jasmine, could see through Harold because he lied to her when she first met him. She didn't like him, and Harold didn't like her. Jasmine also knew how devastated I had been to lose DSM, so she wanted to protect me from having the same thing happen again.

I had some trepidation of my own but simply hoped everything would work out. I learned many valuable lessons in the process. One was that it's best to disentangle oneself from a bad situation as soon as possible rather than going through the dark tunnel, looking for a light that most likely doesn't exist.

About this time, I was asked by the Nebraska Republican Party to run for Nebraska State Auditor against a popular Democratic incumbent. I had widespread support among all the party leaders I spoke to. I was excited and set to run, even making speeches, when at the last minute I made a final call to a woman in the party I trusted. What she told me convinced me not to run.

**

While building BMI helped to give my life meaning and definition, things continued to go downhill in my relationship with Harold. However, when I look back, I think of April 11, 1991, as the night God saved my life and I was finally able to break out of the hypnotic state that had me remaining in this abysmal, depressing, life-depleting relationship.

Earlier that day, I was notified by a woman who identified herself as Harold's wife. I was entirely shocked. To my knowledge, she had divorced him and moved out of state in June of 1988. When I confronted Harold and told him I had decided to end our romantic relationship if he was indeed married, he snapped. He proclaimed that he would kill me and immediately grabbed me by the neck and strangled me.

His attack was swift, targeted, and deadly, like a cobra. My world went black...before I felt myself peacefully floating in a soft white light. I felt I was watching a movie about myself, gently swinging by my neck, vaguely aware I was hovering between life and death, but feeling only love and grace. It was as if I were in the embrace of God. No fear, simply an inexplicable knowing that I was taken care of and protected and loved. In those moments, which were probably only a few minutes but that felt like I was suspended in an eternal timelessness, everyone and everything was part of an inextricable whole. Connected. I could feel that what each of us did affected everyone else. Then...bang! The blissful feeling and white light vanished, and my eyes sprung open. I had been unconscious, and now I was conscious again. I found myself lying on the kitchen floor. Harold was bent over me, still trying to strangle me and get a better grip on my neck.

Years later, I learned that I had been seconds from death. I can only say it was a miracle that I was able to get to my bedroom phone, lock the door, and get 911 on the line. Two white male police officers responded to the call. One spoke to me, and the other to

Harold. The one speaking to me seemed bored and stopped writing after the first sentence. I didn't think anything of it, as I had no experience with calling the police in a domestic-violence crime, and I had already told the 911 operator from my locked bedroom what I had experienced. I had red marks encircling my neck. I was unable to stand without wall support, and I only later learned that I'd suffered a traumatic brain injury, which caused seizures, and damaged my vocal cords. I should have been taken to the hospital for examination and observation as strangulation can lead to internal swelling and asphyxiation. One officer apologetically said he had to issue a ticket to Harold, due to the red marks around my neck. The officer wrote a ticket out; the banality of this activity made it feel like he was writing a parking ticket. Harold was not arrested. The officers left, leaving me with my perpetrator.

I wouldn't learn until after 2014 that Harold's ticket had led to a "no contact" order being issued by the judge, and there was a hearing a few months later. Instead of attempted murder, the ticket was only for third-degree assault and plea-bargained down to disturbing the peace. The attorney for the case was a real-estate attorney I'd thought was a friend to me. In 2018, I spoke with the officer who'd arrested Harold. He informed me that he'd issued the ticket for third-degree assault because he had not been allowed to ticket for attempted murder/felony strangulation in 1991. In 2004, Nebraska finally passed a law to allow for that.

I moved back to Lincoln to care for my aging mother in 2013, which is when I found out about Harold's hearing. I had no idea about it until he tried to contact me twice in 2014, and I told my neighbors to be on the lookout for a strange man. They told me to call the police. A young white male officer responded and, for the first time, I was able to tell my story. I sobbed it out and he patiently listened, then made a few phone calls. Some of the violating crimes I described to him had no statute of limitations. The first thing the detective told me was, "It's not your fault." It was such a far cry from the officers I'd dealt with prior to that. And it was so comforting to hear these sincere words. I would carry them with me as a reminder of all I'd lived through...and almost as an antidote to the self-blame I'd piled on myself for too long in the past.

**

Unfortunately, while I knew that this momentous experience of almost dying was the last straw and I wanted Harold out, he refused to move. Now, I had no idea what to do. Our businesses and lives were merged, and it seemed that I was revisiting the same territory I'd known so well with Donald. I felt helpless. He promised that once a year had gone by since the start of our lease, he would give his notice and move out. I gave notice in the spring of 1992, when the year was over, but true to form, Harold went back on his word and refused to do what he'd said he would. I felt stuck, because the leasing office told me that even if I moved out, I was still liable for all the rent and any damages, as mine was the primary name on the lease. I kept paying half the rent, but unbeknownst to me, Harold was bouncing all his checks.

At this stage, the leasing office told us they could evict us, or we could leave voluntarily. I asked the leasing agent why I couldn't just stay and Harold alone could be evicted. She explained that since both names were on the lease, both of us would have to go.

I was already building my house on a lot I'd bought in Lincoln, and I'd asked my mother if I could move into her house while I was waiting for mine to be finished. I moved in with her in August of 1992 and remained with her until March of 1993, when my house was done. Aside from the fact that I would still see Harold in the workplace, I felt that I could finally exhale the pent-up emotions of fear and uncertainty that had been holding me hostage for so long.

CHAPTER 11

HINTS OF A BETTER FUTURE

Shortly after Harold strangled me, I was asked to serve on the board of a domestic-violence organization in Lincoln. I took the crisis training to learn more about domestic violence and the cycle of violence, and why women seemed to be so powerless to leave a domestic-violence situation. By this time, I was dating a kind CPA who lived in Kansas City.

I was still unable to admit I had been in a relationship in which I was a victim of domestic violence...but the patterns I had experienced firsthand were beginning to make more sense in the context of the abuse cycle, which I was learning about in great depth.

After the abuser seduces and gains the trust of their target, the cycle starts. The cycle of violence as it is described goes through four distinct stages: 1. Tension builds up as the abuser becomes more agitated and starts blaming the victim for their problems. 2. Any type of physical or emotional abuse occurs. 3. The abuser attempts to mend things with the victim, often by appealing to their forgiving nature and apologizing. 4. This is the honeymoon period, where all is calm and it seems the abuser has changed for the better.

After Stage 4, everything begins all over again, sometimes culminating in greater violence than had previously been experienced...and often, in tragedy.

Domestic violence happens to all kinds of people. Women ages 16 to 24 are three times as likely to be victims of domestic violence compared to other age groups. Victims usually don't know much about domestic violence, so they are unaware of the cycle or the fact that abusers often intentionally prey on "susceptible" people. At first, abusers idolize their future target, making them feel admired and loved. They gain trust by sharing intimate details of their own life. They seduce and isolate their target from the people around them, developing a relationship of codependency. They introduce the threat of violence to see how the target will react (that is, will the target pull away or will they excuse the behavior?)—and then they escalate the violence.

One in three women are abused in the United States. What few people know is that the most dangerous step in a relationship in which a woman is experiencing domestic violence is when she leaves. Often, the outcome is murder.

Shame keeps women silent, and silence perpetuates abuse. Although I learned about all this, it wouldn't be until many years later that I would absorb the fact that all of this happened to me, with Donald and with Harold. And with Harold, that fated evening in 1991 would prove not to be my final encounter with the cycle of violence.

During the honeymoon period, it will appear to the victim that her abuser has genuinely changed and is back to the charming, caring person he pretended to be during the seduction phase. This is what happened to me—well after he'd strangled me and I'd moved out, with the belief that the nightmare was finally over.

In late 1993, I allowed Harold to move into my house on the lake with me. He spent hours telling me how sorry he was about everything he had done, how he missed me so much, and how miserable he was without me. My dating relationship had ended with the Kansas City CPA, and Harold begged if I would give him another chance, he would prove how repentant he was. He started doing thoughtful things, like bringing me flowers at work. I truly believed he was a changed man.

He wasn't.

Harold was no longer physically violent, but he was a master of manipulation and his abuse was often insidious in the way he managed to get into my head and make me doubt myself. He began coming up to me nearly every morning as I was in the kitchen preparing breakfast, and he would softly say in my ear, "Are you going to be lovable today?"

At first, without thinking, I would say, "Of course," not truly realizing or asking what he meant. I would come to learn that it meant whenever I did something he didn't like, he would refer to me as "unlovable." The effect of his seemingly innocuous question was that it implanted a sense of self-doubt. The longer it went on, the more I doubted myself. I began to think, *Maybe I really am not lovable. Maybe he's the only one who would ever want to date me.*

I knew I never wanted to marry him (or anyone else), but I still had the misperception that a person needed a boyfriend or girlfriend to be whole.

My mother and her third husband, Dale, married in September 1994, at which point a twinkle of hope that I could move on to something better came over me. Now that my mother was married, she had someone to take care of her, which perhaps meant I could be free.

New realizations that seemed to be urging me toward major lifestyle changes were sweeping into my life. For one thing, I was diagnosed with mononucleosis. It appeared as a cold that never went away. When I asked how in the world I could get mono at almost 38 years old, my doctor told me it was caused by stress. She informed me the only way to heal was to rest, and she said that if I stopped drinking alcohol, I would heal faster. I quit alcohol cold turkey, and my life transformed.

Being sober, I realized that my social life revolved around associating with Harold and his friends, who were a bunch of drunks. Listening to their sexist, racist "jokes" made me sick to my stomach. And how they laughed and made fun of others irritated me. When I had been a social drinker, I was oblivious, numb, and figuratively asleep. With sober eyes, I was jarred awake and had to admit I was running with a rough crowd: the kind of people who didn't add to the good of society, who didn't do volunteer work or have any kind of altruistic inclinations, and who used and abused alcohol. They also didn't appreciate that I was no longer drinking and complained that I wasn't fun to be around anymore.

When I stopped drinking, I knew I needed to make my plan to safely escape my relationship with Harold, but I had no idea how to do it. Moreover, my fear of being alone in my house at night had not gone away. In addition, my neighbors across the street, a nice couple close to my age, started inviting Harold and me over to their home on a regular basis. One evening, the wife confided to us that a counselor had told her she had low self-esteem. Harold shared with her that I was petrified at being alone in my house at night, probably in some kind of move to comfort her. She was stunned at this revelation, and I felt embarrassed and betrayed. I also saw a glint in Harold's eye, and given all I'd learned in my domestic-violence crisis training, I sensed Harold might start targeting our neighbor—so I made a mental note of it. By now, I knew his patterns well, and his wife had once written a letter to me that said, "You aren't the first woman my husband has cheated with, and you won't be the last."

I was beginning to recognize that the light at the end of the tunnel, which I'd been unconsciously awaiting for years, might never come. Maybe I had to be that light for myself.

**

In early 1995, one of my neighbors, Mark, approached me to set up a website for me so I could sell projectors on the newly commercial World Wide Web. We were using the new website Mark created by April. We were the only company in our entire industry, including the manufacturers, with a web presence. I was the only person in my office who was excited about the Internet. I could see unlimited potential and couldn't wait to see how it went. At first, I received about two emails per day. The first big sale was to an international school in Malaysia. My Proxima rep said they already had a dealer in Malaysia, but they hadn't worked with this account, so I could. The school sent a purchase order for 40 projectors. Then Proxima had a huge price drop. I emailed the school to let them know I'd like to pass on the lower prices to them. They emailed back and told me to keep the extra profit, as it was too much work to cut a new purchase order. It was too good to be true. They wired the money, and Proxima drop-shipped the 40 projectors to Malaysia for me. I was so grateful to Mark for asking me if he could make a website for me to see how it worked.

It was standard industry practice for companies and government agencies to ask for three dealers to send their "bids" for pricing. It turns out many dealers were colluding and would name one another on purpose. It turned out the dealers were "bid rigging"—deciding in advance which of the three would "win" the bid, deciding in advance what the price would be, and bidding above the agreed-upon price.

These same companies and government agencies searched on the Internet—and my company was the only name that appeared, so I would get a bid request out of the blue. I was not part of the three "colluders" and became a fourth-bid responder. When I got bid requests outside my territory, I filled out the bids at full retail price. To my surprise, I was winning all the bids I applied for. The dealers who lost the bids to me were upset and complained to my Proxima rep. When he called me to check it out, I told him I was just as surprised as he was, since I bid full retail price. He was also shocked.

I won several large bids at full retail price. Another way dealers tried to rig bids in their favor was to specify a requirement for onsite training. At the higher price, I was winning bids, and I had plenty of profit built in to afford to fly in, do training, and visit any of my friends who might live in these areas.

I was also swimming in many other adventures at the time. In March of 1995, I traveled to China with five other Nebraska women to promote Chinese/American friendship. I met with business leaders and government officials to investigate starting a Proxima distribution company in China. We traveled to Beijing and had a banquet in our honor at Beijing University. We'd all packed books about women to donate to the library at Beijing University for their Women History Studies program. We also toured schools and met with business leaders. I was fascinated to learn that Chinese students were given tests to determine their future. Had they only used test scores as a determinant of future career options, only women would have been able to become doctors, as they consistently scored higher; instead, China allowed for a 50/50 split, meaning that men could score lower and still become doctors. When I asked one of the Beijing University administrators if he felt that compromised the quality of doctors, he got upset.

In being on this trip with other women, my eyes were opened to the fact that I had neglected my own happiness and the power of fulfilling friendships with like-minded people. It was the first time in a long time I felt part of a group of women who were doing good in the world and whom I could also proudly call my personal friends.

**

In my commitment to have more fun, I splurged on a new ski boat in June of 1995. I was able to custom-select the colors. I chose white with purple and shocking-pink stripes on the exterior, with purple carpet for the interior. These were the same colors I'd had in my favorite childhood bedroom. The boat cost $30,000, which I paid with cash, as I had with nearly everything else I owned, including my home and car. This boat had a 454 horse power inboard engine that stayed quiet, and it could pull a skier out of the water in no time. It went from 0 to 60 miles per hour in 60 seconds. The lake I lived on was 350 water acres and about 1 mile by 1 1/4 mile big, so I could drive across the lake in record time.

Harold offered to register my boat for me, but the next year, when property taxes were due and I hadn't received a bill, I went in person to the registration office at the DMV and learned Harold had secretly registered my boat in both his name and the name of someone I believed was his former wife. They were recorded as "husband and wife" in the registration. I had to bring my original bill of sale to correct the registration. When I told Harold what I'd discovered, he was dismissive and didn't take responsibility or apologize. If I called Harold out, he would often attack me for being selfish or unlovable, and I would end up feeling guilty, like I was the source of the conflict. By this time, I knew I had to be careful and keep my assets safe from Harold, or he would simply take my property.

Another highlight was when Maxine Moul, Director of Nebraska Department of Economic Development, called to invite me to speak and be part of Governor Nelson's CEO Roundtable at their fall Nebraska Diplomats weekend. It was such an honor to represent small businesses in Nebraska. I was inducted as a member of the Nebraska Diplomats that year.

In addition to Maxine, I have been blessed with many role models and mentors. Alice Dittman, bank owner and president that I have known for years showed me how to be a gracious leader.

Later in 1995, what started as a severe pain in my leg culminated in a November 10 MRI that revealed a herniated disc in my lower back: the result of lifting a 40-lb. projector out of my trunk by myself as I wore high heels. My doctor recommended surgery immediately, but I had a five-day trip scheduled to Paris with the same friend who had organized our trip to China, so he gave me painkillers instead.

During my Paris trip, my friend asked me personal questions about my relationship with Harold. She wondered if he was supportive of me in our relationship. She was diplomatic but candid and even asked with authentic curiosity what I saw in him. Sadly, I realized I couldn't answer this question. As I tried in vain to rationalize or justify my relationship, I became aware I was lying to myself.

When I got back home, I was in too much pain to sit at my desk. I had to work standing up. I covered the surface of my desk with cardboard boxes to raise the surface to standing height, and I worked that way for several months. When I was driving, I got out of my car at stop lights to stretch and gain relief from the pain.

One of the lucky ramifications of my herniated disc was that I knew I had to work a lot less. Instead of maintaining my workaholic schedule, I went to the pool at 7 each morning, then went to work and left at 5 p.m. I told all the office staff they had to leave at 5 p.m., too. The transformation was remarkable. Everyone seemed happier to be at work, and our sales and profits skyrocketed.

I did many demonstrations of the projection equipment for salespeople in my office, and Harold asked if I could do one for him in Omaha. When we arrived, he told me he didn't feel well and would need to sit in the audience with the prospective client. This demonstration was held in the company auditorium with a stage and stadium-style seats. There were about 20 people seated. I set up the equipment, asked them questions to learn their needs, showed them the equipment, and answered all their questions. Harold sat quietly the entire time, not saying a word. After my demonstration, I walked off the stage to the crowd and he said to me loudly, "You did a very fine job, Karen."

I replied, "Thank you." I then met with some of the prospects, and one woman asked me how long I had been demonstrating equipment.

I said, "I started my projection-equipment company in 1988, so I've been doing this for several years." I handed her one of my cards with my CEO title. She looked so confused that I asked her, "Are you OK?"

She responded, "Harold told us you were in training and he was here to evaluate you." I tried to hide my dismay, but I was flabbergasted. I was grateful for the head's up, and that I had my title on my cards to avoid future misinformation. I couldn't believe that after all these years, I was still dealing with men's egos!

Back at my office, I called a board of directors meeting and presented a resolution to confirm my title as CEO or President retroactively from 1991 to present. It passed unanimously.

**

True to form, even as my personal situation maintained a level of direness and gloom, I found ways to let my spirit shine through and to support other women in moving forward with their dreams. I founded the Karen Dunning Fund endowment in late 1995 by working through the University of Nebraska Foundation. The endowment was for the benefit of the UNL Women and Gender Studies Department to do with what they felt best. The director at the time chose to use it to distribute scholarships to students in the program. The faculty chose the recipients for the scholarships and announced them in their annual awards ceremony. I have been honored to attend many ceremonies over the years and to have met so many gifted students and professors.

I had already planned to sell my company within five years or so and move on to a brighter future...hopefully, one that would allow me to disentangle from Harold altogether. My office manager, Annalise, had become a dear friend of mine. We maintained that friendship even after she quit her job with my company to work in a law firm, and I supported her in her decision to pursue her dreams. In 1995, when I knew I was close to the end of my five-year commitment to BMI, I called Jodi and told her I planned to sell my business to pursue other interests and would like her to come back to work for me so I could teach her how to run it. I was hoping she would buy my part in the business. To my delight, she said yes and came back to work for me in early 1996.

In 1996, 3M announced I had won an awards trip to Hawaii for purchasing a large amount of 3M projection equipment. I had planned to take one of my employees with me, but at the last second,

Harold decided he should come. Unfortunately, my employee felt she had been misled and quit soon after. I was still struggling with my herniated disc and was under treatment for it; at the time, I was only allowed to lift 1 lb. I asked Harold if he would please lift my bags for me at the airport, and he assured me he would.

The 3M trip was a lavish affair on the Big Island of Hawaii. All the top projection-equipment dealers were present. I had known most of them since 1989, well before I merged with BMI. On the awards night, Tom, the 3M manager I'd worked with since 1985, called my name for one of the top dealer awards. As I walked up to get my award, Harold brushed past me and I almost lost my balance. As Tom was handing me my award, Harold reached around me and tried to take it from me. Tom grabbed it back and said, "Geez, Harold!" and firmly placed the award in my hands. I thanked him and walked back to my table, attempting to smile and pretend I was OK. I wasn't. I was embarrassed by Harold's blatant display, and now all the top dealers had seen it firsthand.

After dinner, I was riding on the tram to return to my room, and Harold started yelling at me, at which point other dealers came to my aid. One woman pulled me aside and whispered, "Would you like us to walk you to your room?" I was scared and wanted to say yes, but I knew if I accepted help, it would be worse for me later. Instead, I whispered back, "He'll be passed out soon." Luckily for me, he was.

At the airport in Honolulu back to the mainland, with my injured back, instead of helping me with my bags as he'd promised, Harold refused to help me; he loudly announced to the passengers in line behind us, "Can you believe it? She packs a bag and can't even lift it!" I explained in a loud voice to the United Airlines counter agent, "I herniated a disc in my back and was given a 1-lb. weight-lifting limit, which is why my friend here had told me he would lift it for me." I was furious. To add insult to injury, Harold now seemed to want others to look upon me with the same disdain he did, but he didn't recognize it only made him appear even more awful.

In March of 1996, I was named Entrepreneur of the Year by the University of Nebraska College of Business Administration Center for Entrepreneurship for all my years of building businesses and contributing to my community. I was thrilled and honored to be recognized and rewarded for doing what I loved—what truly came naturally to me.

I received numerous congratulations from friends and family. I thought Harold would be happy and proud of me, but he became angry and jealous, so much so I told people not to congratulate me in front of him. I had taught Harold about the computer supply industry when he was my employee at DSM, and also taught him and other BMI employees about the presentation equipment business, after successfully becoming one of the largest Proxima dealers in the US and largest 3M dealer in Kansas City when I started CPI in 1988. He tried to take credit for the success of the presentation side of the business, despite the fact that he'd been opposed to it from the very beginning, when we merged companies. Annalise remembered how angry he'd gotten when I ordered more projectors. In fact, as the bookkeeper told me, Harold told her not to pay any invoices for "Karen's projectors." I only found out after my vendors called to tell me invoices were past due. After that, I had to micromanage accounts payable and other important business functions, as Harold seemed to be purposely doing things to sabotage the company...just as Donald had.

I recall reading a recent article that talked about narcissistic rage that described Harold's outbursts to a T. I can still recall how the amount of vitriol in his emotional explosions never matched the situation at hand. He was so out of control, it was frightening. The article mentioned something else that was a familiar pattern to me: Often, out of fear, the victim of domestic violence begins going along with whatever the abuser says or does and no longer confronts them about anything anymore, as they simply wish to avoid being the target of rage. This is what happened to me. I knew Harold's anger was completely unwarranted, sometimes even absurd, and if I weren't so afraid of being alone at night, perhaps I would have taken the step to break up with him once and for all. Ultimately, I let my fear stop me from what my heart had been telling me for so long.

**

In August 1996, the nightmare that was my relationship with Harold came to its end. One evening, as we sat on the dock enjoying the lake, he asked me a strange question: "Have you ever slept with a black man?" My answer was no, but this provoked a shocking revelation on his part.

He went on to talk about the black women he'd slept with in excruciating detail. By this time, I assumed this was another fishing tactic to get me to have sex with him and multiple partners. I became increasingly disgusted when Harold gleefully described orchestrating gang rapes of junior-high girls while in college and living at a fraternity house in Lincoln. He spoke about a black junior-high student whom he said had called him "Boofink" and detailed how he would pick her up at her home, lie to her father, bring her to the fraternity house, rape her, and invite his fraternity brothers to rape her, as well. He described spraying her with deodorant between boys. I became sick to my stomach, but he clearly didn't have a problem with the gruesome story he was telling me, as he was laughing while reminiscing—almost as if he were hearkening back to a happy moment.

"That poor girl, she must be so traumatized! You need to turn yourself in," I insisted.

He continued to laugh about it, as if I couldn't possibly be serious. He admitted that he'd inundated all his victims with beer so they were entirely disoriented and didn't know what was going on.

I escaped inside my house, threw up, and prayed: "Dear God, tell me what to do to get away from this person."

The next morning, I woke up, and for the first time in years, I felt completely free. I intuitively understood there was nothing that Harold could possibly say or do to maintain any power over me. I had my answer. I knew exactly what to do. I would dump Harold, sell my house, sell my business, and move to California. Suddenly, a plan that had felt so vague and reserved for some far-off future was beautifully clear.

I called my therapist friend Barbara and told her about it. She said I was proposing a lot of change at once and advised me to see a particular counselor to make sure I had my head on right. I immediately went to Sandra, who would be my counselor for the next two years, until right before I left for California. It was the best gift I ever gave myself. Sandra taught me that I get to choose—and my choice is always love. She also helped me to recognize that not everyone feels, thinks, and behaves the same way as I do, and that I have to recognize not everyone has my best interests at heart. Overall, Sandra's insights helped me to move from victim to victor in my life.

I told Sandra my plan to end my romantic relationship. I noted that I didn't know how to do it safely, as he was clearly a vindictive and dangerous man. She said, "He has changed your reality, and I will teach you tools to use to stand up for yourself."

The next question she asked me was, "What do you desire in a relationship?"

I was genuinely surprised and responded with a question: "Do you mean I have a choice?" All these years, I thought I had to make relationships work by molding myself into someone else. To go along to get along. It must have been subconscious programming. I felt fortunate that I was finally getting an opportunity to dig beneath the surface and to change those toxic beliefs, wherever they'd come from.

The journey was enlightening and fascinating. I had so many "ah-ha" moments that helped me to empower myself so I could move from being a victim to knowing I was a victor...a survivor.

Finally, I recognized that I had total and complete control over myself, that I was not responsible for other people's actions. I was only responsible for my own actions. I met with the counselor once a week and went over what had happened the week before, and she would ask me lots of questions and suggest responses to the situation if it occurred again.

I had originally planned to sell my business and then break up with Harold but, as I learned new tools and recognized just how unhealthy my relationship was, I kicked him out of my house once and for all in October of 1996. He refused to completely leave, so it wasn't until my birthday, December 3, 1996, he finally moved the last of his items. By now, he was living with a former neighbor, who had also been his lover for the past year, unbeknownst to me. When he moved out of my house, he stood by with a broken leg and ordered her to remove a large picture off the wall, which she did unquestioningly, even when I informed her the picture was mine and she shouldn't listen to Harold. She was so brainwashed that she was acting like his loyal servant. But he was out of my hair, and it felt terrific. It was the best birthday present I could have hoped for.

To my delight, I have never been afraid to be alone at night ever since I stood up for myself and ended my toxic relationship with Harold.

Ending things with Harold opened up a new window in my life. Suddenly, the dark corner I'd painted myself into over the course of our relationship was drenched with light and possibility. I began to feel like *me* again, not simply some contorted version of who he'd wanted me to be. I started playing my piano again and doing things I loved. I stopped sitting around in bars with barfly friends, and I began dancing. I focused on my business and my volunteer work, which gave me great joy.

Some of my so-called friends had a negative reaction to the new and improved version of Karen. They accused me of being a victim when I asserted myself, stood up for what I believed in, and voiced my opinions. Because I was seeing a counselor every week, I was able to stay on my own path instead of allowing their judgments to sway me. I felt validated in my decisions, and I knew that I would no longer hitch myself to someone else's boat the second they needed me. I would not abandon my own boat or let it wander down the river of my life without me.

**

In 1996, I had another wonderful experience that helped to set the stage for the life I knew I wanted to move into: one in which I could use my gifts for the greatest good. I was the only business owner in Nebraska invited to attend the White House Economic Summit, held at Kellogg School of Management at Northwestern University in Evanston, Illinois. The summit's purpose was to teach women business owners how to access all-important capital market resources to enable them to expand and grow. Women-owned businesses were not receiving their fair share of this important resource to grow their businesses, and since women-owned businesses were the fastest-growing market segment at the time, the White House was determined to do its part to educate business owners through seminars, networking events, and one-on-one counseling sessions. The summit was attended by several hundred business owners from across the United States. I met the U.S. Treasury Secretary, Small Business Administration officials, U.S. Senators and members of Congress, and others.

I also became acquainted with a company that developed entrepreneurial seminars for girls ages 13 through 17, called An Income of Her Own. The purpose of their seminars was to give girls a new perspective about their futures. If a girl is exposed to possibilities and caring women business owners, she has a better chance of seeing and expanding possibilities for herself.

When I returned to Lincoln, I shared what I learned with the

Lancaster County Commission on the Status of Women. I asked the director if the Commission might be interested in doing the administrative work to bring An Income of Her Own's seminars to Lincoln if I raised money for a one-day seminar. The seminar would be for a hundred girls, and the total cost would be $10,000. The Commission said yes, and I raised the $10,000 by enlisting many of my customers to sponsor a girl for $100 each to attend the conference. The first bank I approached donated $5,000 to sponsor 50 girls. In March of the following year, the one-day seminar was attended by a hundred girls, selected by their teachers and counselors, who attended Lincoln Public School junior highs and high schools. Twenty local women business owners donated their time to act as role models for the girls. The founder of An Income of Her Own flew from California to Lincoln to facilitate the event. It was remarkable.

By the time 1997 came around, I felt a new sense of purpose. I loved being single, and I felt safe and free in my own home. My personal life had improved dramatically as I let go of even more toxic relationships and continued to learn coping tools from Sandra, my counselor.

At work, however, I was still interacting with Harold, although I could now see him exactly for what he was, with a newfound sense of clarity and empowerment. Harold seemed to be doing whatever he could to sabotage BMI, and he had already threatened me by saying he would tear it apart. Our office was receiving multiple calls from angry clients about the false promises Harold had made them. I was working overtime to smooth ruffled feathers and fix what Harold seemed intent to break.

Annalise was our office manager and was reporting to me every word Harold said to other dealers about me. Sandra was also helping me to formulate my language in my responses to Harold's horrible behavior. I was "documenting" everything he said and did, much to his increased anger and hostility. I was determined to sell out and keep the business viable, but there were definitely days when I was tempted to walk out and never come back, leaving all my money on the table.

Now, I was ready. I had more than fulfilled my verbal commitment to stay at BMI for five years and was itching for a quick sale, so I made plans to move to the West Coast. I'd already had an evaluation from a professional company specializing in business valuation, as well as one from Merrill Lynch and another from a company in San Diego. My goal was to sell my business for $400,000. I went to my bank to arrange financing for whoever purchased from me. Based on my current financials, they could loan me $400,000. Perfect.

On February 21, 1997, I was honored to be asked by my neighbor, Mark, to participate on a panel and speak about my Internet experience at the International Association of Business Communication's (IABC) Internet Workshop. It was held at the University of Nebraska–Lincoln at the Wick Alumni Center. I sang the praises of Mark, who originally asked me if he could set me up on the World Wide Web to see how effective it was. Because of his efforts, my business was selling all over the United States and in many parts of the world. I detailed how I was able to convert one email from a school in Malaysia into a $40,000 profit. One of my recommendations for participants was that they reserve their website domain names as soon as possible to avoid the disappointment of finding their desired name already taken.

In April of 1997, I went to California to be certified by An Income of Her Own as a trainer to present my own seminars. I loved speaking, and I also loved sharing my own insight about what it meant to own my businesses, as well as the level of freedom it had afforded me. That month, I spoke at the leadership conference of the Nebraska Family, Career & Community Leaders of America (FCCLA), a national vocational student organization that belongs to the Department of Education. Appropriately, my seminar was titled

"You Can Be Your Own Boss."

**

In April of 1997, Harold called me into his office when I returned from lunch. He was clearly upset as he informed me that someone had called him to say they'd seen me at lunch with another man— and apparently, he was heartbroken.

I was astounded. "Who called you?" I asked.

"I'm not telling," he responded.

"Are you spying on me?"

He remained silent, so I continued, "I broke up with you last October. My personal life is none of your business, so stop following me."

I was irritated by Harold's childish displays and attempts to regain my affection. However, I had unknowingly created a legal situation whereby neither one of us had the authority to fire the other. We had equal power: I as CEO and him as President. I had worked with an attorney to cement my title, as I knew Harold would likely try to fire me if he became upset enough. The attorney devised a plan whereby either of us could be fired if we violated company resolutions. Knowing Harold, I recognized that he would be likely to shoot himself in his own foot through his sabotaging behaviors, so I held out the hope that I'd someday be able to fire him.

For all of 1997, Harold kept telling me he couldn't get over me and couldn't bear to see me dating anyone else, as he was supposedly deeply in love with me. I wasn't convinced. I knew this was probably his way of purposely stalling on buying me out of the business. All the while, he was stringing on women who thought he was their boyfriend. I had zero interest in Harold's personal life but, as Annalise told me everything, she included all the sordid details— including the fact that he was telling other people lies about how I wanted to get back together with him.

I was also approaching what felt like the end of my work in the presentation-equipment industry. One customer, a trucking firm, called me because their projector kept turning off. Their regular salesperson wasn't returning their calls and they needed their projectors on constantly, as they used them to dispatch their fleet of vehicles. I went over and saw their projectors had been installed in a small enclosed space, where they were overheating and turning off. They told me their salesperson said it would be fine. It reminded me of my IBM days, when the systems engineers had to fix all the problems created by salespeople who overpromised and underdelivered, then let someone else clean up the mess they'd created. At IBM, they called this "putting out fires." As CEO of my company, the buck stopped with me, and I felt responsible for the errors of the salesperson.

It was a good time for me to sell out to someone who was excited about the design-build aspect (meaning a dealer would help their client with the entire installation of their projection equipment) of the business.

Still, I was dealing with major issues, including the fact that Harold was charging personal expenses on the company credit card and not paying for them, and then arguing about it. Also, while Harold had a company car, I didn't. Way back in 1991, I also discovered that Harold had doctored and manufactured minutes to a board of directors meeting. A second page was added, with false activity reported. I remedied that by requiring that every page of minutes contain my original signature in order to be considered valid.

Annalise was still considering buying my stock, but she had some big concerns when it came to sharing a business with Harold. "Even when I know the truth, after he twists it I think the truth is a lie and the lie is the truth." She ultimately decided that she would not purchase my stock but would purchase his stock if I would stay.

Annalise also observed that Harold always did and said the opposite of whatever I said or did. With this new epiphany, I went to Harold and told him I had changed my mind about selling my business and desired instead to purchase his stock. As Annalise predicted, he did the opposite—now, after years of dissuading me from leaving the business, he suddenly wanted to purchase my stock.

Soon after, our bookkeeper came to me to show me extensive personal charges on our business credit card—all charges that Harold had made. I called my attorney and had the locks at work changed; when Harold came to work, I told him he had violated our resolution and was no longer an employee. He threatened me and stormed out. A couple hours later, he came back with his familiar voice of false care and said, "I know we can still work together."

I was well past being manipulated by Harold ever again. I firmly replied, "No, we can't. I will let you buy me out for $400,000, and you have until Friday to arrange your financing and buy my stock. If you can't arrange your financing, I will buy you out on Friday for the same amount." My attorney also drew up a Board of Directors Special Meeting notice to vote on removing Harold as an employee of BMI in case he didn't buy my stock.

I had already written the non-compete clause for whoever was bought out to abide by.

I told all employees what was going on and that I would be selling my stock, resigning, and moving to California. They gave me a heartfelt send-off with cards, a cake, and many thanks for all they had learned from me. I knew that I, too, had learned from them, and I was truly honored by their devotion and caring. Finally, it felt as if I'd be getting the proper ending I never got with IBM or DSM.

On August 4, 1997, with August 7 as the date of the final transfer. Harold arrived with his attorney, whom I knew. I greeted him warmly. He said hi but seemed sheepish. Was he embarrassed to be representing my former business partner? The signing and check exchange was short and quick. Then Harold brought up my DSM non-compete and implied I was untrustworthy. I reminded him that the only point of scrutiny in that case was when my attorney directed me to let Mutual of Omaha know they could acquire HP toner from him, directly benefiting *him*.

The day I signed papers and received money for my stock was a great relief. I had also written a verbally agreed-upon thank-you and farewell letter to be sent to all my customers, informing them I was resigning as CEO and selling my business. I learned it was never sent. Instead, Harold wrote up a letter with false claims that I refused to sign. I was deeply saddened that my customers would not be getting the thank-you and farewell letter I had written, after all. My customers were all so important to me, and it was upsetting to learn that even years later, some of them still thought I owned the company and still believed it was woman-owned, as they had never been told the truth.

When I sold out, BMI was in the best financial shape it had ever been in. It had zero debt, an established line of credit, and a well-trained team—and was poised for a successful transition to design build, so it could adapt to the ever-changing industry. I was proud of what I had created—and I was ready, willing, and able to embark on my next adventure.

As I returned to my lake home the day I sold my business, I was floating on air. I danced and twirled about in my living room, practically touching the 12-foot ceilings. I felt sparkly, strong and safe.

I had ended my time with BMI in the best possible way, and I was finally free.

CHAPTER 12

FINDING MY OWN PATH

After breaking the cycle of violence for the final time, my life became more joyful and vibrant than it had been in years. I continued to go to counseling and learn more about myself, and I felt as if I were discovering dimensions of my life I had never known. It was exhilarating, like I was falling in love with myself for the first time.

Once I sold my business, I took a couple weeks to relax and enjoy myself. It was perfect lake weather. I took my Baja boat on a river trip with friends, then sold it to a family with three young daughters who loved the purple carpeting and pink and purple stripes. I went dancing with friends and meeting new people, and I continued to work on my volunteer boards. I was also taking flying lessons, and I started taking voice lessons with a talented and highly regarded musician and vocal coach. The relief of being out of a toxic personal and business relationship did wonders for my appearance. I looked and felt great.

I was also at the end of my three-year term as Vice President of the Lincoln Lancaster County Commission of the Status of Women, an appointment I'd received from the mayor. As a commissioner, one of my duties was to see what needed to be done to gain equality for women. The other commissioners were a diverse group of women, and we had lively discussions at our monthly meetings.

I was also serving as the board Treasurer of Planned Parenthood as at the same time. The mayor had converted from a Democrat to a Republican and claimed to be a born-again Catholic. He went from supporting Planned Parenthood funding of sex education in schools to opposing it and taking a staunchly pro-life stance. I had known him and his second wife years ago when they were both married to other people. She had worked with me at IBM, and I was the chair of her successful election campaign for Lancaster County Commissioner. They had even set me up on a date with one of his friends after I filed for divorce.

I recognized a disturbing trend in local politics that year. The Republican party in Lincoln went from moderate to far right. The Catholic Church started busing Catholics to the annual Republican County Convention and actively voted out any Republican who desired women to have personal control over their own bodies.

I had been active in the Republican party starting in 1972 in junior high. I had been asked by the Republican Party to run for Nebraska State Auditor in the early 90's. I was all for the Equal Rights Amendment, and also for everyone to have the right to privacy. The Republican party had always stated it was on the side of personal freedom and limited government interference. It made no sense to me that the Republican party was now actively trying to interfere with my personal rights. My civil rights and my body had been violated on several occasions, and the laws had never supported me. In fact, they seemed to have been designed to favor perpetrators. I was standing up for myself and all citizens by telling the government to stay out of my personal business. I was so disheartened to see the strong influence of the Catholic Church on the party, so I stopped being active.

In the meantime, I was still dealing with Harold's antics. After selling my BMI shares, I met with a realtor to list my house and had a big party to celebrate my new freedom. My realtor's guest asked me whose house it was and, when I told him it was mine, he didn't believe me. He told me that Harold had claimed to own the house. I said, "No, I've been the only owner. I built it and paid cash for it and moved in in 1993." He still didn't believe me. My realtor, who had looked up all the tax records, assured the guest that I was the only owner.

That is how convincing some manipulators can be. The truth

becomes lies, and lies become truth.

My future was wide open at this point. I was approached by several dealer friends to see if I might work for them: Epson asked me to interview for a National Sales Manager position; Proxima asked me to interview for CEO or a VP Sales position; a local business owner asked me to consider being CEO of a company he owned in Lincoln; one of my customers, at a company called Paragon, asked me to work for him on the West Coast selling a proprietary assessment tool designed for large retail stores and the hospitality industry to improve their customer service; and yet another business friend asked me if I might stay in Lincoln and become CEO of his company. I still didn't know what I wanted to do, but my heart had already decided on the West Coast quite a while ago. In 1997, I invested in An Income of Her Own, which converted to a for-profit company called Independent Means (IMI), headquartered in Santa Barbara, California. I had already gone through the training and seminars in California, and I knew I loved mentoring girls in entrepreneurial skills.

Still, I wasn't prepared to make any immediate decisions. I had started a new company right after leaving IBM, and I'd embarked on yet another business even before the ink had dried on my disastrous divorce settlement. I wanted to be intentional about my next direction.

In December of 1997, I prepared for a four-week trip to New Zealand and Australia. By coincidence, my brother's family was flying to Australia to spend time with a family his wife had stayed with 30 years prior as part of a high-school study-abroad program, so I had the added bonus of joining them for Christmas. I flew into Auckland, New Zealand, and met with a travel agent who mapped out a driving route to tour the South Island. Driving on the left side of the road was a challenge, but away I went, exploring and admiring the scenery along the way. It felt amazing to return to one of my first loves: travel and discovery of a new place. I met many local residents and learned about local customs. At the time, there were 3 million inhabitants and 30 million sheep. After New Zealand, I flew to Australia, spent time with my family, and toured much of the eastern coast of the continent.

It was a wonderful reprieve from Lincoln. When I got back home in January of 1998, I knew it was time to move forward. My house was already on the market, so I busied myself tying up loose ends, saying my goodbyes, and resigning from volunteer boards.

I had an estate sale to pare down my belongings and started packing. Soon enough, I was on my way to Los Angeles to apartment-hunt and meet with friends. I reserved an apartment in West Los Angeles a few miles from the ocean, with an ocean view.

I accepted a sales job with my former client, Paragon, which would begin when I got to California. The job allowed me the freedom of living anywhere I wanted on the West Coast. Paragon's assessment tool was fascinating to me and, while I would work for them, I'd be their only employee on the West Coast, so I had total control of my schedule.

I could feel it in my bones: I was finally ready to move on to the next phase of my life. No regrets, and no backward glances.

**

It was spring of 1998, and this new era of my life ushered in a fresh breeze filled with spiritual-growth opportunities and expanded lessons. I was taking plenty of time to know myself and to enjoy the new rhythms of my life.

My 24th-floor apartment overlooked the ocean and had a wide balcony. Every morning, I rode the elevator to the street level and swam laps in the Olympic-size pool. A regular group of five women, all over age 60, hung out poolside every morning, having coffee in the shallow end.

I loved LA. I felt so anonymous. No one knew my name!

One of my goals was to learn the entertainment industry so I could be instrumental in developing more positive roles for women on TV and in movies. I called Stan, the founder of AMC Theatres, one of my former projection-equipment clients, and asked him if he knew anyone I could talk to. He did. "Call my West Coast man, Bob, and tell him I sent you."

I called Bob and went to his office. He was the former president of Paramount Pictures and knew everything and everyone, including all the A-list stars. He was candid and told me I was too lowly for their consideration, but what he could do was make me lunch and dinner reservations at the best LA restaurants at the prime table. I soon learned that was a huge favor. The first time I called him to make a reservation was at Spago. When I arrived, the valet graciously took my car and I was escorted in like royalty. The staff fawned over me and took me to a table in the power position with a bird's-eye view of the restaurant. As A-listers arrived, they paused to look at this woman seated at the prime table. I was amused by the spectacle and wondered why in the world anyone would care who was at what table!

I had started voice lessons in Lincoln, and I continued them in Los Angeles. My Los Angeles teacher had studied at Julliard and was an opera singer. He gave me daily exercises and arias to learn. His home in the Hollywood Hills was spacious, with two concert grand pianos in the huge music room.

I also met up with some cabaret singers from New York City who adopted me and invited me to attend open mics with them. The first night, I sang my favorite song, "Your Song" by Elton John. One of them said, "Forget the lessons, you simply need to get out and *sing*!" I didn't have any real aspirations of quitting my day job and becoming a singer, but I decided to do both: keep taking lessons and keep getting out there to sing.

As for my work with Paragon, I was truly grateful for the opportunity, which had given me a place to land upon my big move out west, but I quickly discovered that my heart was in the entertainment industry and I resigned a few months later upon returning from an international trade mission to China.

So, how can someone completely new to the entertainment industry find their way in? Networking! Nebraskans are quick to help other Nebraskans, and they are scattered all over the place. There was a large contingent in Los Angeles, and one introduction led to another. I was introduced to Lew, chairman of the UCLA screenwriting program; he also had extensive industry experience. Lew in turn introduced me to Todd, founder of the Nebraska Coast Connection, which held monthly networking meetings designed to help people in the entertainment industry. Most of the attendees were from Nebraska, knew someone from Nebraska, or liked Nebraska. Todd told me the first meeting had several hundred attendees. As of this writing, he is still hosting monthly meetings, now via Zoom during the pandemic.

Another Lincoln friend encouraged me to contact the actor Ed Asner. I did, and we made a lunch date. When we came back from lunch, he called his agent, told her about me, and arranged for me to meet her. I met with her, and she connected me to opportunities to serve with nonprofit organizations in LA.

I also joined Women in Film (WIF), a networking group composed of women and men who supported women in the film industry. They had many meetings and networking events each month. I met many talented individuals who were working to create film projects to improve opportunities and roles for women and address serious issues in the film industry, such as sexual harassment, especially against women, and the perennial "casting couch," whereby roles are given to women only if they sleep with a director. We also addressed sexual violence on screen and in person, such as casting women characters as powerless, representing businesswomen as ruthless bitches or moms as passive, and not casting movies and TV shows that reflected what SAG called the American scene. For example, in 1988, women were underrepresented and men were overrepresented on TV and in movies. I decided to join the committee to create public service announcements (PSAs).

Later that year, I was accepted as a member of the Screen Actors Guild. My acting career began in a role as a female doctor extra on the prime-time series *Chicago Hope* for one season. I also acted in movies and other TV shows.

The way the industry worked is that actors would sign up at the casting companies, which hired background performers for various shows and movies. Central Casting was the largest agency at that time, so I signed up with them. They would take a prospective actor's photo and gather other information. Sometimes they submitted your name and photo for a potential job, but in the beginning, the best way to secure a job was to regularly call the casting help line and listen for the available parts. If any of them were a fit, you would call the casting agent for that job—and if they felt you had the right look for the part, they would book you. Usually, the parts on the line were for the very next day.

I called on a Friday evening, and the line asked for a 40-something female doctor for *Chicago Hope* the following Monday. I immediately got in contact with the casting agent and told her I'd like to be considered. Actually, I pleaded: "May I be the female doctor, please?" It was a prime role.

Usually, the casting agents liked to give the better roles to actors they already knew and had a relationship with. I was brand spanking new. She asked me lots of questions about what type of clothes I had, how reliable I would be, and what my overall experience was. She seemed skeptical at first, but she warmed up as we spoke and she finally said, "Oh, all right, you can have the role."

Chicago Hope was filmed on the 20th Century Fox lot, which was only a 20-minute drive from my apartment via surface streets, so I was never in LA traffic and didn't have the hassle of driving on the interstate to get there. In the acting industry, each role had a "call time" for arrival. One must be early and ready to go on set before the call time. If you were late, even by a few seconds, you were often sent home.

When I showed up at 20th Century Fox, the guard directed me to the parking lot for extras. I was friendly and thanked her. Then I walked to the area outside the stage where *Chicago Hope* was filmed. First, I was checked in with the assistant director as to my name and role, then directed to wardrobe, where there was a line of extras with the clothes they'd been instructed to bring. The wardrobe manager liked what I was wearing, so there was no need for me to change and I was admitted inside the building, where filming took place.

Chicago Hope was a weekly hour-long drama. Each episode took about eight days to film. Each day, the actors were presented with the script for that day, known as "sides." Usually, extras didn't get copies of the sides, nor did they get to watch what occurred during the filming unless they were needed for that particular scene. When I became a regular extra on *Chicago Hope*, all of that changed.

For now, I was simply a non-union extra, the lowest position on the set. We were not to approach or speak to the big stars unless they spoke to us first. As I stood in line for the wardrobe check-in, Mark Harmon happened to walk by and I quickly said, "Harley says hi." Harley was one of my friends from high school, who happened to be a successful actor in LA. When I'd told her the good news, she'd asked me to pass on her greeting to Mark. He stopped and came over to me, and I introduced myself to him. He was gracious and kind—unusual in comparison to some other actors, who could be somewhat frosty and removed from the extras.

When I was on set, the stars were so skilled that we rarely had to do a second take for each of the three camera angles. If it was a guest star, sometimes they became so nervous that they forgot their lines and we had to start over numerous times. "Back to one," the director would call, and we'd have to remember our exact steps and where we were on a certain line of dialogue.

In between scenes, anyone who was not needed would be escorted by the second assistant director back to the extra holding area. It was a dimly lit room with wooden chairs. Extras milled around; some played cards, read books, or talked quietly. This was in the era before cell phones. I had a pager and a Palm Pilot with addresses, so I could type notes while I waited, but I mostly met the other extras and learned about their experiences: how long they had been doing this and what their future goals were. Many of them were "$2 million away from my first film." It seemed everyone was looking for someone else to fund their dream film that they'd direct, produce, and act in. One extra lived in an RV and drove from set to set. Most were non-union in the holding area. The union extras were treated a little better and could hang out in the craft service area, where there were snacks and lunch for the actors.

At lunch, we all went to the craft service area. The more prominent actors usually ate separately in their trailers. The crew lined up first, then came the union extras, and lastly, the non-union extras. Sometimes, there would be a line for union extras with what looked like delicious food, while the non-union extras were left with hot dogs.

In the afternoon, I decided this was a fun way to spend my day and told the second assistant director I was really enjoying his set and hoped I would be asked back. I recall him saying, "You *look* like a doctor." After that, anytime the script called for a female doctor extra, I would be called in, usually three to four times a week, so I became part of the regular group of extras on *Chicago Hope*. There were about ten regular extras, and some had been there since the original pilot. They were a close-knit group and welcomed me into their ranks, giving me useful pointers. We were not confined to the holding area but were free to stay on set during filming and get to know the crew and actors. The crew found out I was interested in learning more, so they would point out why they were using certain lights or camera angles. It was a congenial team. The weekly dramas had different directors come in for each episode, so I was exposed to various directing styles. The actors were all skilled and professional, and I learned by osmosis from them.

As a regular extra, I received my own name badge, as well as a stethoscope and lab coat. When they asked me what type of doctor I'd like to be, I chose cardiologist, as my dad had died of a heart attack. One morning on my way to *Chicago Hope*, I was in my apartment elevator going down to the parking garage wearing my TV name tag and lab coat. A sweet elderly couple entered the elevator and said, "Oh, we see you're a doctor."

I smilingly replied, "Yes, a cardiologist."

They looked at my name tag. "*Chicago Hope*. Now, where is that?"

I replied, "It's on TV."

They looked confused, so I surmised they hadn't seen the show.

Each morning I drove into 20th Century Fox, I was always friendly to the guard. One evening when I left, she said, "I have to tell you what happened this morning. The car behind you saw you pull into the parking lot for extras and asked me, 'How in the hell does an extra afford a Jaguar?'"

I asked, "What did you say?"

She replied, "I told them, 'She's a darn fine extra!'"

**

Every set has its own unique personality. Some of the TV shows I was on after Chicago Hope included *ER* and *LA Doctor*. I also appeared in movies: I was a featured disco dancer in *Gun Shy*, and I also appeared in *The Doris Duke Story* and *Bowfinger*, which was a 24-hour shoot in the famous Mann's Chinese Theatre. Steve Martin did comedy for the thousand extras as we waited between scenes. Many of the extras were asleep in their chairs, and crew members would walk up and down the aisles to wake people up for filming.

For long-term acting success, it was essential to be in the union. The various sets helped me acquire enough SAG vouchers to qualify for membership. The union had requirements for sets to hire so many extras; if they had to hire more, they could hire non-union extras for half the pay. Sometimes the sets were unable to book enough SAG members and could fill them in with non-union extras. Sometimes a set needed fewer than 20 extras for a day but still couldn't find enough SAG extras, so they could hire a non-union actor and pay them SAG wages, providing the lucky extra with a SAG voucher. With three SAG vouchers, a person was eligible to join the union. It took me three months to qualify for SAG membership. The average back then was about 18 months.

The American Federation of Television and Radio Artists (AFTRA) was the union for soap operas, radio hosts, and TV news anchors. The unions were separate at the time, but there was pressure to combine the unions into one larger union, so SAG-AFTRA was born in 2012. I joined AFTRA and was immediately booked on the soap opera *The Bold and the Beautiful*. The experience was night and day from a typical SAG set. I was still an extra but, when I arrived, I was escorted to my own private suite, complete with refreshments. I was the only extra on the set and had a prominent role, with many on-camera views. Everyone treated me as a special guest. The wardrobe department outfitted me with an expensive suit and matching shoes, even hose and undergarments, and did my hair and makeup. The day was over in about 5 hours, versus up to 12 on many SAG shoots.

Besides my weekly voice lessons, I took numerous acting classes. I attended the Groundlings Improv classes, regular acting classes, cold-reading classes designed to help with the audition process, hosting classes designed for newscasters, and voiceover classes.

I had done extensive speaking about my business experiences, in addition to some motivational speaking. I decided I'd like to add humor to my speeches and took a standup comedy class with Judy Carter. The weekly class of about 15 students, most of whom were in their early twenties, was held in Judy's home studio and culminated in a combination of all her classes performing at the LA Improv. We learned the basics, and each week we were expected to have written more of the routine we would eventually perform for our class and to receive critiques from our teacher and fellow students.

Every week, we brought a tape recorder to class so we could record ourselves and listen later. One technique was to rant into your tape recorder at home, which might eventually surface some material that could be incorporated into our routines. I did my rants and brought material each week, and no one ever laughed. Not once. My material was not funny, and I was often advised to "dumb it down." I was told that audiences were usually drinking and out for a good time, and they didn't want to hear anything too serious. It was so dumbed down that by the end I didn't like it—and I still wasn't getting any laughs. I had no desire to invite anyone to my performance at the LA Improv, but Judy said it was important to have support in the audience, so I invited my college-age niece. There would be 90 students, performing 5 minutes each of stand-up comedy, for 2 to 3 days in front of friends and agents from the industry. The day of the event, I called my AMC mentor, Bob, and told him I was performing.

He barked, "Let's hear it."

I dutifully went through my routine, and he barked more loudly, "That's not funny!"

I replied, "When I pause for laughter, it will be."

I arrived at the LA Improv, and when my niece and her friends arrived, I found them a good table and started a tab. I told them, "As soon as I say my line, I need you to laugh fast, and laugh loud."

My turn came. I started my routine and said my first line. I heard a loud "Ha, ha, ha!" coming from the direction of my niece's table, and then, laughter rippled across the entire room. I waited and delivered line after line in that manner. The five minutes went by quickly. I was invited to sit at a table with one of the agents, who asked, "Is that really the first time you've ever gone up?"

"Yes," I said.

The next day, I was notified that 2 students out of 90—me and a young man—were selected by agents to submit their tapes. This was the company that represented Jerry Seinfeld, I was told. Nothing came of it, but I continued to do standup at open mics around the LA area with my comedy friends for the fun of it. I didn't really care whether I would eventually hitch my wagon to a star—I was simply enjoying the newfound burst of creative freedom that was now my daily reality.

CHAPTER 13

A NEW WEST COAST EXPERIENCE

One of the most exciting things about being on the West Coast was the newness of the culture, which was so different from the salt of the earth mentality I'd been accustomed to in the Midwest. I was suddenly being exposed to all kinds of new mindsets and philosophies, from the New Age vibes of the yoga and healing enthusiasts to the creative innovations of the entertainment industry.

One of my friends invited me to a seminar in LA. When I arrived, I discovered it was all about healing family relationships. There were hundreds of people in attendance. Some had not spoken to family members for years and had forgotten why they had stopped talking. The last assignment was to call our parents and tell them how much we loved them. They warned us not to be surprised if we received no response. Regardless of the other person's reaction, our goal was to simply express how we felt.

I grew up in a family that held emotions tightly and rarely discussed them. After the class, I called my mom and told her I loved her...and as I'd expected, there was dead silence on the other line. But after a few months of my consistently ending the call by saying I loved her, she eventually told me she loved me, too.

Unfortunately, I was also dealing with some unfinished business from BMI. I had started the BMI profit-sharing plan when I was CEO, and as expected, I received my required distribution from the time I worked for BMI in 1997. The money, about $12,000.00 was deposited as I expected in May of 1998. However, on my next statement, I noticed that the deposit had been reversed. I called BMI to find out what happened; I was told that Harold had changed his mind and taken my money. I explained with as much patience as I could muster that such a maneuver was illegal and violated IRS rules, but still, Harold refused to give me my money. I called the company that had drawn up our plan, and they told me I had to get the paperwork from BMI. BMI refused to give it to me, as required. I had to get an attorney involved in the matter. As it turned out, I never did get my distribution. I recently learned that what Harold had done was an IRS violation and was told I could still complain to the IRS, since it was an IRS-sanctioned profit-sharing plan. Back in 1998, I didn't realize this or even know to call the IRS. I recall thinking, *It's only $12,000, and perhaps it got redistributed to some of my former employees.*

I also received many concerned calls from friends and former clients, as well as my mom, after a misleading article was published in a Lincoln paper effectively changing the history of BMI and even taking credit for starting my presentation-equipment side of the business. Again, I contacted an attorney. I knew I had no control over what a person might tell the paper or others, but I also knew I had a right to tell my truth.

In 2002, I received more phone calls regarding another article about BMI. In it, Harold once more took credit for the projection-equipment side of the business and everything else—no mention of me or how two companies had merged together. I like to avoid conflict, but my friend, Barbara, the counselor, told me it was important for me to tell my truth, so I wrote a factual and diplomatic editorial, and it was printed. Harold must have had a narcissistic rage attack, as the employee I spoke to at the paper was clearly rattled. She said a man had called, yelled, and threatened to sue the newspaper for printing my editorial, as I was a "liar." I told them I wasn't surprised, as he had threatened me in the past. I had any supporting documentation they might need and knew where to find evidence within the company, too.

By this time, I'd broken my cycle of domestic violence, but I had one more lesson to learn before breaking the family cycle of dealing with con artists.

Before I left Lincoln in 1998, I encountered an extremely handsome man—the most beautiful man I had ever met. When I told him I was going to California he decided that he, too, was going to California. We decided to go together. I dated him for a short time. He was sweet while sober, but the smallest bit of alcohol changed him into an unpleasant person.

The silver lining was that I went to Al-Anon, a worldwide fellowship that offers a recovery program for friends and family members of alcoholics. This led me to make the choice to end our relationship, as I knew that it would never change and would likely worsen if I remained.

I called his mother to tell her, and she said, "I love my son, but he's a con artist. The family debated telling you but chose not to because we figured you're an adult".

This was practically the same language my mom had received when she divorced Albert when I was in high school. I felt great relief in knowing that I could finally trust my discernment.

**

In 1999, a Lincoln friend called me about a dot-com opportunity. The company was based in Iowa and needed a West Coast sales rep for a revolutionary product that was still under development. The owners flew out to interview me and explain what they needed. I could live anywhere on the West Coast if I took the job.

The product was a software program that analyzed word patterns. It was being used to analyze stories schoolchildren had written to help detect those who might be at risk for committing crimes, such as the Columbine shooting, which had happened earlier that year. The program could use word patterns to predict the future success of job applicants, too, and that would be the major planned use. The company had offers from large consumer organizations that wanted to use the product to better market their products, but the owners of the technology thought it could be misused and were rejecting the offers, at least for now. I would be paid a base salary, and when the software was complete, I'd be on base plus commission.

At the time, my true dream was to sing, but I was in an avoidance pattern around it. People would call me to do something business-related, since I was good at it, and in many ways, I didn't know how to say no. I figured that if they were asking me, it must be part of my life path. I hadn't really laid out any goals and was simply bobbing along the river of my life, so I was now ready to jump off my boat and onto someone else's at the drop of a hat.

I visited a friend in the Bay Area and drove across the Golden Gate Bridge to Marin County. The banks of fog, dappled with sunlight and surrounded by greenery, were so picturesque. I thought, "If I can find a place to rent here, I'm going to move."

My first stop was a realty office. The agent asked what I was looking for, and I noted my criteria: privacy, quiet, a gorgeous view, a garage for my car, and a washer/dryer in the unit. She gave me a key to an in-law unit in Larkspur, the next small town over. She then gave me directions to the apartment, told me to check out the surrounding area and visit downtown, have a cup of coffee, and return before she closed at five. The unit was perfect for me. It had a sweeping view of Mt. Tamalpais and was located in a beautiful neighborhood, within walking distance to downtown. I had easy access to San Francisco to the south and wine country to the north.

When I told Ed Asner I was now in the Bay Area he told me I must meet his nephew, Gavin, and his niece, Hilary. I called Gavin, who was a San Francisco City supervisor. Gavin was none other than Gavin Newsom, the current governor of California. His sister Hilary asked me to serve on a steering committee for her annual golf charity fundraiser.

I was working for the dot-com company but since there was no product, there was nothing for me to do. My friend who also worked for the company would compare notes with me: "Did you get a paycheck?" Yes. "Have you heard from anyone from the company?" No.

We felt so guilty getting paid for nothing that we both decided to quit. When we called to tell them, they said, "No, we need you on the team to get financing. If you must do something, take people to lunch, go to conferences, and network." That's what I did for a full year. With no product, I was limited to only the salary, which was $5,000 a month, and never the commission, which was supposed to be "unlimited."

As part of my networking for the job, I met numerous people in Silicon Valley, and I decided to learn the venture-capital industry. The VC firms were creating the dot-com opportunities, and I desired to learn how the industry worked and how the VC firms chose which companies to invest in. Silicon Valley was creating instant millionaires simply by investing in their companies. I recall feeling that if I had been given $10 to $20 million with my other companies, I could have done so much more and helped so many more people.

I called a friend who introduced me to the owner of one of the biggest industry leaders. He told me he wasn't hiring, but he did need people at the dot-coms his business funded. He told me about a few, and one in particular intrigued me. He called their president and said, "I'm sending a woman over. Place her wherever she wants."

I went over to the company he referred me to, and the president detailed six main business areas. I chose business development, a glorified name for sales, and used my two-week vacation from my first dot-com company to see if I liked it there before resigning.

At this new dot-com, we sold the data to companies such as Google. Business development was a team with no individual quotas. I was disturbed by what I learned was happening with consumer data and how most of the young employees didn't see an issue with invading privacy. There were laws, but there were many legal loopholes for bypassing the laws that consumers weren't told about. In those days, the dot-coms had so much money thrown at them that inflated incomes and lavish parties were the norm. The day I started we hadn't even discussed my salary. They asked me how much I'd like to be paid. I told them and they said, "Fine."

I already had a six-week trip planned to go to Scotland and England, and they said they'd pay me for that time; I'd also be getting stock, healthcare, and other benefits. I learned so much and called on numerous companies but was also commuting two hours minimum each day. When I quit, I was even paid the sales bonus for my team.

At this point, I decided to focus on my mentoring for girls and women. In August of 2001, I applied for and received a trademark for MENTORmania, for educational services and courses in the art of mentoring others around professional and personal development. I was interested in learning about the mentoring programs provided by various companies. My thought was to aggregate all the mentoring programs on a single website to disseminate information about mentoring and mentoring programs. At this time, I was still attending conferences with my press pass and doing mentoring research. I even purchased stock so I could meet with company leaders at stockholder meetings and ask them if they had a formal mentoring program. I was most impressed with the leaders at Cisco, Hewlett Packard, and Google. They were genuinely interested in mentoring all levels of employees, and they all referred me to people in their companies I could speak to for further information. One of the most enthusiastic individuals I met was Mark Cuban after he spoke at a conference about how he got started.

I attended mentoring conferences and met the executive director of the California Mentoring Association. It was located in Tiburon, close to where I lived, so I volunteered there for four hours a week and helped with a fundraiser by putting on a movie premiere with George Lucas.

At this time, I spent many hours playing my keyboard, singing in open mics, and going to local venues to listen to music. I also found a small Methodist church and sang in its six-person choir, which included the minister. Marin County was home to exceptional musicians, many of them famous, who often performed in small venues, sometimes unannounced.

I met my first Marin County friend, Kim. She introduced me to her friends, and that was how I met Luke. I was drawn to him immediately. He was kind, engaging, and genuine. Like my first love, Cam, Luke didn't try to impress. He asked me about myself, but he didn't fall all over me attempting to win me over. His friends adored him, but he wasn't the center of attention. He had a way of being that was secure yet open. He later told me he played rugby and that rugby players were usually good people because they didn't have to prove they were physically strong—they were already secure in their strength and manhood and were comfortable showing their sweet sides, as opposed to bullies, who put up a front of being tough because they were secretly insecure. I found this insightful.

After I dated Luke for a while and disclosed that I was ten years older than him and had been married before, he asked me why I had gotten divorced. I simply told him, "It didn't work out," as I wasn't comfortable reopening old wounds. Luke was fine with that and didn't press me for further details. Later on, I told him I left because Donald had punched me, but I didn't offer any details.

Luke said with the utmost sincerity, "I would never do that."

I replied, "I know that. Those types don't come around me anymore."

I also appreciated that Luke seemed to have a genuinely good relationship with his mother. One of Luke's hobbies was raising orchids, and when I inquired as to how he'd gotten started, he explained that his mother raised orchids. He wanted to have something he could share with his mom, so he also raised orchids and helped with hers, too.

His mom informed me when her husband left her and Luke was in junior high, Luke assured her, "Don't worry, Mom, I'll do the barbecuing from now on." And sure enough, Luke stayed true to his word.

I loved that I'd finally met a man who was devoted to other people and committed to being a bright light for others on this planet. He personally sponsored an annual chili cookout to raise money for charity and, every Christmas season, he rented a San Francisco cable car and had a caroling party for over 60 friends and relatives.

I fell in love, quickly and deeply. And given that Luke was so wildly different from Donald and Harold, I knew I'd broken another pattern in my life of choosing the wrong men.

After dating for a year, Luke and I bought a house together. It was on 1.5 acres with a sweeping view of the valley below and all the hills clear to Mt. Tamalpais. Our driveway was 250 feet long and ran up the side of a steep hill. Below us were two houses and another shorter driveway to the street. The neighborhood had a swimming pool, hiking and horse trails, and a private school at one end and a public grade school near the entrance.

At some point, we got engaged. At first, Luke didn't care one way or another if he had children. But when his friends started having children, he reconsidered. I thought I would see what happened, and then I had what I thought was a period that lasted over a month. My doctor tested the tissue and informed me that I'd had a miscarriage. On further testing, it was determined I would need to be on fertility drugs to maintain any hope of having a child. Luke had no desire to adopt and, at the age of 44, I wasn't comfortable being on fertility drugs.

We chose to end our engagement and remain friends, which was one of the most difficult decisions of my life. Finally, here I was, getting to enjoy the "storybook romance" that had not been my fate for so many years. I knew I loved Luke, and he loved me. But the glaring fact that I didn't really want children and he did was staring me in the face. It didn't seem fair for either of us to succumb to something we didn't want—whether that was me going through the fertility treatments, or him staying with me despite the fact that our chances of having biological children together were slim. Finally, I told him that if he truly wanted children, he should be with a woman closer to his age.

I always felt safe and protected when I was with Luke, and I will always have a place for him in my heart. After my mother died, I called Luke and told him about it, and he assured me that I could call him anytime to talk if I needed to.

After Luke, I only dated one or two men seriously but none measured up to him. It's unclear as to whether a serious relationship is in my future at this point in my life, but if there's one thing I've learned, in the midst of life's twists and turns, anything can happen.

**

By the time I quit my second dot-com, I was in touch with one of my former IBM branch managers who was now president of 3Com. I had originally contacted 3Com to sell data to them, but after they met me, they asked me to interview for a job in South Korea. I turned that down, but I did say yes to a consulting job managing the installation of a new wireless network at 3Com Park. The goal was to have tablets in all the suites at 3Com Park to enable the box holders to order food, see statistics, and communicate between boxes.

Software and hardware engineers were developing the products, and a dot-com advertising company was working with the public-relations rollout. The company wanted to use high-school students to train the box holders and their guests on how to use the tablets. I was to manage all the aspects, attend the football games, and oversee all the suites to make sure the rollout was going smoothly. We had meetings with the team members and the 3Com Park manager. The executive at 3Com warned me that there were many egos involved, so I was not to mention I was the manager of the entire project and also getting paid the most.

At one joint meeting, where I was one of only a handful of women, I made a comment and one of the men from the advertising company sarcastically said, "Oh, and I suppose we'll learn you're secretly in charge."

I hid my smile, but it amused me and I almost said out loud, "And being paid the most, too."

I did other consulting, but only when people specifically called me and asked me to. I even received a call from Annalise, my friend and former BMI office manager, to ask me to buy back BMI. I was honored but I diplomatically refused. 3M set me up to sell projection equipment, and I used the proceeds to fund my mentoring and musical pursuits. My real goal was still to sing and play my piano. I started taking music and real-estate classes at the College of Marin, and I purchased a new piano. I received my California real-estate license for fun due to my love of looking at houses, but my primary focus was music. I sang in numerous choirs and formed an a-cappella singing group called the Harmonics. Over time, we added guitar and sang mostly folk songs. We sang throughout Marin County and at the Civic Center, as well as for Democratic political events. I also became a music tutor for the College of Marin and tutored mostly adult students in voice, theory, ear training, and piano. I had a good ear and could easily and tactfully suggest ways for the vocalists to communicate their songs. It was such a joyful experience to see my students' eyes light up when they grasped a concept. Plus, hearing about all the music they were working on amplified my own learning experience in a beautiful way.

**

Amid the relative peace and stability of my life, an unexpected source of stress arose. What had begun as a friendship with neighbors escalated into a full-blown two-and-a-half-year lawsuit, complete with a trial.

What I learned from being sued by my ex-husband, I was able to apply here.

First, I read a book written by a famous lawyer who noted that in a civil suit, if the law is on your side, you must stick with the facts and refuse to be emotionally sucked in. If the law is not on your side, you should be as emotional as possible so as to suck the other party into becoming emotional, and then both parties would look crazy and the judge might rule in favor of the party who didn't have the law on their side.

What happened is that the two neighbors who owned the houses below ours decided they should park on our driveway, even though we all had an acre-plus of land and plenty of off-street parking. I went to the county to see what to do and received a lecture that our property had a designated turn-around for safety, that parking was prohibited, and it was my responsibility as the landowner to keep the area free of parked cars. If there was a fire or other emergency, I would be 100 percent liable for any problems, no matter who was parking on the property.

I explained this in writing to my neighbors, but they were not satisfied and insisted on parking in our driveway, anyway. We couldn't seem to come to an agreement.

Even before we broke up, Luke and I decided to sell our house (we were both conflict-averse), and the realtor told us we needed to fix the cracks in our steep driveway to attract buyers. We decided we would do the design and gain approval from the county for a new driveway design; then we'd sell our house and let the new owner choose to use the permit to redo the driveway or not. The neighbors were opposed to Luke and I even submitting a driveway beautification project to Marin County to obtain a permit, so they filed numerous complaints with the county.

My coping skill as we went through the ordeal was to learn a new song every time the neighbors did something that was disturbing. I learned many songs.

We finally received approval, and the neighbors sued us before we could get our house on the market. They filed a lien prohibiting us to change title, so we were barred from selling our property until the lawsuit was settled. They and their friends would yell at me as I drove up my driveway, "Why don't you *move!*"

Instead of relying on advice and blindly using any attorney, as I had in my divorce, I systematically interviewed 12 attorneys. The one I chose had a reputation for being a real asshole. His track record, professionalism, and no-nonsense manner resonated with me. His daughter also worked with him, and she was just as driven. They applied to my homeowners' insurance company, and the insurance company paid all our legal bills.

The entire lawsuit was an eye-opening experience. My job was to "not engage" with my neighbors and to photograph every instance of a property violation.

I engaged the help of an energy healer who helped me set the intention of controlling my own property and keeping me grounded. A Feng Shui professional came over and did healing on my property. She told me she sensed the neighbors above my house on the hill (whose back property touched mine and whose homes were on a different street) were in dispute and when that was resolved, my situation would be resolved, as solutions start at the top and flow downhill.

She told me every time I drove up or down my driveway to chant, "Harmony, Harmony, Harmony."

One time, as I gazed upon the view from my home, I noticed a Catholic nun getting out of a car to visit my neighbor, and the verse, "Love thy neighbor as thyself," popped into my head. At first I thought, "My neighbors must not love themselves, or they would treat me better." Then, "If my neighbors don't love themselves, maybe I don't love myself, either. Perhaps my neighbors are my lesson to learn to love myself."

From then on, I asked in every situation, "What would a person who loves herself do in this situation?" This taught me to stand up for myself with no apology.

I had learned about "projection" during counseling. An example would be when a man accuses or tells others that a woman is cheating on him when, in fact, he is cheating on her. Maybe all the cruel things reportedly being said about me were really projections of how my neighbors felt about themselves and had nothing to do with me.

It turned out that the neighbors above me *were* having a property-line dispute. They had apparently resolved their dispute, but Marin County had so many rules that they were required to send adjoining property owners a letter about their dispute. If I didn't like the situation, I could make a public comment. I called the neighbors who were having this dispute and went to visit them to see if their issue would negatively affect my property. It wouldn't.

At this point, just as my Feng Shui energy reader had predicted, things began to fall into place for my own legal issue. Our judge ordered three separate court-ordered mediations, which came to nothing, and then a five-day trial. By then, I had 1,200 photos and hours of video. My attorney was a master at trial, as well as depositions. When we were notified that we'd won our case, I was elated. I called my mom, who asked, "What does this mean?"

I said, "It means I can sell my house!"

My house was staged and up for sale. We had a cash offer in two days. The sale was finalized on June 1, 2005, which turned out to be the peak in Marin County, right before the housing crash. I was ready for my next adventure.

CHAPTER 14

BREADCRUMBS FROM THE UNIVERSE

After my house sold, I put everything in storage and drove my Jaguar to Lincoln for my high-school reunion. (Shortly after that trip, I would move to an apartment in Marin County a few miles east from the house I sold.) I stayed with my mom in our family home. I saw as many friends as I could schedule and shared time with Annalise, my former employee and business manager I had trained to run BMI.

At the woodsy reunion, I got bit by something that turned out to be a tick. Two-and-a-half years later, in 2008, I was diagnosed with Lyme and Ehrlichiosis. Shortly after getting the bite, I had a rash and took a picture of it. By the time I arrived back in California from my reunion, the rash was gone and I didn't think about it. As I started getting symptoms, I traipsed from doctor to doctor. They thought the rash was a spider bite and tested me for lupus and other diseases, but everything came out negative, even the Lyme test.

During this health journey, I learned many methods of alternative healing. I learned how to do Reiki and meditation, as well as how to ground and run energy. I also got acupressure and craniosacral therapy, and worked with a Feldenkrais practitioner. A choir friend introduced me to someone who sent me a Kombucha mushroom, and I started making Kombucha tea. I also learned about the healing of singing bowls. Not to mention, I read all the books I could on organic food and healthy diet. The film *The Future of Food* educated me on what was happening with genetically modified organisms (GMOs). I stopped eating sugar and felt much better for a while.

This path of healing was new to me, but it didn't feel unfamiliar. During one of my Reiki trainings, I noticed that all of the students had a luminescent glow in their eyes, like a divine light was shining from our hearts and out through our gazes.

At this time, I continued singing with Harmonics, as well as the world-famous Glide Gospel Ensemble in San Francisco. I became a soloist in addition to choir soprano, and I performed in operas and musical concerts, in addition to playing my piano.

I was still taking music classes at the College of Marin, but I was experiencing a brain fog and fatigue that made it difficult to learn. I didn't know I had Lyme and that it was progressing.

**

Although my health seemed to be deteriorating, my engagement with my inner world was expanding. I recall learning a song about unconditional love that made me realize I didn't know what unconditional love felt like. "Who have I loved? Who has really loved me?" I queried out loud.

I decided that it was my father's fault. He'd died when I was only five years old, and his sudden departure had felt like abandonment.

"Why did you leave me? How am I going to learn how to love?" I was practically shouting.

Just then, an apparition of his face appeared before me, almost like a hologram.

"What are you doing here?" I asked, shocked.

"I came to help you," he responded.

I had been so sick for several months that I thought it must be my time to die. "Did you come to take me with you?"

"Not now," he replied. "There are many things for you to do here first." And just as quickly as he'd come, he was gone.

Suddenly, I wasn't sick anymore, and I knew who to sing the song to: myself. I knew that once I learned to love myself unconditionally, I would be able to love and be loved.

The next day in voice class, I stood in front of the class to sing my song. I asked, "Who believes in unconditional love?"

One student called out, "There's no such thing!"

I responded in all sincerity, "I believe there is."

As I sang my song, I could feel for the first time in years a connection between my words and my heart. Before that, I'd always been told that I had a beautiful voice, but it lacked deep emotion. This day, I had both. As I sang in Italian, I noticed that many of my classmates had tears in their eyes. They had allowed me to touch them with my voice.

Before this experience, I was always coached to give more in my performance. This time, my teacher came over to me, still standing in front of the class, and said, "That was wonderful. You're on the cliff with your toes hanging over, but you didn't fall off. Next time, you can pull it back a little."

I realize now that some of the missing connection and my tendency to hold back emotion came from the experience of domestic violence, but some of it could directly be attributed to my experience of singing in junior high, when my voice teacher belittled, mocked, and yelled at me during my first solo performance in front of a group. Ever since then, I'd been afraid to express myself, as it could open me up to physical harm and emotional abuse. As I felt the relief and gratitude wash over me during that class, I knew I'd broken yet another pattern. I'd become even more free.

**

After completing my College of Marin associate's degree in music in May 2006, I moved to Olympia, Washington, one hour south of Seattle, to be closer to my family and to privately study piano, singing, and jazz. I was only there for a year before moving back to California, whose weather I preferred. Over the years I spent on the West Coast, I kept moving up and down the shoreline, going wherever my heart took me.

On one of my visits to Marin County when I was still living in Olympia, my piano teacher gave me a CD of various concert pianists and invited me to play his prized Steinway concert D piano. This was the Steinway he'd hand-picked from Hamburg. He was dying of cancer and told me he wanted me to have his piano after he died.

I was shocked—my piano teacher couldn't possibly die! I didn't cry, but I felt like it. And also, I would find my own piano. I'd already been looking for a Steinway D with ivory keys.

As I listened to the CD, Franz Liszt kept playing over and over in my head. I told my piano teacher that I wanted to learn how to play this particular piece. He was not encouraging. He said it was very tricky to master, and not many people could play it with the intended emotion. He recommended that I take a look at the Sherman Clay piano store before I headed back to Olympia.

I went, and they showed me a Bosendorfer piano, which I wasn't familiar with. The salesperson told me it was designed for Franz Liszt. It was the finest piano I'd seen, as it had been hand-made in Germany. It was beautiful, and it played beautifully; it also cost $160,000. And while I wanted ivory keys, the new ones had plastic keys, as ivory was no longer allowed to be used for pianos.

I was driving in my Jaguar on I-5 from Marin County to Seattle, listening to Liszt's "Consolation #3" on repeat, and daydreaming about learning to play this piece and do it justice. As Mt. Shasta came into view, I started to feel a tingling sensation throughout my body. I suddenly felt the presence of my grandmother in my car with me.

Immediately, I asked her if she would go find Franz Liszt and ask him if he would teach me how to play the piano and connect my emotion to my playing. I also asked her to find Maria Callas to help me with my singing.

My cell phone rang at that moment. It was strange, as only a handful of people even had my cell-phone number.

"Hello?"

"Karen, you called me a few months ago looking for a Steinway with ivory keys. It's not a Steinway, but I have a piano for you—it's a Bosendorfer Imperial with ivory keys, and it's available for you to play tomorrow in Seattle."

I was overjoyed! I set the appointment and hung up.

"Thank you, Grandma," I whispered. By this time, my face was soaked with tears because I knew I was supposed to have a Bosendorfer piano and would have no need for my piano teacher's Steinway D. In fact, I was certain that he would live to play his own piano.

I pulled into a rest stop, tears still streaming down my face and bright-red nose running. I was a total mess, but I felt exhilarated. The other travelers stared a little too long at me, but I didn't care or even try to wipe the tears away. This was who I was and this was how I felt, and I was OK letting them see me.

I had a feeling of gratitude for being a witness to the power of the universe. It was a feeling I will never forget.

My piano teacher went to surgery for his cancer, and the surgeons said they couldn't find the tumor in his esophagus. It had shrunk from 2.5 inches to a tiny speck. He is still alive today, playing his Steinway D. And soon enough, I had my 1,225-lb. Bosendorfer and would learn to play "Consolation #3."

**

In 2007, I met a woman who had Lyme disease. She shared her experience, and it sounded similar to mine. I showed her the photo of my rash, and she said, "That's a Lyme rash. Here's the lab, and here's the doctor in San Francisco trained to treat Lyme."

At that time, there were only two labs in the U.S. that could properly diagnose Lyme once the bacteria entered the soft tissue. If Lyme is caught early when it is still in the bloodstream only, a six-week course of Doxycycline will usually stop it for good. But in my case, it had been years and I had over 20 serious symptoms. My test was positive for two tick-borne diseases, Lyme and Ehrlichiosis, increasing my symptoms exponentially.

My doctor suspected I had Lyme disease as early as 2000, and in

2005 the Nebraska tick further infected me with Ehrlichiosis. These bacteria can cross the blood-brain barrier, causing cognition to be affected.

The doctor started me on Bicillan shots once a week. I could purchase the medicine from the pharmacy for $60 a shot, and a nurse administered it. It was not covered by insurance. If the nurse wasn't available, I went to the hospital infusion center and they provided the drug and administered the shot for $1,200 a week, meaning I was spending nearly $5,000 a month that was not covered by insurance.

I was on weekly Bicillan shots for 12 months, and slowly but surely, I began to regain full cognitive capacity. The nurse administering the Bicillan told me it was used for another spirochete bacteria—the one that caused syphilis. Two doses cured syphilis.

All in all, I was taking various antibiotics for three years and greatly improved, but I was not 100 percent better, as I wished to be. Not to mention, I now also had to heal from all the side effects of the antibiotics.

By this time, I had moved back to Northern California from Olympia, Washington. Since I worked and studied at the College of Marin, the tutoring center told me I qualified for a free cognitive evaluation that was normally worth $5,000. I went every Saturday for several months to get tested for four hours at a time. My IQ was 132, the same as it was in grade school when I marked two answers wrong on purpose. The biggest finding was that I could not place the pictures of the four seasons in correct sequential order. After they pointed this out, I could see how easy it was, but I was stumped at first.

As I healed, I regained other skills—some I hadn't even realized I had lost. For example, we all have the innate ability to keep an internal beat, to "hear" a tone before singing it, to feel the "one" beat in a song. I had lost all of that, so when I sang with other people, I was not able to keep time with them and I couldn't sing a scale or find the starting note. I also lost the ability to play my piano. I could see the notes on the staff, but I couldn't remember what they were or where they were on the keyboard. I took all the piano classes offered, starting at Piano 1, to relearn how to play piano. I could hear sounds in my French class, but I couldn't distinguish what they were enough to imitate. Common words were difficult to "find" or spell.

Even with all I had lost, the cognitive tests showed I was considered "above average." Still, things I had once easily grasped were hard for me to learn. This was frustrating and demoralizing. I had become like the students who didn't seem to care or try, but I *did* care and I *did* try. The experience instilled in me a newfound compassion for all students who struggled. I learned from the doctors that no matter our struggles, speed, or ability, once a person "learned" a concept, no matter how long it took, they would have finally gotten it. It gave me comfort to know I could still learn, but that it would simply take longer than it had in my past.

The gifts of Lyme were many. I could no longer do the millions of things I had once done at the same time, and I was forced to choose what was important to me. I was exhausted and couldn't say yes to everything, so I thankfully learned to say no. I learned to care for and have compassion for myself. I learned to ask for help. I had over-given most of my life, and now I was giving back to myself.

I had jumped off my own boat and my own path and destiny to help others—and now I was staying on my own boat. I did only what I loved and what I considered fun.

Just as I'd experienced with my decision to quit drinking alcohol, not everyone appreciated the new Karen, who no longer dropped everything for them. I let go of relationships that seemed unhealthy or didn't nourish me. I attracted people for what I felt to be my next level of life lessons. I was grateful for everything I could do. There was no room for lamentation or regret.

**

I attended a large New Year's Eve party in 2008 in San Francisco with several hundred people. While on the balcony watching the midnight fireworks, I felt like I might faint. The next thing I knew, I opened my eyes and was on the ground with a doctor and my friends nearby. I discovered that I'd had what is called a generalized tonic-clonic (grand mal) seizure. Upon medical examination and brain scans, the neurologist traced it to when I was strangled to unconsciousness by Harold in 1991 and hit my head on the floor with such force as to cause a traumatic brain injury. My brain was sensitive to light and movement—including from 3D movies and fireworks.

I also had a vocal cord examination to find out why I was sometimes unable to sing on pitch. The scope down my throat showed that damage to my vocal cords had caused the issue, and there was no immediate remedy. Again, it could be traced back to my strangulation.

It was a devastating discovery. I had always dreamed of singing, and I'd worked so hard practicing...only to be told that there was no cure. I almost gave up, right then and there.

One of my voice teachers experimented with me and told me to "accent" every word, which helped me to stay on pitch. She informed me that she would never advise this to anyone else, but it helped get more air through my vocal cords. Since I never knew when I would be on pitch or not, it was nerve-wracking to sing in front of people because I didn't know what would come out. I decided I would sing anyway and enjoy the notes that *did* come out. It was yet another testament to my determination to never let my past get in the way of my dreams.

**

My determination led me to even more wonderful opportunities. When Glide was invited to sing at an event for Barack Obama, we were also asked to stay and enjoy the reception and refreshments. We were welcomed with open arms. Obama's words were inspiring and gave me great hope for my country. I even registered as a Democrat to vote for him in the California primary.

I wanted to be sure he was the real deal, so I went to the Democratic Convention in Denver. I stayed with a friend of my brother Steve and rented a car to drive and park close to the convention. I had no ticket and was not a delegate, but I did know a few people. I figured that if I was meant to be there, a ticket would show up; if not, I would be content to hang out with the people selling t-shirts. I met up with Nebraskans, Californians, and Washingtonians I knew, and I attended events every day, meeting people and making my own assessment as to the organization and caliber of the Obama folks. As I met people, they gave me their convention tickets to get on the floor with other delegates.

On the second-to-last day, I asked a new contact if they had any extra tickets for that evening. They said they'd check. On the tram back to the California delegation hotel, I received a call—there was a ticket, but I would need to go and pick it up. The patrons on the tram helped me find the building where I picked up the ticket. When I arrived at the convention, it turned out I was seated in a section with supporters who told me they'd donated $100,000 to sit in this particular section. My seat also included a separate suite complete with wait staff and food and beverages.

As I went back and forth, I met up with a pregnant woman I knew. She was walking with her husband and was exhausted. No one from her state would give up their seat for her. I told her I had a suite and she should come with me. I arranged for her to sit in my section, too, because a few people had left to sit with the Clintons in their box.

The next day was the final night of the convention, when Barack and Michelle would speak. I had a public ticket, but that morning, the pregnant woman called me and said they were going home early and she'd like to give me her delegate ticket for the main floor because I was the only one who'd helped her the night before.

I arrived early; the California delegation seats were in the front section of the stadium. The first two rows were roped off, so I sat in the third row. When security came to rope off more rows, they told me I could stay in the third row. As the crowds streamed in, the California delegates filled in around me. I made friends with those nearest me, who included former governor Gray Davis and his wife, as well as the mayor of Los Angeles and other luminaries. It was an enthusiastic crowd and a memorable experience.

At every turn, I was impressed with the Obama staff I met, and I knew without a doubt that he and Michelle would be an asset for the United States for years to come. When he spoke, his words were sincere and patriotic. As a couple, they exuded love and devotion for each other, their children, and their country. It was a memorable moment that would impact me for years to come, and that would remind me of the power of finding stability and hope in moments of uncertainty and rapid transformation.

I was elated when Obama was elected president, and I attended his inauguration in 2009 with my sister, Linda. I rented a condo within walking distance to nearly everything. The morning of the event, we woke at 4 a.m. to walk to the inauguration. It was bitterly cold, and I wore a purple ski mask. We were not allowed to cross the street but were directed through a tunnel designed for cars and now converted into a pedestrian walkway. We were delayed but, due to our early departure, we weren't stuck for long. Even so, with such a large crowd and extra security checks, we barely got to our area before the ceremony started.

The enthusiasm and courtesy of the crowd impressed me most. There were millions of people and, as I was told, no arrests. I had never seen so many happy, smiling people. It seemed we were turning the corner to forming a more perfect union.

**

In 2008, I was asked to run for U.S. Senator for the state of California, as well as U.S. Senator for the state of Nebraska. The woman who asked me to run in California was an elderly Republican party leader I happened to be seated next to at a Marin Symphony gala dinner. As we spoke, she suddenly blurted out, "You need to run for the U.S. Senate, and I will help you." She suggested that I run for Barbara Boxer's seat. I went to her house, made a few phone calls to the few Republican friends I had left in Nebraska, and seriously thought about it. A spiritual Marin woman I knew discouraged me. She said, "You are too pure to be in politics."

In Nebraska, friends of mine from both parties suggested that I run both for the 2008 open seat and again for the 2012 open seat. When I learned I had Lyme disease in 2008 and needed to focus on healing, I decided not to move back to Nebraska and run for the U.S. Senate. For the 2012 election, there was an open seat, and a Republican newcomer was running—but so far, there was no viable Democratic candidate. I called Bob Kerry, the former Democratic governor of Nebraska, who had since moved to New York but was considering moving back to Nebraska to run for U.S. Senate. I called Bob and told him if he didn't run, I would.

When Bob Kerry decided to run in the 2012 US Senate election in Nebraska, I chose to focus on music and stay in California.

**

In 2009, I experienced yet another transformational moment in my life. I attended the week-long program at the Hoffman Institute. I'd heard about this program from three different people and listened to their informational weekly call, which convinced me to attend the eight-day program known as The Process. I wasn't sure if I had the strength to do it due to Lyme, but I felt compelled to go.

During that week, I was guided to examine what the Institute called "negative love patterns"—that is, coping mechanisms developed in childhood that we all carry into adulthood. While the coping mechanisms were instrumental to our survival as children, we often discover that they are ineffective and even harmful as adults.

Over the course of that week, I learned to clear out old trauma and recognize and replace ineffective and unhealthy patterns so I could open more space in my heart for loving, healthy relationships. I learned to truly forgive myself and others, and to love myself and develop self-compassion and self-empathy.

One exercise I learned was a daily check-in with my Spirit, Body, Intellect, and Emotion. I asked each if they had any messages for me. Some days I didn't have any messages, but some days I did—and I always listened to the message I received. I learned that it was a powerful way to discern what was truly inside me, and to ensure I stayed true to myself and my spirit-guided path. The more I did this, the more I recognized that things had a way of falling into place. It seemed that the universe was conspiring to bring me the joy and fulfillment I'd been seeking for so long.

One morning, my message from my Intellect was to write songs. I walked to my grocery store and ran into a musician friend I hadn't seen for a while. He asked me what I was doing. I said, "I'm writing songs."

He responded, "I've got the book and the teacher for you."

When I called to meet with the teacher, he asked me to tell him about my songwriting journey. He listened as I told him about my Hoffman Institute experience, my spirit guides, and my message to write songs.

I was astonished and validated when he smiled and replied, "You are meant to study songwriting with me. I, too, went to Hoffman, and I wrote music for their meditations."

CHAPTER 15

DANCING WITH PURE LOVE

While attending a Nebraska Diplomat's event in Nebraska, I was introduced to Craig, who was a professor in the University of Nebraska–Lincoln Business College and Director of the UNL Leadership Institute. He asked me to join the board of the UNL Leadership Institute. I attended meetings and met the other board members; we were all presented with what the Institute was doing, as well as the training they were developing and the research they were undertaking. It was all fascinating to me, as I'd always been interested in a deeper understanding of the qualities of good leadership, individually and collectively.

When Craig was hired to be the Dean of the Business College for American University in Yola, Nigeria, he asked me if I might consider coming over for a short stint or longer to teach classes in entrepreneurship and leadership. My involvement with the university, as he told me, could end up having a massive impact on young Nigerian students, who were the future of their nation.

Given that music was still my number-one priority at the time, my first question was, "Can I bring my piano?"

He said yes, so I interviewed with the president of American University and at age 54 was hired as a professor of practice to teach entrepreneurship for up to three years.

As I prepared to move out of my townhouse in Northern California, I realized it was not realistic to bring my piano to Africa. Instead, the school would provide me with an electronic keyboard. I visualized where I'd like my beloved Bosendorfer to live in the meantime. I saw it at TRI Studios, owned by Bob Weir of Grateful Dead fame. I knew my piano would be well taken care of in his state-

224

of-the-art studio, and only used for special recordings. I put out some feelers, and soon enough, the studio manager called me and wrote up an agreement; my Bosendorfer had a new home, and I was embarking on a new adventure.

In August of 2011, after three weeks of packing and moving things out of my townhouse in Kentfield, California, into storage, I flew from San Francisco Airport to Frankfurt, Germany, and then to Abuja and eventually Yola, Nigeria. I took four huge pieces of luggage, including a travel guitar. Everything arrived in Yola intact. I was met by a large, friendly group from American University.

Sadly, my time in Nigeria was cut short after I contracted malaria, even though I had been taking anti-malarial drugs to prevent it. I had also brought my mosquito net, as recommended, but the maintenance department hadn't gotten around to hanging it.

Despite my short time in Nigeria, I learned many valuable lessons. My students were both Christian and Muslim, and everyone seemed to get along with one another. The tribal leader was Muslim and had dictated that all religions were to be respected. I heard from some of my students there were parts of Nigeria outside the leader's jurisdiction where there was conflict between religious groups. For example, one female student told me that in the town where she'd grown up, the religions were integrated throughout neighborhoods, but today's neighborhoods were almost all segregated by religion, and it was rare for a Christian to visit or live in a Muslim neighborhood, and vice versa.

My highlights in Nigeria included meeting and learning from my students, singing the U.S. National anthem for the tribal leader and US ambassador at the matriculation ceremony, attending Ramadan events and a four-hour Christian church service, and learning about efforts to provide women with more opportunities through microfinance loans and expanded equal rights.

While I was there, I was struck by the disparity in wealth that I saw. My students were from among the richest communities in

Nigeria. One student told me his monthly allowance was equivalent to $10,000 U.S. In contrast in the markets and neighborhoods, I saw children begging, as well as a slew of partially built houses with no hope of ever having running water.

In September of 2011, I wrote the following blog to share a bit more about my experience:

My purpose in coming to AUN as a Professor of Practice in Entrepreneurship is to teach future leaders of Nigeria and make a positive impact. As each day passes, I learn and accept that what I came to do is not possible due to the artificial constraints in place.

Nigeria faces many challenges that only Nigerians can choose to face or ignore. Corruption is accepted and constant, power blackouts occur numerous times a day with guards turning on the generators that profit the rich elite, running water is for the rich, malaria is endemic, poverty is widespread, and children beg in the streets. Oil profits benefit the rich elite, and the basic infrastructure suffers. Nigeria suffers at the hands of its own leaders.

Nigeria is ripe for a revolution of the poor masses to rise up against their rich, selfish leaders. The age of consent for a woman is 12 years old, meaning 12-year-old girls are forced into marriage and having babies, and often, both baby and child bride die. The Lamido (tribal leader) has 60 children. His father before him had 64 children. One in 10 babies die, according to a local female leader—and this is the second-highest infant-mortality rate in the world.

As a white person in Nigeria, I am on a pedestal of a hierarchical society. I am allowed to live in a big house with a driver and a chef, running water, and air-conditioned rooms. I still suffer the incessant power blackouts and power surges that explode my computer power supply and render technology useless. I am victim to the local scams of paying for stolen cell-phone cards with no recourse. I am charged four to ten times more than a Nigerian because I am white, and I have to live in a gated compound with armed guards because I am white. I am told not to ride a bicycle on the streets due to the danger, and I work at a university with 425 guards for a student body of 1,500 students. AUN is home to the children of the rich elite. AUN entry standards are lower than other Nigerian universities.

A few weeks after I arrived in Nigeria, the Nigerian terrorist organization Boko Haram took responsibility for bombing the UN building in Abuja, killing 18 people. I resigned from AUN on September 4 due to health reasons. That same evening, two AUN students were assassinated with bullets through their heads while shopping in Jimeta.

I pray Nigeria's leaders will take heed of the words of their beautiful Nigerian Anthem: "To serve our fatherland with love and strength and Faith, one nation bound in Freedom, peace and Unity, to build a nation where peace and justice reigns."

**

After I returned from Nigeria, I spent time in the Seattle area with my family, then in the Bay Area to visit friends and my Bosendorfer piano at TRI Studios, before returning to LA. At the Hoffman retreat, we'd done a class skit, and afterwards the instructors told me to "get yourself to LA—you are a great actor," which stayed in my head. The truth is, I decided to go back for the perfect weather, although I did do some music, acting, and standup comedy in my free time.

It was a period of returning to familiarity, and I loved it. I connected with a number of musicians and even made up my own recitals to perform. Much to my delight, I met a handsome young man in my building who ran a comedy club open mic nearby, to which he invited me. To my dismay, he had a girlfriend, but I liked both of them, so it was fine!

I ended up moving into the same building I'd lived in when I first moved to California, but it had changed substantially. When I first moved in, the pool was a regular meeting place for five retired women having coffee and me swimming. Now, the apartment complex was full of 20-somethings with amazing bodies, and the pool was a prime venue for social gatherings. I continued to meet singers, actors, and standup comedians, and I also acted in shows like *NCIS LA* and *Madmen*.

On a Saturday morning in June of 2012, I asked my Body, Intellect, Emotions, and Spirit what messages they had for me. I heard, "Go to the shelter and get your poodle."

I asked if I could wait until after lunch.

"Anytime today" was the reply.

I knew enough to recognize that I should listen to the message. After lunch, I headed to the pet shelter in West LA and announced to the volunteer greeter that I had come to adopt my poodle. She practically scoffed and said, "We don't have any poodles here and, even if we did, you couldn't adopt one today. You'd need to pay for it, then wait a few days while we do a health check and any medical care needed, and pick it up later."

Undeterred, I calmly said, "I'm here for my poodle."

The volunteer brought out a few small dogs for me to visit with, and each time I said, "This doesn't look like a poodle."

She would reply, "It isn't a poodle, because we don't have any poodles."

Suddenly, a door to what looked like the shelter's clinic swung open and a veterinarian walked out with a black poodle on a leash. She looked straight at me and said, "Here's a poodle, and he's already been medically cleared, so you can take him home today."

I was delighted, and the volunteer started talking to no one in particular. She said, "She came in for a poodle, and now she has a poodle," as if it were some sort of miracle.

I adopted my first pet ever, then went to the pet store and bought food, a bed, a crate, squeaky toys, and whatever the sales reps told me a dog would like, before taking him home to my LA high-rise apartment. It turned out that my apartment complex had an entire area devoted to dogs, so he and I met other dog owners. My new dog liked to stand on his hind legs and dance and walk around, so I named him Dancer. We went walking every day, and I took dog training lessons with him. He was incredibly smart, fierce, and loyal. Much to my surprise, he didn't like men and barked at all of them. *There goes my love life*, I thought.

Bringing Dancer into my life was a profound experience, because he was a great teacher. He taught me how to be in the moment. He would pick up a pom-pom, skip around with it for a while, then get distracted by a bee and drop the pom-pom.

He and I drove from Los Angeles to Superior, Nebraska, where I attended Lew Hunter's two-week screenwriting class. Dancer attended all the classes and is prominently featured in our final class picture. After Superior, we went to Lincoln and stayed with my mom, who is a cat lover, but not fond of dogs. Fortunately, Dancer won her over.

After Nebraska, we drove to Seattle, where most of my family lived, and I decided to stay there. I wanted to get to know my young great-nephews better, and to spend some more time with my brother, sister, niece, and nephew. My doctor brother, Steve, let me put my huge concert grand Bosendorfer Imperial, which I'd named Anton, in his office so I could play it in the evenings. During the days, Dancer and I went walking to the parks and explored the area.

I had an overseas trip planned to Vietnam and was referred to a pet resort where Dancer would stay while I traveled. When I returned from my travels and picked Dancer up, they said he had a great time. I had paid extra for him to be well taken care of. I noticed he didn't bark as much for several weeks and wasn't chasing his squeaky ball too often. I was also concerned that his paws seemed tender. The vet told me he had an ear infection. Dancer seemed to recover. Then I had a trip to Nashville for five days. I lined up an in-house pet sitter, but she canceled the day of my trip. I documented what happened next in an email to a friend:

I called the pet sitter and took Dancer to the Pet Resort. I checked on him by telephone and was told his feet and ears were fine and he was having a great time. When I picked him up two days later, the receptionist took a long time to get him and was crying. She said his ears were all messed up and smelled infected, and his paws were all bleeding, rubbed off completely. She told me she didn't know how it happened and hated to think about how much pain Dancer was in. He bled all the way home and for days after. I took him to my two vets and it turned out he had methicillin-resistant Staphylococcus pseudintermedius (MRSP) bacteria, which is highly resistant to antibiotics. I took him to a specialist and they tried to save him, but it was too late. He could barely walk, so I carried him most of the time.

He was put to sleep July 1. He was only four years old.

My grief has been deeper than anything I've ever felt, partly because he died in such a painful way and partly because I didn't do my homework and find a pet sitter I was comfortable with. I believed the Pet Resort staff, and it turns out they lied about all his visits. They'd said he was fine and having a great time, when in fact, he was so stressed out that he'd jumped up and down until his paws bled.

My big lesson and message is to always use in-house sitters, never boarding kennels. I hope you will help me spread the word.

My vet advised filing a formal complaint with the City of Seatac, so I am in process. I took the public tour last week to gather information and see if I could find out what really happened to Dancer. The crying receptionist, Sierra, toured me and recognized me as Dancer's mom. I didn't tell her he was dead. There was a dog in extreme stress—jumping on his hind legs and scratching his paws on the fence and barking nonstop. I asked if Dancer was doing that and she said yes, all the time, and even worse during the last visit because they placed him between two dogs. I was sick. No wonder his paws were getting thinner all the time and he couldn't chase his ball, and by the last trip his paws were bleeding...and they did nothing.

I found out they didn't even take the dogs outside to go to the bathroom. They made them defecate where they played, then hosed the floor with chemicals and had them come back onto the floors still wet. At night, the dogs were locked in the sleeping area for 12 to 14 hours, so they had accidents right where they slept.

It was horrific, and I learned a good lesson. I had no idea what questions to ask, and the Pet Resort was highly recommended by my neighbor. She is also appalled and says I need to complain for Dancer's sake, too. There were many unhappy dogs, and not one toy. A little white dog was shaking in the corner of his cage with his paw up—in need of medical attention. I said that, and Sierra responded, "He's just scared." I know they will lie to these owners, too, and tell them what a great time their dog had.

I reminded Sierra that Dancer's feet were bleeding when I picked him up. I told her he was not allowed to jump on his hind legs and bark in stress, and she said she would update my file. I asked for a copy and was told she had to get permission from the owner. I called the next day, and someone named Lisa read my record, which had the caution about no jumping, etc. She said she would fax the schedule and Dancer's records after the owner gave her permission. On Friday I went to my vet and they called again for me and finally got two pages of summary with parts crossed out in black marker (the part about jumping and barking), but no detail. They can't/won't tell me who cleaned Dancer's ears, etc.

I am getting messages from Dancer. He tells me to wait on getting another dog—time for a human relationship first. He tells me to think about how much I love him versus how much I miss him. He said it's not about me but about the natural cycle of life: Love, Loss, Rebirth. He came into my life to teach me a lesson about unconditional love, and to help me to fully grieve my past losses so I can move on to rebirth.

Dancer communicated I was stuck in loss, and his death was the only way to get me unstuck: by feeling deeply and completing my stuffed grief. His contract was up; he had one year with me.

He says he's having a great time in heaven, where he runs faster than on Earth, and is watching over me. He met my dad and is in good hands. He sprinkles love on all the kennel dogs and flits over them like a ballerina.

He told me tonight that he forgives me, and someone (him) has to go into battle at kennels. Dogs who suffer and die due to kennels win a purple heart for doing battle against kennels. He knows I will do something to help other dogs. He tells me to file a complaint to shut the Pet Resort down, but not to pursue legal action. He tells me to let the authorities handle everything, and to stay in the moment.

I have faith that this is a divine plan, and someday I'll understand why Dancer was the sacrificial lamb. I'm grateful for 365 days of pure love.

CHAPTER 16

WHEN EACH PERSON HAS PEACE,

THE WORLD HAS PEACE

In all my experiences of work, travel, and learning more about myself and my passions, my original goal of making world peace possible was never far from my heart. In 2012, I created and sponsored a worldwide peace song contest to add peace to the world and to encourage more positive influences. A former client referred me to a friend of his to help spread the word on the Internet.

I was grateful to everyone who submitted songs. The winner received $500 and the chance to be recorded in audio and video at a private studio in San Rafael, California. I announced my contest winners, Colby and Awu, on World Peace Day. To me, their song embodied peace, and their harmony and tone were exquisite. I also loved their story. They'd met when Colby was in Cameroon, where Awu was from, when he was working on a humanitarian project.

It was delightful to be a part of something bigger than myself, and I was inspired to write more songs about peace, as well.

Of course, I continued to learn and grow in my musical pursuits. In 2013, I went to a concert of the Total Experience Gospel Choir. Afterwards, I introduced myself to the founder and director, and mentioned I had sung with the Glide Gospel Ensemble, at which point she invited me to sing with them. They would be singing backup with the band Heart in Key Arena and another arena outside Portland, Oregon. I went to the weekly practices and sang at every outside event offered, including Seattle's famous Bumbershoot, and with Heart.

Of course, shortly after all of this, I would go through the grief of losing Dancer, who passed away in 2013. I was so grief-stricken I thought I couldn't possibly adopt another dog and go through that pain all over again. I attended a grief support group at the Seattle Humane Society. I thought that if I ever did adopt another dog, I'd like a little girl who was about ten pounds so she could travel on the airplane. I wanted a non-shedding dog with a calm and sweet disposition.

August 1 was my grandmother's birthday. When I asked for my daily messages, I was told, "Go to the Seattle Humane Society for your dog." I went—and much to my delight, there was a small, calm dog in a large kennel. Most of the other dogs were barking. I asked about her and was told that she was already reserved, but I could be second in line to adopt her and play with her until the new owner showed up.

When the woman who had reserved her showed up, she let me keep playing with her. After a while, she said, "I think she loves you more than me, and I have some vests to give you that I think would fit her."

By this time, two more parties were in line to adopt this dog. I said, "Are you sure? You're number one on the list."

She was positive.

When they showed me the dog's paperwork, it turned out that she had been living in a Los Angeles kill shelter when Dancer died. She was eventually flown to the Seattle Humane Society with 35 dogs. She weighed only 7 lbs. and her ribs stuck out, but I could see the light in her eyes had been undisturbed. I decided this dog had come to me by grace, so I named her Grace. She became my service dog to help me with seizures and PTSD from my strangulation by Harold in 1991, and from my experience of being held down and punched by Donald years before that.

Soon after I adopted Grace, I decided I needed to spend more time in Lincoln to help my mom. By this time, her husband was living in a skilled nursing facility due to Parkinson's, and Mom was living in an independent-living apartment complex. She was still driving daily to visit him, but complaining to me how scary it was to be driving.

In the fall of 2013, I rented a U-Haul and towed my car from Seattle to Lincoln, where I rented an apartment. Then I bought my family home in Lincoln to help my mom and stepdad. I used the same real-estate attorney for the paperwork from years ago, when I had my Nebraska real-estate license hanging part time. He seemed genuinely surprised to see me.

During this period, I split time between Seattle and Lincoln. Grace dog and I flew back and forth on Alaska Airlines. The Omaha airport was so small that they always remembered Grace and greeted her warmly every time.

I'd already talked with my other siblings about caregiving for Mom, but none of them were interested in taking on this task. As the oldest daughter, I felt I should do it, but I didn't know what I was getting into. I attempted to change my mindset to "I am grateful to be able to have this gift of time with Mom and Dale, and to be helpful and add to their lives." I was told by others who had helped their parents that it was difficult but worth it in the end. They also told me to pace myself, because otherwise it would be all-consuming. One woman limited her visits to twice a week at two hours a time. There were other relatives in Lincoln, but they were rarely if ever available to help when I asked them for it.

Some days I spent over 12 hours driving my mom and stepdad to various medical appointments and functions. I thought this must be what it felt like to be an over-scheduled parent juggling their life to take their children to events, and never having time to themselves. I was exhausted but assured by other adult children who had walked this path before me that it was one of the greatest gifts I could give, and the rewards were too numerous to detail.

I took Mom and Dale to church—the same Methodist church in

which I'd grown up—and I even sang in the choir. An extra bonus was having Grace dog sit with the choir. During the summer, when the choir didn't meet, I had the pleasure of singing solos at church. While in Lincoln, I was cast as Chava in *Fiddler on the Roof* at the Lincoln Community Playhouse. Mom attended with friends, and I was delighted to see how proud she was to show me off after years of discouraging me from singing in public for fear that I might not be "good enough."

In June of 2014, my stepdad died. He and Mom had been married nearly 20 years. His children lived out of state, so I had the benefit of spending extra time with Dale. He shared many personal things with me and, after he died, I felt that I received closure not only after his death, but also closure from my father's death so many years before.

Before he died, he was supportive of my singing. He'd asked me to sing "Amazing Grace," at his funeral, an honor I cherish.

In the ensuing years, I poured my heart and soul into music. In Spring of 2016, I went to an immersive three-week musical training in Cuba. Together with my group of musicians, we visited music schools, had drumming lessons, and saw many musical events in casual and formal settings. We met a number of friendly Cubans and learned from all of them.

One of our hosts was an ophthalmologist and her husband, who lived in a high-rise in Havana with gleaming wood floors and sweeping views of the ocean. Their apartment encompassed the entire floor. The family lived in one section, and we stayed in individual suites with our own living room, dining room, and wrap-around veranda. Our host explained that all citizens had free education through college, in addition to medical care, housing, and food. They were able to keep all the income they earned, as there were no federal income taxes.

In addition to music, I wanted to expand my acting skills, so in Fall 2016 and Spring 2017, I attended intensive full time classes at an acting school in New York. I felt the extra training could help with my singing delivery. Grace dog and I flew to New York City with two suitcases for the school year. I shared a condo near Central Park with the owner, a retired theatre actress. The classes were held Monday through Friday and were time-consuming and stressful. I had a lot to memorize, and the other 30 students were all younger than me.

One of the most memorable and life-changing events for me was writing a monologue that was meant to reveal something about ourselves. I wrote a funny piece called "World Peace is in the Laundry," and for the first time ever publicly disclosed my experience of being strangled and punched. It was exhilarating to share something so personal that had been kept a secret, even from my closest friends and family.

World peace is in the laundry! One person at a time....When each person has peace, the world has peace.

I know war is easier than peace. Right now, men only have war. At least women can cry and sob. Tears are as cleansing to humans as rain is to earth, but I have a better way. My laundry-bashing parties.

War is expensive. Laundry bashing is free, and open to everyone.

Oh, I could spew my anger and hate on others. I know what it feels like to be held down and punched in the face by someone who vowed to cherish me, or to feel someone's angry hands wrap around my neck and squeeze...leaving me hanging by my neck like a limp sheet on a clothesline.

Suspended between life and death, heaven and earth, I suddenly felt what I can only describe as divine love. Now, I know I must love myself before I can love others.

My power is internal and a permanent gift from God. I can forgive, and forgiveness sets me FREE. I can't sing on pitch sometimes, but here I am, alive!

Grandma taught me to turn my hate and anger to love and peace by beating and bashing pillows. Now I have laundry-bashing parties. Everyone gathering over food and drink, all the pillows lined up, our beautiful valley, the trees above, the greens of our shaggy native grasses, the fragrant flowers...all of us immersed in nature, and people bashing, bashing, bashing! Everyone free to bash and beat the laundry over and over and over and over, and suddenly they feel better. They don't know why, but I do!

They have turned their hate and anger into love and peace by bashing laundry. And when each person has peace, the world has peace.

World peace is in the laundry.

**

By this time, my mom was 94 years young. Physically, she was in good health and used a walker for balance. She had been diagnosed with dementia several years earlier.

One day, she brought down the figurines she had painted years ago and asked me if I would like them. I looked at them and said, "Mom, these are the figurines I was looking at when Dad grabbed me off the rocking horse and brutally spanked me."

She had tears in her eyes as she said, "I know. I've always felt really bad about that, and I'm sorry."

It was the first time she'd acknowledged remembering what happened. It gave me a closure I wasn't even aware I'd needed. In the past, she'd simply told me she couldn't remember the violent event I'd described, and that she couldn't imagine my dad would do something like that. All these years, I'd wondered if I really did remember what happened or if I had made it up. Now I knew, and I was comforted; finally, another adult was validating my memory as a young child.

I took the figurines home and held a short ceremony for them, "from dust unto dust." I felt like smashing them on the concrete driveway, but I tossed them in the trash instead. I felt a little guilty but also relieved I wouldn't be seeing them again.

I was still splitting time between Nebraska and Seattle at this stage. While I was still in New York, I'd contracted a nasty virus from several of my acting classmates that turned into such a severe cough that I cracked my rib while doing a 20-minute yelling exercise in acting class. It was painful to breathe, move, stretch, or bend; even walking jarred my rib.

In Seattle, my rib healed but I still had heart pain. The exam revealed that my heart had a valve problem, and I was referred for possible open-heart surgery. The test also showed a small mass in my liver, but no one followed up on it. I also didn't have any obvious symptoms, so it didn't occur to me that it might be serious.

The stress of flying back and forth to Nebraska to help my mom, all while maintaining vigilance around the possibility of seeing my past abusers in Nebraska and trying to get the facts of my 1991 strangulation from the Lincoln Police Department, was taking a toll on my health. So in 2018, I sold my Nebraska house and drove a U-Haul back to Seattle with Grace dog. This is where I would be settling permanently.

It was a relief to spend 100 percent of my time in Seattle with extended family. I lived next door to my nephew and his wife and their two young children. They invited me to share dinner with them every evening, and I did dishes. It was fun to get to know all of them. I had the spirit of a toddler, so we laughed, played, and sang together often.

The mild weather was also perfect for being outdoors, and I felt comforted by the towering trees, flowers, and water, which filled me with the kind of serenity I knew I needed. I started singing and playing my guitar at a local cafe on a weekly basis. I went to songwriting meetings, met local songwriters, and sang in open mics. Grace dog came, too, and was very popular.

In 2019, I started singing with two churches and for a short time played piano at church when the regular pianist was out of town. I also transferred my Nebraska Rotary membership to Mercer Island, Washington, and presented a five-minute summary of my life experience, including my experience with domestic violence. By this time, I had shared my experience with my mom before I left Nebraska, as well as my brothers and sister and nieces and nephews. I'd also written about the abuse on my blog, so I had supportive comments from friends and loved ones.

Overall, it felt like my inner world was beginning to match my outer world, and I was no longer afraid to hide any part of myself.

During this time, my heart was out of synch and I was told I needed open-heart surgery. When I received a second opinion, the doctors ran two additional tests and said it was a moderate problem, so there was no need for surgery. I also had the mass in my liver checked for cancer in May of 2019. The biopsy came back negative.

However, that was far from the end of my health issues. In August, I experienced severe pain and another ultrasound. The mass in my liver had grown, and the recommendation was to have it surgically removed. It turned out that the biopsy I'd received was wrong and I'd had cancer the entire time, but this wasn't clear until after surgery. By the time they could schedule surgery, the mass was the size of a large grapefruit and they removed 40 percent of my liver. Before my surgery, I realized I might not even make it through the procedure due to my heart. I finally realized this was a life-or-death situation and sent instructions to some of my friends and family members about what to do and what parts of my life I wanted to share in the chance that I might be incapacitated.

Getting through surgery was a major accomplishment. Thankfully, my liver regenerated and functioned beautifully within a couple months. However, by May of 2020, a scan revealed small tumors in my lungs. I was told that average survival with no treatment was medically reported to be up to one year; with treatment, the average survival was two years.

The shock was immediate. It had never occurred to me that I wouldn't be able to heal. I wasn't afraid to die and I took the news matter-of-factly, but I had so many projects I wanted to complete and my prognosis seemed to leave me little time to do so. We discussed the option of immunotherapy to possibly extend my life by a year. My gut response was that it seemed like a lot of medicine for only one extra year, and my most heartfelt wish was to have a good quality of life—and I knew the treatment had a number of possible side effects. I told him I'd think about it.

He said I'd have a certain amount of time with no symptoms, and at some point, I'd find it hard to breathe and would have to go to hospice. I hated the idea of a slow decline, so I asked him if I could opt for death with dignity, and he said yes; in fact, now that I'd brought it up, he could discuss it with me. He told me that when I had less than six months to live, I could go to hospice and opt for death with dignity instead of long-drawn-out suffering.

For a while, I thought, *Surely this prognosis is wrong, because I feel so good!* However, when I broke the news to my brother Steve, who was a doctor, I began to accept the possibility that my time on this planet was truly limited.

As I shared the news with a few of my networking groups (now via Zoom due to the pandemic), I learned that some of them were healers. Many of them told me, "It's a diagnosis, but God has the final word," and other heartening comments that helped me change my mindset. Instead of being despondent about my life ending, I could genuinely enjoy the goodness in my life and do whatever God had put before me with the time I had left.

**

That spring, I went through another major rite of passage. My mother died at the age of 97.

Mom was in Nebraska in a skilled nursing facility, and no visitors were allowed due to COVID. I saw her via Skype and told her I loved her. She died that night.

Although I felt heartbroken that I could not be with Mom in her final hours, a number of energy healers and mediums shared important information with me after her death. One energy reader told me that Mom was so sorry and hoped I could forgive her. Mom also wanted me to always speak my truth because she felt I was hiding my greatness and strengths. Mom herself had lived in a box her entire life, and she'd learned so much from her children about what it meant to take a different path.

Later that year, in August, another medium, Susan, confirmed that Mom was deeply apologetic. Now that she had crossed over, she had a greater understanding of the bigger picture than she had when she was alive. Susan informed me, "She says of herself, 'I could have done better. I tried my best.'" Of course, whether I could communicate this to Mom myself or not, I forgave her. I fully understood that my mother had wounds, just like we all do, and that she'd had no way to heal them while she was alive.

The readings I received were deeply healing for me. I understood that my mother hadn't allowed herself to feel the full range of her emotions, as she had learned that was dangerous. She couldn't receive love because she didn't feel she deserved it, so she rejected it and unconsciously pushed others away. Susan told me that I had the power to heal, and that my mother was open to communicating with me directly in the future, which made me feel overjoyed.

In August, I also received another message that delighted me, from the Masters, who are spirit guides that Susan channels. She calls them in before a reading, and they download a message to her that she types up verbatim prior to meeting with clients.

We are so delighted to have this opportunity to be in communication and dialogue with you today. You are a bright light on this planet and have brought much joy and liveliness to all those you have encountered. You have a generosity of spirit, a desire to connect and know others deeply, and a commitment to bringing joy to the world through your actions and activities.

We recognize that there have been many trials and tribulations on this journey. These have provided opportunities for your soul to grow and expand in ways that you could never have imagined. You have entered this world in this lifetime to integrate much of the duality and polarity that is inherent in the physical experience. You have experienced both sides of many issues and situations…the love and joy, along with the heartache and suffering.

From these experiences, you have become stronger and stronger in your own sense of personal power. Much of your life has been dedicated to this exploration of personal power. You have experienced many situations that have increased your own sense of personal power, often as a result of moving through the feelings of powerlessness that first arose in response to a specific situation. In addition to exploring this concept of personal power for yourself, you have been a champion for others, supporting women, in particular, in recognizing, owning, and moving into the world with their own sense of personal power.

You have been a role model for so very, very many people as you have lived the principle that power is not a result of aggressive tactics, or domineering behaviors, or using power over others to control and manipulate people and circumstances. You have embodied the true nature of power by recognizing that it is the integration of the masculine and feminine energies, the receptivity and the action, the strong and soft, and the spoken truth aligned with active listening.

You have been integrating all of these principles in an effort to find your own "middle way," your own sense of oneness and wholeness. Congratulations, for this is the primary purpose of a soul's evolution on this planet…to remember…to return to the knowingness that comes from remembering that you are one with spirit, with the divine, with the infinite, with the universe, the creative source of all that is. You are the spark of the divine. When you remember, truly remember this truth, you are one with yourself and all that is, union with the divine. This union with the divine heals the wounds of the physical experience and assists you in moving forward on your journey to complete wholeness.

Your health challenges have been a symbol of this reunification process. The old emotional wounds that you have been wanting to heal were captured in the cells of the body, concentrating in certain places. The liver is the place where the body detoxifies and eliminates the impurities that are circulating throughout the body. This mass was removed to aid in the purification process, and you are ready now to release and fully heal these old wounds.

Now is the time to fully embrace your own sense of integrated personal power, in partnership with spirit. You are surrounded by love and light. Do not be afraid. Simply see yourself as the loving, beautiful, powerful, light being that you are, who has been playing in the physical realm to explore every possible experience that you could in one lifetime. That was your intention for this lifetime, and you have been succeeding! Now, you are ready to choose a future that is filled with the love and light that is your true self and your true nature.

It was so affirming and supportive to receive this message. And now that I found myself in this new place in my life, this middle ground between life and death, I felt more receptive to receiving guidance from the universe.

In September, the Masters delivered another message to me:

It is with great pleasure that we have the opportunity to communicate with you again today. We see you making great strides in your efforts to heal yourself from the trauma and painful experiences of your past. As you work through these experiences, you bring much light and expansion to the cells of your body. Rather than pain and suffering, your cells begin to resonate and crave the emotions of love. It is truly a chemical process triggered by emotional, psychological, and spiritual energies cascading through the body. The more that you shift the emotions of the body from fear, frustration, uncertainty, anger, pain, and suffering, the more that your body begins to come alive with love, light, peace, and joy. These emotions trigger chemicals that energize the cells and organs, whereas the former emotions trigger chemicals that are destructive to the physical body and organs.

So you are doing a marvelous job making this shift from the pain and suffering of your past to find the peace and joy in the present moment. For all things exist in the present moment. We would suggest that this is an important consideration for you at this time. There is much emphasis in the medical community on the predicting of future events. We suggest that this is an opportunity for you to recognize that there is no time that exists except in the present moment. When you live in this present moment, and we mean fully live in this present moment, your awareness of new possibilities expands and the potential for a different future to be created exists, in the here and now, present moment.

So, this is a wonderful opportunity to practice the reality that is true for all humans on this planet. There is no time except this present moment. Whenever you are NOT focusing on this very moment now, you are out of your body, out of your conscious awareness. For living in the past causes pain and suffering, while living in the future causes fear and anxiety.

The truth is that the best way to live is to live in the present moment, for in this moment, everything is possible. The love, peace, joy, and happiness that you experience right here, right now, is the very energy that creates your reality in the next present moment. As you string one present moment to the next present moment to the next present moment, you reinvent yourself completely. That is when the miracles occur...when you transform who you used to be and become what you truly are...a peaceful, loving, beautiful, gorgeous ray of light shining brightly on your immediate surroundings and radiating out to the world at large.

You are a master and have chosen to be here on this planet, at this time, to experiment with mastery. You are so incredibly powerful! Massively powerful...more than you can ever imagine. The diagnosis that was presented to you was simply an opportunity for you to align with your true mastery, to embrace the powerful being that you really are. For when you embrace who you truly are, you become a force for creation that is magnificent. You can create anything and everything that your heart desires without stipulation.

We see that you have felt powerful in certain arenas in your life, but not so much in others. This is a time of great integration for you. For you are bringing all of your experiences into alignment so that they bring the wisdom that integrates every aspect of your being into one cohesive, authentic being...a mighty and powerful spiritual being mastering this physical experience.

Now is the time for you to rise up and assume your true place, your true nature, your true and authentic self. You are a teacher, a way shower, here to assist other people, particularly women, to transform themselves by recognizing and aligning with their own true nature and true sense of personal power. The world is ready and waiting for what you can offer...the wisdom that you bring to others, particularly women. As you assume and step into your own power, that has a tremendous ripple effect out to the world. You do not yet realize how much of an impact you have on the mass consciousness as you integrate all of the wisdom that you have gained in this experience. Once you complete this personal transformation, you will be amazed at how your external reality changes to match in every way!

So live in the present moment, recognize and embrace the power that comes from the wisdom that you have amassed, and BE the master that you are!

With much love to you, the Masters

As time passed and these messages of hope and love came pouring in, I felt my mother's presence even more acutely. In January of 2021, I asked, "Mom, are you enjoying heaven?"

I could feel her response of joy and delight. The message I heard was, "Yes, the food, the flowers...every color of the rainbow. We get to send them to delight humans and see them smile. Every laugh is a healing. Every outrage is a stumble. Every hate is a bumble and a tumble. The music is perfect fifths, and we sing and harmonize. Eyes, wise, prize. Healing is dealing, not stealing. Healing is peeling. Healing is feeling."

I could feel the wisdom and playfulness in her words, and I felt tears of joy rise into my eyes. I felt a sense of light, as well as a deep gratitude for my mother, who I believed was giving me what I needed to break the human cycle of pain and suffering while I was still on Earth. I felt that I had received the Masters' message on a cellular level.

I received more messages from my mother, such as, "Take away judgment and everything is divine. It's that simple. Follow your heart and be light. A knot in your stomach equals NO. The feeling of skipping like a child equals YES. Your heart knows yes and no. Maybes are not from your heart. How we love ourselves in between is up to us, and if we love our self, we are connected while living on Earth. This is the way of the word."

I had another message from the Masters on March 16, 2021. It read:

We are delighted to join with you again today. You have made such dramatic and significant progress in your personal and spiritual evolution. You have taken many steps to reflect upon the experiences that you have gained and the wisdom that you have accumulated throughout this lifetime.

You traveled to the peaks of the mountains, up rugged terrain and treacherous slopes, to emerge the victor as you plant your flag on the top, looking out over the beautiful vistas that you have conquered.

There is no need to worry about any specific achievement or desired outcome that you have held in your mind as a "goal" to be achieved. For every step that you have taken, every word that you have written, every page that you have shared with others, has been a process of release.....review, learn, release. Review, learn, release. The process of reflection has offered you the chance to see your life and its unique opportunities and obstacles from a more elevated perspective so that you could observe the patterns of learning, the patterns of discovery, that you have chosen for yourself in this lifetime.

You have exceeded even your own expectations as you have observed the massive amount of learning, experience, and wisdom that you have gained. Of course, it was always a choice....to learn, grow, and evolve from your experiences or to retreat into the pain and suffering. You have risen to the occasion and have stepped above the experiences to see the grand tapestry of your life, every thread interwoven into a magnificent piece of artistry. Each thread, in and of itself, held no true significance until it was intertwined with other threads of various colors, textures, and dimensions. As you wove each thread into the tapestry, you weren't able to see the image that you were creating of the "whole." Now as you reflected back on each thread, the "whole" began to emerge into a beautiful image, the vision for your life that you created before arriving.

Now that you can see the "whole" in great relief and detail, you can appreciate the need for every thread. For without each and every single thread, the picture would not be complete, the image would be deficient. There would be gaps or "holes" in the overall experience.

So we commend you for your bravery, your persistence, your

resilience, your sense of wonder, your delight in discovery, and for your continued commitment to learn, grown, and evolve as a spiritual being playing in this playground called planet earth.

Now you have owned your personal power in an integrated way, so that you are "whole" and "complete".....no gaps, no regrets, no doubts about who you truly are.....a beautiful, brilliant, and powerful spiritual being, who has transformed your life and the lives of many, many others during this unique journey.

With much love to you, the Masters

Not long ago, the chaplain from my hospital's integrated care team scheduled a Zoom call with me. She asked me how I felt about dying and if I had any fear.

"I'm not afraid, but I have so many loose ends to finish if possible, such as writing my book, publishing my songs, and sorting files," I said. "I know that before I die, I want to forgive myself for having been conned by abusers...and I want to forgive them."

I told her I had been informed that the liver is where anger is held, and I sometimes wondered if my unresolved anger and prolonged silence about my abuse had created my illness. We talked about it in great depth, and finally, she asked me a simple question. "Karen, do you love yourself?"

As I sat and thought about that question, a feeling of warmth and peace spread over me. I understood then and there that any regrets or questions that might have remained unanswered didn't matter in the presence of this deep, all-encompassing grace that was holding me...that had made it possible for me to tell my story.

"Yes, I love myself."

And I knew I was telling the truth.

CONCLUSION

I have the following words taped to my mirror on a piece of paper. "I am whole and complete. I am love and joy, peace and grace. I was born this way."

They are a reminder that enables me to greet each morning with joy and wonder.

When I walk with Grace dog, I sing songs I make up, thanking the trees for oxygen, the leaves, and everything I can see, feel, and hear. One day I sang so loudly that a man called out, "You have a beautiful voice!"

I laugh a lot. I smile a lot. I wake up with a sense of gratitude and humility. I thank God for waking me up. I thank my bed, even my water faucet, for all they do. I've called nearly everyone I know to tell them how grateful I am for having them in my life. Some people I tell about my health and some I don't; some can handle it, some can't.

The side effects from immunotherapy were severe enough that I only had a few rounds before discontinuing treatment. Since October of 2020, I have been on the "God plan." The silver lining is that I can now take more natural herbs, which previously conflicted with the immunotherapy drugs, and I have no side effects.

I feel exuberant, alive, and strong.

I am grateful that my cancer diagnosis was a powerful catalyst in my life that enabled me to pour my efforts into heart projects on which I had been procrastinating. I view it as a godsend.

Aside from my natural lifestyle, which includes acupuncture and eating whole organic foods, I am on numerous prayer lists. I meditate daily and receive energy healing and clearing sessions every three weeks. I also play my piano daily and make it a priority to learn new things that keep my body, mind, and spirit agile and youthful.

I know without a doubt that when I meet my creator, it will be with many lessons learned and the pain of my past transmuted into wisdom.

Most of us are running subconscious programs 95 percent of the time, and our bodies are running our show on autopilot. If we desire to heal, we must be aware of our unconscious programs and become a new person. Otherwise, we will simply repeat old patterns and reenact old traumas. As we integrate new patterns and become more aware of the programs that are sabotaging us and preventing us from experiencing the wholeness and joy we all deserve, we literally experience an energetic rebirth. Our energy changes, we see things differently, and we generate new possibilities.

Nothing is written in stone. While I have made peace with dying, I am well aware that the divine plan may have something different in mind for me...and I'm open to it.

I think of an affirmation from Dr. Joe Dispenza that I often repeat to myself in meditation: "I bless my past that it may turn into wisdom."

Whatever the case, I can look back over the story of my life—all the people, places, situations, and experiences—and feel a genuine awe and reverence for all of it. Yes, even the dark nights of the soul and the moments of feeling I'd hit rock bottom and there was no way out. I can look back at the people I'd believed were horrible and recognize that they were all my teachers—and I can be grateful for every one of them. They, too, were helping me to transmute my understanding of myself so that I could eventually choose love and wholeness over fragmentation and fear.

I understand today that any of the obstacles I encountered were there to remind me of my true and infinite nature, which is love. I am not to blame for what happened, and I understand that it was not my fault.

I never saw Harold again after I left Nebraska—except one time when I was in Las Vegas. He was walking in one direction while I was going in the other. He appeared drunk. He happened to be with my former employees, so I am guessing they were there on business. They greeted me effusively, and I responded in kind. Slurring his words, Harold said, "Hey, I know you!" It was interesting to see this person, who had seemed to have so much power over me at one point in my life, and feel nothing more than the polite regard one would feel toward a stranger.

"That was a lifetime ago," I said, smiling. I kept walking.

After my divorce and Donald's subsequent lawsuit, I didn't see or speak to Donald again but, in 2009, I had a dream in which his mother beseeched me, "Forgive my son." I called my mom and told her I was going to forgive Donald. She said in a disgusted tone, "You're a bigger person than I am."

I sent him a note that said, "I forgive you and I ask for you to forgive me." I also sent him back an autographed print of Woodrow Wilson, who'd attended Princeton, just like Donald. The print was one of the things I'd received after the divorce settlement; I'd never liked it, and I knew he did. Donald had previously refused to return a painting I'd commissioned in college in Spain, of the Cathedral in Seville, from my Seville Spain artist neighbor. I thought that perhaps if I sent him Woodrow as a peace offering, he might finally send me my painting.

Not long after I sent him the note and print, I received an email from him thanking me for Woodrow and telling me my painting was thrown away. He made no mention of forgiveness, but I felt better all the same. I was sad that my painting was lost, but not surprised.

I see now I would rather be me than anyone else in the world, and I wouldn't change my past for anything because it got me to where I am now.

I bless my past and turn my past to wisdom.

I also learned a valuable meditation from Dr. Dispenza that he calls "Reconditioning the Body to a New Mind." He explains a special way of breathing that cleanses our body and resets our mind.

If I get up from the meditation as a new person, I am healing myself and freeing myself from unconscious programs of stress, fight, flight, fear, and freeze, which all add to illness. The key is to embody elevated emotions such as love, joy, gratitude, and peace. This is the key to healing: recognizing we are already whole and complete. We just need to remember this and embody it in every moment.

My sincere hope is that this book can be a reminder of sorts for you, if you have forgotten, along life's winding and ever-changing road, who you truly are. May you hear me whispering these words to you, as I am in this moment: "You are love, you are loving, you are lovable. You are whole and complete. Everything you touch turns to gold."

APPENDIX

SELECT AWARDS, ARTICLES, AND LETTERS BY DATE

Partial Awards List

Lincoln East High School Distinguished Alumni, March 26, 1986

Leadership Lincoln Class 1 Graduate September 1985–May 1986

Inc. magazine's Inc. 500, #250, Karen Dunning, CEO, announced 1987

Inc. magazine's Inc. 500, #185, Karen Dunning, CEO, announced 1988

YWCA Tribute to Women Award and program speaker, October 6, 1994

The Chancellor's Club, University of Nebraska–Lincoln, 1995

Karen Dunning Fund Endowment, University of Nebraska–Lincoln, 1995

Governor Nelson's CEO Roundtable Speaker, 1995, and trade mission, 1995 and 1998

Entrepreneur of the Year Award. University of Nebraska–Lincoln College of Business Administration Nebraska Center for Entrepreneurship, March 26, 1996

Partial Articles List and Articles by Date
Dunning, Karen. "'Real World' Satisfying Experience." University of Nebraska–Lincoln College of Business Administration *Probe* magazine, May 1981.

IBM Lawsuit CV84-L-661 October 2, 1984

"People to Watch." *Lincoln Sun*, 1985.

Piersol, Dick. "United Phone Book grows up, up, up." ©*Lincoln Journal Star*, November 24, 1987.

Letter from Lincoln Mayor Bill Harris, December 16, 1987.

Harrell, Ann. "Women overcome stereotypes in starting their own business." ©*Lincoln Journal Star*, January 3, 1988.

McConnell, Curt. "Fast-growing Data Source Media plans to double sales in 1988." *Midlands Business Journal*, Jan. 29–Feb. 4, 1988.

Associated Press. "Magazine ranks three Lincoln firms in top 500 fastest-growing companies." ©*Lincoln Journal Star*, November 22, 1988.

Barnes, Jeffrey S. "Computer Products Inc. addresses office printing needs." *Midlands Business Journal*, May 12–18, 1989.

Computer Products, Inc. 3M Desktop Presentations advertisement and photo. ©*Lincoln Sunday Journal Star*, February 25, 1990.

"1990, Success Spotlight: April 15 Means Big Returns for Nebraska Dealer." *Proxima POST* newsletter, Spring 1991.

"Lincoln's business people offer their advice." ©*Lincoln Journal Star*, March 18, 1991.

Lincoln Police Department. Public Incident Report Case 91-032330. Assault: Non-domestic "Grabbed and choked by neck," April 11, 1991.

University of Nebraska–Lincoln College of Business Administration Center for Entrepreneurship speaker, 10th Nebraska Conference on Productivity and Entrepreneurship, April 4, 1995.

"1995 Governor's CEO Roundtable Assembled." *The Courier* (Nebraska Department of Economic Development, Nebraska Diplomats) and Governor Nelson letter, December 1995.

"Four owners named Entrepreneurs of the Year." ©*Lincoln Journal Star*, April 15, 1996.

"Women's Studies Awarded Endowment—Karen Dunning Fund for Women's Studies Established." University of Nebraska-Lincoln Women's Studies Program newsletter, Spring 1996.

Beutler, Patty. "Girls Just Wanna Have Funds." ©*Lincoln Journal Star*, March 15, 1997.

Karen Dunning news interview. Channel 10/11, CBS Affiliate, Lincoln, Nebraska, April 8, 1997.

Todd, Daniel. "Enhanced graphics boost Business Media's sales." *Midlands Business Journal*, Spring 1997.

Griess, Karen. "On the Waterfront." ©*Lincoln Journal Star*, June 20, 1997.

Kaiser, Rebecca. "Focus on 4: Karen Dunning." *Strictly Business* magazine, October–November 1997.

Dunning, Karen. "Power Presentation and When to Use Them." *Strictly Business* magazine, November 1997.

Dunning, Karen. "Women: Flex Your Economic Power." *Lincoln–Lancaster Women's Commission Quarterly*, Winter 1997/98.

Korbelik, Jeff. "Aiming for the Stars." ©*Lincoln Journal Star*, March 21, 1999.

Dunning, Karen. "Company History." ©*Lincoln Journal Star*, March 16, 2002.

Glide Gospel Ensemble on *Conan O'Brien Show*, 2005.

U.S. Senator Ben Nelson recommendation letter to President-Elect Obama, December 17, 2008.

Pohlman, Marty. "Hunter's Screenwriters Colony in full swing." *The Superior Express*, September 27, 2012.

Dunning, Karen. "Grace, Service Therapy Dog, Reporting for Duty." *Lincoln55+ Seniors*, Fall 2016.

Dunning, Karen. "Escape cycles of abuse." ©*Lincoln Journal Star*, March 2, 2015

Beach, Natalie. "#USToo: The United Shame of America." *O* magazine, March 2018.

University of Nebraska College of Business *Probe* magazine,
May 1981.(Karen Age 24)

"Real World" Satisfying Experience

By: Karen Dunning

IBM Systems Engineer
Karen Dunning keeps
her customers informed
of new technological
developments.

I have found the business world to be as fascinating and challenging as I thought it would be. I've learned many things - both through my own experiences and those of others.

I celebrated my second anniversary of working for IBM as a Systems Engineer last December. It has been both rewarding and challenging. I would like to recap some of the events that lead to my career choice.

Since I was young, I have been fascinated with business and always wanted to know how it operated. When I was growing up, with two older brothers and a younger sister, my mother was constantly supporting us - a super motivator. We grew up knowing we could do anything we wanted if we tried hard enough.

College has many things to offer to those who will let it. Due to my strong interest in business, I studied finance and real estate. I wanted to go into banking and did not want to wait four years to begin working. I have worked at various jobs since I was fourteen and at a local retail store during most of my college career. I was also involved in my sorority, many clubs, and had an active social life. I have always thought of college as a place to learn and grow. My junior year was spent studying in Seville, Spain and traveling in Europe.

When I returned to the United States I was ready to finish college and begin a career. Since I graduated midyear, I spent most of that first semester in job interviews. As a finance major, many avenues were open to me. I was most interested in banking, sales and insurance. As a member of Phi Chi Theta, a busi-

ness fraternity for women, I was fortunate to hear Lynn Roper speak. She was one of two women stock brokers in Lincoln at that time. I was very impressed with this woman and her accomplishments; so I arranged a personal interview with her for advice on how to succeed in business.

She suggested that I search for a company with a good training program. She recommended certain books to read concerning women in business and advised me to interview with as many companies as possible. I also talked to other people. One of my banking professors felt that being a Bank Examiner would be a great way to learn banking. One of the bank officers I talked with in Lincoln warned me about negative attitudes toward women. These people were all a tremendous help to me.

SPARKLY AND STRONG

"Real World"

Assertive Attitude

Armed with a positive attitude, a resume and knowing what I wanted; I set out to land a challenging career. I was looking for a career that was challenging with rewards for a job well done, the right salary, and a certain amount of control. I interviewed mainly through the University of Nebraska placement center and local Lincoln businesses. I found that the more assertive I was, the more confident I became and the more job offers I received.

I feel that the benefits of interviews are threefold: 1. finding out more about yourself; 2. finding out more about the company; and 3. the company finding out more about you. I really checked out the companies I interviewed with and especially their attitudes toward advancement and women in business. When I was in college, I thought the business world treated all applicants the same and used the same criteria for everyone. I soon found out how wrong that was. I had both good and bad experiences. I would like to tell you about a couple, not to dwell on the subject, but to make you aware of what can happen. Some of my interviewers asked questions which were clearly illegal and irrelevent, such as: "Do you plan to marry and have children? If so, when? What if your husband won't let you travel?". I clearly stated that I wanted a career, and even if I did get married, I certainly would not marry anyone who had such backward attitudes toward women in business. One company man, after I responded in this way said, "Well, of course you would say that - that is a very good answer for a woman." I replied, "If you thought I would say that anyway, why did you bother to ask?" That left him speechless. Needless to say, I got the job offer!

Company Discriminates

If someone had told me what I am about to tell you, I would not have believed it. The most blatant case of discrimination during my interviewing came from one of the local Savings and Loans. In one of my banking classes, a male classmate had told me about an opening as a loan officer at the Savings and Loan Company he worked at. I was excited about working there. I had had a savings account there since I was eight and the people were always very friendly towards me. I went immediately to the personnel office and stated that I would graduate in December with a Finance degree, and wanted to interview for the loan officer position my friend had mentioned. She said, "The only opening for you is Receptionist." I replied that I did not study finance to be a receptionist and felt that my talents could be better utilized as a loan officer. She told me that I would have to take a typing test. I told her I had never learned how to type on purpose because I did not want to be a secretary. She said, "Everyone who has applied for jobs here has taken a typing test - even our President." Well, if the President took it, I could too, so I took the test and scored a miserable ten words a minute. She told me never to come back to that institution until I learned to type, but to fill out an application in the meantime. As I filled out the application, this woman dictated a letter to be sent to five men. It went something like this: "I enjoyed talking to you about our opening for a loan officer. I would like you to come in next week for a second interview to further discuss this position." I could not believe what I had heard. I got up, went into her office and said, "I just heard you dictate those five letters, I know you have an opening for a loan officer

and I would like to be considered. She said, "For you the only opening is for a receptionist." I was furious. Imagine, having a finance degree and only being allowed to interview for the position of receptionist! I did not report that incident then. I was afraid of how it would affect my chances of ever getting a job in Lincoln.

Discussion Helpful

One banker told me I could be a teller at $600 a month, that their bank was very competitive with other banks, and that the officers were making $12,000 a year, the highest paid in Lincoln. Of all the banks I talked to about loan officer or management traniee positions, I did not get a single offer. I was insulted and hurt, but I did not let that get me down. I knew what I had to offer and what they were missing. I would not work for any company with such discriminatory attitudes and for the salaries they were willing to pay.

I traveled to various cities and interviewed with many companies. I received so many job offers I did not know what to do with them all. I narrowed them down to the three most promising: Systems Engineer for IBM; bank examiner for the comptroller of the currency; and internal auditor for a large local insurance company. I discussed the pros and cons of each offer with Lynn. She pointed out factors that I had not even considered and was immensely helpful. I urge everyone to discuss career plans with a successful business person.

I chose a career with IBM for the following important reasons. IBM offered the best opportunity for me to utilize my skills. I would be selling and installing computers with a specialization in banking, finance, distribution and construction. I would be responsible for many

8

259

accounts, could plan my own schedule, have extensive training to enable me to do the job right, and travel. IBM cared about my career path which would be unlimited. IBM pays well for a job well done, and recognizes accomplishments. At that time, there were few women in the fascinating field of computers and business.

Training Important

I started my career with IBM on December 26, 1978 as Systems Engineer for the General Systems Division. I was responsible for selling and installing computers for various businesses and acting as a technical consultant on business operations with cost effective business solutions. My first year was spent mostly training in classrooms or on the job. I spent seventeen weeks in training in Atlanta, Georgia, the head quarters for my division and the location of most of the education centers for new employees. These classes were an experience in themselves. There were four classes. The first three were five weeks long for both Marketing Representatives and Systems Engineers. The last class was two weeks long and was for Systems Engineers only. They were comparable to seventeen weeks of finals. We were graded on everything daily, which caused a lot of pressure. My classmates were from all over the United States, most had never met anyone from Nebraska before. The instructors were all past proven System Engineers or Marketing Reps. I was impressed with the caliber of students and instructors; I have become very close to many of the IBM people I met.

The first class taught us the basics of how a business runs, contrasting manual operations with the advantages of using computers, how to make effective sales calls and presentations and how to justify business computers.

The second class was very technical in nature. We learned many

details of our computers, got to know the product line inside out and learned several programming languages. We also learned the importance of having superior products, programs and customer service.

The third class was an overview of the many application programs which IBM offers, such as manufacturing, retail, finance, distribution, construction, law firms, hospitals, and medical groups.

The final class was for System Engineers only and covered how to manage territories, more sales call techniques, more programming, and the importance of customer service.

Proving Competence

In between classes, I was responsible for special projects and was free to accompany others on sales calls to improve my skills. I was on an uphill learning curve that entire first year - both in learning my job and in working with others. When I started, there were no higher ranking women role models for me to follow. I had to learn to cope with people who really question the ability of women to do a complete job. More than once, a male coworker would say to a male customer, "Karen was hired to satisfy EEO requirements," or some equally obnoxious statement. The solution for me was to pursue my work with as much energy as possible, proving that I was more than capable for the job.

In one of my first classes, I had a male advisor tell me he could not believe how well I was doing, especially since I had three handicaps: 1. I was young; 2. I was a woman; and 3. I was straight out of college.

I read a few books such as, *Business As A Game* by Albert Carr and *Wising Up* by Jo Foxworth. I began to realize that business really is a game and if you want to win you have to play by the rules. You have to know what you want, set goals

and time frames, and not be afraid to ask for such things as well-deserved raises and promotions.

New Responsibility

After a year of training, I was promoted to Associate Systems Engineer. With this, came the responsibility of managing a territory. Mine started with twenty-two business accounts in Lincoln, Beatrice, Nebraska City, Fairbury and Hebron - all current users of IBM equipment.

Besides the training for new employees, IBM offers a variety of industry classes. I went to several concerning construction, distribution and finance. IBM also offers annual conferences in certain industry areas. This past year, I was able to accompany some of my customers, along with two thousand other IBM customers, to the Construction Conference in Washington, D.C. At the conference we were able to learn of new developments in the construction industry and compare different methods of handling business solutions. I found the conference valuable.

Currently, I handle about forty-five accounts with more to come. My customers are very important to me. I concentrate my efforts on learning more about their particular needs and offering better business solutions. The computer industry is constantly changing with more to learn in every area, and it is up to me to keep my customers abreast of all the new possibilities available to them.

Satisfying Career

My career with IBM is everything I wanted and more. The people I work with and my customers are super. Management helps with my career planning. They know I want to go as far and as fast as I can and

continued

9

"Real World"

that I am planning to go into marketing this year. For a job well done, the rewards and recognition are there. My days are fairly flexible - I plan my own schedule as results are what counts. I am free to learn and grow as much as I am capable of.

In addition to a satisfying career, I feel that community involvement is very important. I have been a member of the Nova Chapter of Business and Professional Women for over two years. We have month-

ly meetings with very informative speakers. The group is made up of many talented business women, and I find it fascinating. I also helped on the United Way Campaign, and am a member of the Pi Beta Phi Alum Club and UNL Alumni Association. Due to my interest in Sales and Real Estate, I am also involved with Mary Kay Cosmetics and have an active Real Estate license.

My future plans include getting more involved with the Republican

party and local politics and the business college - helping business majors chart careers, and obtaining a Masters Degree in Business. I really feel that I have had a rich life so far and am looking forward to a very positive and fast-paced future.

My overall advice to anyone is to maintain a positive mental attitude, know what you want, how to get it, develop a detailed plan of action and then go for it. I truly believe that you can be anything you want to be, if you believe it yourself. □

"People to Watch." *Lincoln Sun*, 1985.

People to Watch...Karen Dunning (age 28) of Data Source Media, typed for readability:

When Karen Dunning was a little girl, her ambition was to be a business person. More than that, Karen wanted to be president of her own company.

Today, that dream has come true because Karen Dunning is President of Data Source media, Inc.- a rapidly rising force in the business of computer and word processing supplies.

After her 1978 graduation from UNL with a degree in finance, Karen worked for IBM as a data processing manager. "It didn't take much of a crystal ball to see the market for data processing and computer supplies would be a major area of business growth," Dunning recalled. "Fortunately, I learned that Data source Media, Inc. was for sale here in Lincoln and I bought it.

In this business, I have to wear many hats and I love each one of them. Planning, marketing, buying, sales, servicing accounts – all of these activities are great. And I just love being able to work as long and as hard as I want. It's also nice to know that your products help make the work of so many others so much easier and faster to accomplish."

"I've also noticed in Lincoln that most of the businesses try to help each other. Whenever they can, they try to buy products and services from each other." Dunning observed.

Karen finds time to be of service to her community. She co-chaired the YWCA Tribute To Women, is an active member of LIBA and the NOVA Business Women's Club.

Moreover, Karen chaired Stephanie Armitage's successful reelection campaign for the Lancaster County Board, is an active alumnus of her UNL sorority and is active in the women's ministries of First-Plymouth Church.

The President of Data Source Media, Inc. is concerned about local issues, is willing to work to make positive changes, and is ambitious and highly organized. Those are the qualities that make Karen Dunning a person to watch.

Piersol, Dick, "United Phone Book grows up, up, up" ©Lincoln Journal Star, Nov. 24, 1987

United Phone Book grows up, up, up

The other Lincoln companies on the list, all appearing for the first time, were:

Data Source Media, 3505 N. 48th St., a distributor of computer supplies, ranked

See GROWS on page 5

By Dick Piersol
Journal Business Editor

United Phone Book Advertisers, 1221 N St., led four Lincoln companies ranked among the nation's 500 fastest-growing companies, according to INC. magazine.

From page 1 # Grows —

No. 250. Founded in 1973, the company's estimated sales for 1986 were $1.147 million, and its 1982-86 growth rate was 992 percent. Karen Dunning, president of the company, said it distributes supplies and accessories for a variety of computer companies, including International Business Machines Corp. and 3M, but sells no software or hardware. The company is the largest in this market niche in the Midwest, Dunning said. The company sells in 28 states, but concentrates in Nebraska, Iowa and Missouri. A poll of customers showed the company's strengths to be the quick availability of quality products, service, quick shipping and competitive pricing, she said. The company has 14 employees and additional offices in Omaha and Des Moines and Davenport, Iowa.

To qualify for the INC. list, companies must meet four requirements: to have been independent and privately held since Aug. 1, 1987; to have at least a 526 percent increase in sales over the past five years; a 1982 net profit ranging from $100,000 to $25 million; and greater sales in the fifth year than in the fourth year.

Letter from Lincoln Mayor Bill Harris, December 16, 1987.

OFFICE OF THE MAYOR   NEBRASKA'S CAPITAL CITY   BILL HARRIS, MAYOR

December 16, 1987

Ms. Karen Dunning
Data Source Media
3505 North 48th
Lincoln, NE 68504

Dear Ms. Dunning:

On behalf of the City of Lincoln, I commend you on being included on INC.
magazine's list of the 500 fastest-growing privately held companies in the
nation.

This recognition serves not only to highlight your personal achievement and
entrepreneurial success, but serves also as an example to encourage and inspire
other companies throughout our community.

I wish you a Merry Christmas and continued success in the New Year!

Sincerely,

Bill Harris
Mayor

tjs

CITY OF LINCOLN • 555 SOUTH 10TH ST. • LINCOLN, NEBRASKA 68508 • 402-471-7511

Harrell, Ann. "Women overcome stereotypes in starting their own business." ©*Lincoln Journal Star*, January 3, 1988.

Women overcome stereotypes in starting their own business

By Ann Harrell

In 1984, Karen Dunning was selling computer systems to banks for International Business Machines Corp. She also was searching the want ads for a new business opportunity.

She found it in the form of a retiring salesman who wanted to sell his computer supplies business in Omaha and Lincoln. She bought his Lincoln business — which he ran out of his basement — quit IBM and turned entrepreneur.

Today, at 31, Dunning is the president and majority owner of Data Source Media, a computer supply company with offices in Lincoln; Omaha; Davenport, Iowa; and Des Moines, Iowa.

Data Source Media is among the 500 fastest-growing companies in America, according to INC. magazine. Sales in 1986 were about $1.14 million. They are expected this year to be $2.5 million and next year should be about $5 million, Dunning said.

Buying a business was scary, Dunning said. She wasn't sure customers would follow her to her new company, but she was ambitious and aggressive and believed she could do a better job for the customer with her own business. She also thought it would give her better opportunities.

"I always wanted to have my own business," Dunning said. "I'm not a very good corporate citizen."

Becoming own boss

Dunning is not alone. Increasingly, women who want to control their own futures are leaving other people's businesses to be their own bosses.

Owning a business is challenging, hard work, five local women business owners agreed. It also can mean facing and overcoming stereotypes about women.

But for some women, leaving the corporate world to become an entrepreneur means leaving behind limitations placed on women.

Ten years ago, it was all the rage for the female baby boomers in the workforce to get a master's degree in business administration, said Rieva Lesonsky, editor of Entrepreneur Magazine, based in Los Angeles. They thought it would be their passport to the same jobs, salaries and opportunities their male counterparts were offered.

But they found they were running aground in middle management, and salaries still weren't equal to men's, Lesonsky said.

"They are dissatisfied with what the corporate world is offering them," said Sharon Tiley, communications and news services manager for the American Business Women's Association. "As a result, they are starting businesses."

In the 1970s, the trouble was getting women into corporate suites, Tiley said.

See WOMEN on page 3B

JANUARY 3, 1988   SUNDAY JOURNAL-STAR

RANDY HAMPTON/SUNDAY JOURNAL-STAR

Karen Dunning, president of Data Source Media, 3505 N. 48th St., takes inventory Thursday at the company's Lincoln office.

From page 1B Women

In the 1980s, the hard part is keeping them there. "They have ideas," she said.

Of the nearly 17 million small businesses in the United States last year, about 4 million were owned by women, Lesonsky said. Within 20 years, women are expected to own about half of the country's small businesses, she said.

Cheryl Mapes was a sales manager and later buyer for Brandeis department stores when she left in October 1980 to take a higher-paying job with a smaller chain of specialty shops in Omaha.

The pay was better, but the rewards were not, Mapes said. She quit soon after taking the job, and, although she had other job offers, she moved back to Lincoln to start her own business instead.

Cheryl's Fashions, a specialty store selling women's large sizes, opened in East Park Plaza in April 1981. Sales that year totaled about $183,000, Mapes said.

Today the company has two stores and a warehouse in Lincoln and one store in Omaha. Sales in 1987 will be more than $1 million, Mapes said.

Ability doubted

One problem Mapes faced was establishing credit with some New York clothing manufacturers, she said. Although they had known her when she worked for Brandeis, some doubted her ability as a business owner, and some questioned why she had gone into business for herself.

"You were made to feel pretty low," she said. "I'm sure there are plenty of men who went into this business who didn't get asked why."

Once she proved herself, those people came around, Mapes said. "I'd say I get 100 percent cooperation now."

She emphasized that people in the Lincoln business community have treated her well.

Maria Lemon, president and majority owner of The Editor Inc., Communication Management, founded her company in 1982 with one client and no money. The company produces written material for clients and does consulting in communication management.

Lemon said the biggest frustration she faced as a female entrepreneur was "no cultural background to tell you you could do it and succeed."

Editor Vice President Laura Partsch worked for the state Health Department until 1986, when she left to form Communication Strategies, a home-based writing and editing company. She joined Lemon in January 1987. Partsch said some people were concerned that she would be hurt if the business didn't succeed.

Seen as a hobby

It is hard for women entrepreneurs to be taken seriously, Lesonsky said. Some people consider business a hobby for women, or see it as something she will try until she decides what she really wants to do with her life.

"I think it's part of the old habits about women who want to work," she said. "But it's dying, and it's dying quickly."

Just as economic realities erode stigmas about women in the labor force, so they make it more acceptable for women to start their own businesses, Lesonsky said.

Dunning said she is often the only woman at industry conferences, and her presence sometimes confuses male peers.

Occasionally, that leads male competitors to tell her trade secrets and business ideas, thinking she needs the help or won't know what to do with them, Dunning said.

"They learn later," she said with a laugh. "I'm sure they wouldn't do that to a man."

Different treatment

Competitors and vendors may be more likely than customers to treat a woman business owner differently, Lesonsky said. Some male business associates may assume the woman's presence is a sexual come-on, adopt a fatherly role or try to cheat her, she said. But customers are concerned about whether they are getting what they want for a fair price.

Some women entrepreneurs interviewed said they see less sexism now that they are successful businesspeople. Success is like a badge, they said. As you prosper, more and more people want to work with you, sell to you and buy from you, they said.

Strong self-esteem, determination, good role models and a supportive family all were mentioned as contributing to success for women in business.

"I don't think I would have opened my own business without the support and encouragement of my family," said Tari Hendrickson Sweeney, 30, president and owner of the three Paper Parade stores in Lincoln. Her mother, Cecilia Hendrickson, is the principal of Hawthorne School in Lincoln. "If people have good models to observe and learn from, that will put them ahead of the game."

Learning to network

Networking skills also are crucial, although the women agreed that it is harder for women to learn them.

"A man's networking is done on almost a subconscious level," Lesonsky said, while women's groups are more formal. "I think it will evolve to a more informal state."

For Mapes, it was easier at first to form associations with the women who are part of her buying office in New York. Becoming acquainted with the men took longer.

"Once I got over being the new kid on the block, I got some nice networking with both men and women," she said.

The business owners advised other women interested in becoming entrepreneurs to research their product and market, be prepared to work hard and not be afraid to take reasonable risks to make their companies grow.

"A lot of people said it would never work," Mapes said. "It's very rewarding to have a nice-sized business now and to be able to look back and say, 'It worked.'"

Fast-growing Data Source Media plans to double sales in 1988

by Curt McConnell

A new in-house computer to streamline operations, two new sales offices in Iowa, the hiring of a marketing director and the move to a larger Lincoln headquarters should all help Data Source Media reach its 1988 sales goals, said Karen Denning, president of the computer supply company.

In its December issue, Inc. magazine gave DSM its midway spot on its list of the 500 fastest-growing companies in the United States. The 15-year-old Lincoln firm, which Denning bought in 1984, placed 250th with growth of 992 percent during the previous five-year period.

Denning said that growth will continue.

After achieving sales of $2.5 million in 1987, the firm is targeting a sales goal of $5 million for this year, Denning said, RE-aching that goal will require another kind of targeting, she said.

"Rather than just send out fliers to everybody, we're going to be more selective," said Denning, who located DSM in its own building at 3305 N. 48th St. a year ago.

"When we were little, we sent the flier to anyone."

DSM's previous location at 11th and K had 1,000 square feet originally, Denning said. The firm doubled its size at that location shortly before moving into its current 9,000-square-foot building, which has a loading dock and "a big yard so that we can build on in the future when we need to."

Just over a year ago, DSM had six employees, com-

Continued on page 14.

Office Manager Pam DiPaolo, left, and Denning.... "We need to have a really big market share to sell enough products for our manufacturers."

Midlands Business Journal, January 29–Feb 4, 1988.

14   MIDLANDS BUSINESS JOURNAL   January 29-February 4, 1988

Data Source Media

Continued from page 1.

pared to the 15 on staff today, said Dunning, who in January hired Bruce Christenson of Des Moines as the firm's marketing director. DSM's Des Moines sales office opened last February, shortly after the opening of another sales office in Davenport, Dunning said.

Data Source Media sells supplies in bulk to 26 states, but its biggest markets currently are in Iowa, Kansas and Nebraska as well as the cities of Lincoln and Omaha, she said.

DSM's inventory of 2,200 kinds of computer ribbons, printwheels, diskettes, paper, labels, hardware, copier supplies, forms, laser printer toners and other supplies is up from 600 items four years ago, Dunning said.

"The sales offices' function is to take care of our customers. Our philosophy is that we want to have the best quality products and service in the industry and we want to have buying power that will help us to serve clients pricewise," she said.

"The next place we'd like to look at (for a sales office) is Kansas City," according to Dunning. "We really want to be a regional computer supply company." DSM also has a sales office at 84th and L Streets in Omaha, she said.

To be more selective in finding new accounts, DSM is targeting its mailings toward government agencies, schools and the nation's 1,000 largest companies, Dunning said.

The firm's new IBM System 36, installed last March shortly after the move, "allowed us to have multiple terminals," Dunning said. "We use them to put in all orders and track customer histories. That's probably the big thing, that we've become more streamlined and automated to handle the growth."

Besides making the Inc. 500 list, Dunning said one of the firm's top successes to date was in getting invited to a 3M seminar in 1986, one year after Data Source Media signed up as a 3M distributor. Some distributors work with 3M for up to 10 years before getting invited to the seminar for top producers, Dunning said.

At other distributor seminars, Dunning said, she is

often the only representative of a Midwestern computer-supply company, because "you have a smaller market, so you need to get a bigger market share" in this part of the U.S., she said.

"Just one company in Chicago would be bigger than my very largest account, easily. We need to have a really big market share to sell enough products for our manufacturers."

One of her biggest challenges is giving up some of the day-to-day control so that she can spend her time more efficiently in leading the growing company, Dunning said.

> 'My goal is that everyone in this office can handle everything that comes up without me, so the company can go forward.'

Pam DiPaolo, office manager, has been assigned to make hiring decisions and handle other personnel matters.

"That was a really big thing for me to give up," Dunning said. "But the most important thing I can do is analyze where we've been and where we want to go in the future and how we can remain a company that has good service, knowledgeable people" with the products that are the best possible, she said.

In keeping with that change, Dunning said she makes only a once-a-month appearance at the weekly 15-minute staff meetings that focus on new procedures, how existing procedures are working and the company's strengths or weaknesses. Dunning said her attendance is not necessary because "my goal is that everyone in this office can handle everything that comes up without me, to keep it so the company can go forward and remain in business for a long time."

Dunning said that she has had a bad experience with one employee, one advertising agency and one distributor, all of which have caused her to be more careful in screening.

Hiring the wrong person for a job at one point was not a costly mistake, but "after that we have been very careful about hiring employees, because employees are key to your business, in addition to customers," Dunning said.

The "fiasco" with the ad agency started when "they

didn't understand our business and everything they told us didn't happen," she said.

Because DSM has always backed the products its sells in case of problems, it had to pay for replacing any defective merchandise when one ribbon manufacturer folded, Dunning said. She said DSM has carefully screened every manufacturer since then by looking more closely at its track record and financial background.

In the future, Dunning said she'd like to trim Data Source Media's inventory to what she called a more manageable figure, since "2,200 products is an awfully lot to keep track of."

Due to its new sales offices, which have allowed DSM's sales staff to find more customers, the firm's purchasing volume has increased, allowing it to take advantage of manufacturer's volume discounts, Dunning said. "We can compete with anyone in the country, which is a really good situation for us."

"A really big challenge for us is to make sure, as we streamline and grow, that we don't forget our customers, who are the most important thing to us," Dunning said.

Associated Press. "Magazine ranks three Lincoln firms in top 500 fastest-growing companies." ©*Lincoln Journal Star*, November 22, 1988.

Magazine ranks three Lincoln firms in top 500 fastest-growing companies

By Associated Press

Three Lincoln companies are on Inc. magazine's 1988 list of the 500 fastest-growing companies in the United States.

United Phone Book Advertisers was No. 14 with 1987 sales of $21,076,000 and a sales growth from 1982 to 1987 of 9,795 percent.

Data Source Media, distributor of computer supplies, was No. 185 with sales of $2,506,000 and sales growth 1,527 percent.

International Galleries, offering direct marketing services, was No. 349 with sales of $5,153,000 and sales growth of 893 percent.

11-22-88

Barnes, Jeffrey S. "Computer Products Inc. addresses office printing needs." *Midlands Business Journal*, May 12–18, 1989.

SECTION B/Page 12 Midlands Business Journal May 12-18, 1989

Computer Products Inc. addresses office printing needs

by Jeffrey S. Barnes

A Lincoln firm has been established to serve what its owner perceives as a need in office automation printing.

Karen Dunning, president of Computer Products Inc. (CPI), has geared her firm's product line to automated printing needs. In Nebraska and Iowa, CPI sells continuous feed paper, fax paper and copier paper; business forms, including pin-fed custom letterhead, snap-apart envelopes and checks; copier supplies for 10 major brands; Hewlett Packard hardware and computer furnishings.

She said her favorite product, however, is an image projection device. The user can attach the unit to a computer and place it on an overhead projector, which projects the computer's screen onto an overhead screen. Dunning said

hers is considered the most advanced in the industry with 16-color generation and a universal prism, allowing it to be attached to any computer.

Dunning has also opened a Kansas City office that will serve the Kansas market and sell all varieties of computer supplies (the firm is known as Business Media Inc. in Kansas).

Dunning is a University of Nebraska-Lincoln graduate with a degree in finance. After working for IBM for six years, she became president and owner of Data Source Media in Lincoln, a vendor of computer supplies since 1984. "When I started with the company in 1984, it was losing money and turning out maybe two invoices a day," she said. "By the time I left, it had been on the INC. 500 list (of

Karen Dunning displays projection device at recent infotec trade show in Omaha. Firm also carries computer paper, copier supplies, computer hardware and finishings.

Karen Dunning, president of Computer Products inc.(CPI), has geared her firms' product line to automated printing needs in Nebraska and Iowa.

She said her favorite product, however, is an image projection device. The user can attach the unit to a computer and place it on an overhead projector, which projects the computer's screen onto an overhead screen. Dunning said hers is considered the most advanced in the industry with 16-color generation and a universal prism, allowing it to be attached to any computer.

Dunning has also opened a Kansas City office that will serve the Kansas market and sell all varieties of computer supplies (the firm is known as Business Media Inc. in Kansas).

Dunning is a University of Nebraska-Lincoln graduate with a degree in finance. After working for IBM for six years, she became president and owner of Data Source Media in Lincoln, a vendor of computer supplies since 1984. "When I started with the company in 1984 it was losing money and turning out maybe two invoices a day," she said. "By the time I left, it had been on the INC. 500 list(of fastest-growing companies) two years in a row."

Dunning lost the company in November 1988, however, in a divorce settlement. Under Nebraska law, the company was divided in half and she was unable to obtain a bank loan to pay for her half.

Despite what would seem to be a painful experience in business, Dunning decided to start her own company. "Business to me is fun," she said. "I like building things. I did interview with several companies, but I didn't feel I'd be able to clock in from 8 to 5 every day with someone else being my manager."

A native of Lincoln, she decided to start a company selling items that would not compete with her former company's.

"I think I can expect some results, too," Dunning said. "I learned a lot of things from having my own company. I learned it's smarter to hire excellent people and pay them for their skills, rather than lower-wage people to train them on the job. When I first started, I hired people right out of college; I don't closely supervise, however, and people right out of college aren't very practical. You need people that can take on a lot more responsibility."

Dunning

Dunning said her biggest challenge is in establishing her new markets. "In Nebraska and Iowa, I'm selling products I don't know about to people who have been buying them from others; outside the two states, I know the products but not the people I'm trying to sell them to. Starting small, I'm finding I have to juggle making the sales and buying the inventory."

She said her pluses make up for the minuses, however. "I'm pretty driven, very persistent in the way I do business. If I call on someone, I'm sincerely interested in what they do and what their needs are."

Dunning said she presently sees her best potential in the Kansas City market, and expects to hire a sales representative for that office first.

Computer Products, Inc. 3M Desktop Presentations advertisement and photo. ©*Lincoln Sunday Journal Star*, February 25, 1990.

"1990, Success Spotlight: April 15 Means Big Returns for Nebraska Dealer." *Proxima POST* newsletter, Spring 1991. (Enlarged version below article)

April 15 Means Big Returns for Nebraska Dealer

Karen Dunning, owner of Computer Products, Inc.

Tax time! Those words strike terror in the hearts of most Americans, but not Karen Dunning. Dunning, the owner of Computer Products, Inc., in Lincoln, Neb., and Business Media, Inc. in Kansas City, Kansas, is actually pleased to see April 15th roll around. She recently sold 60 A400 Data Displays to H & R Block. This well-known tax return preparation company will use the Data Displays to train their tax preparers in offices all over the country.

According to Dunning, H & R Block chose Proxima Data Displays because of their quality, reliability, and compatibility with the Tandy computers used exclusively by Block.

Dunning, whose background includes six years in computer sales for IBM, started Computer Products, Inc. in 1988. She began stocking Proxima products immediately. A half million dollars in sales that first year, and a million by 1990, told her she must be doing something right.

"I'd rather be very knowledgeable about one brand of products and steer my customers in the direction of that kind of quality, than stock several different lines," Dunning said.

"Experience taught me that Proxima had the best Data Displays, so Proxima is all I carry."

Dunning, a respected consultant in the LCD field, also supplied Data Display units for the Looking Glass Operation at Offut Air Force Base, Neb. Data Displays for the Looking Glass Operation are used for strategy meetings and conferences between the President and the Air Force.

Dunning considers the Data Display market "fascinating and fun, with tremendous potential."

In an effort to realize that potential, Dunning recently completed a merger between her Kansas location (previously called Computer Essentials, Inc.) and a company that sells computer supplies and accessories. Her Kansas City company is now known as Business Media, Inc. □

April 15 Means Big Returns for Nebraska Dealer

Karen Dunning, owner of Computer Products, Inc.

Tax time! Those words strike terror in the hearts of most Americans, but not Karen Dunning. Dunning, the owner of Computer Products, Inc., in Lincoln, Neb., and Business

Media, Inc. in Kansas City, Kansas, is
actually pleased to see April 15th roll around.
She recently sold 60 A400 Data Displays to
H & R Block. This well-known tax return
preparation company will use the Data
Displays to train their tax preparers in offices
all over the country.

According to Dunning, H & R Block
chose Proxima Data Displays because of
their quality, reliability, and compatibility with
the Tandy computers used exclusively by
Block.

Dunning, whose background includes
six years in computer sales for IBM, started
Computer Products, Inc., in 1988. She began
stocking Proxima products immediately. A
half million dollars in sales that first year, and
a million by 1990, told her she must be doing
something right.

"I'd rather be very knowledgeable about
one brand of products and steer my customers in the direction of that kind of quality,

than stock several different lines," Dunning said.

"Experience taught me that Proxima had the best Data Displays, so Proxima is all I carry."

Dunning, a respected consultant in the LCD field, also supplied Data Display units for the Looking Glass Operation at Offut Air Force Base, Neb. Data Displays for the Looking Glass Operation are used for strategy meetings and conferences between the President and the Air Force.

Dunning considers the Data Display market "fascinating and fun, with tremendous potential."

In an effort to realize that potential, Dunning recently completed a merger between her Kansas location (previously called Computer Essentials, Inc.) and a company that sells computer supplies and accessories. Her Kansas City company is now known as Business Media, Inc. ☐

"Lincoln's business people offer their advice."
©*Lincoln Journal Star*, March 18, 1991.

MARCH 18, 1991

3 *Inside* LINCOLN BUSINESS
Karen Dunning, owner, Business Media Inc.: Take good care of your customers and success will follow.

University of Nebraska–Lincoln College of Business Administration Center for Entrepreneurship speaker, 10th Nebraska Conference on Productivity and Entrepreneurship, April 4, 1995.

Karen Dunning, President, Business Media, Inc.

Karen Dunning graduated from East High School in Lincoln. She graduated from UNL with a Finance degree and studied at the University of Seville, Spain, in international business. She spent six years working for IBM in Lincoln, both as a systems engineer and a sales representative.

In 1984, she became president and owner of a small computer supply company in Lincoln which has grown from $100,000 annual sales with two employees to annual sales of $3 million and 25 employees in only four years. She was included in the Inc. magazine's 500 fastest growing privately held businesses for three years in a row.

In 1988, she founded another company to specialize in computer projection equipment and merged that company in 1990 with Business Media, Inc. Business Media was named to Inc. 500 in 1994. Business Media, Inc., specializes in computer presentation equipment, graphics software, and computer supplies. Business Media has offices in Lincoln, Omaha, and Kansas City.

Enlarged type for readability:

Karen Dunning graduated from East High School in Lincoln. She graduated from UNL with a Finance degree and studied at the University of Seville, Spain, in international business. She spent six years working for IBM in Lincoln, both as a systems engineer and a sales representative.

In 1984, she became president and owner of a small computer supply company (DSM) in Lincoln which has grown from $100,000 annual sales with two employees to annual sales of $3 million and 25 employees in only four years. She was included in the <u>Inc.</u> magazine's 500 fastest growing privately held business three times.

In 1988, she founded another company (CPI/BMI) to specialize in computer projection equipment and merged that company in 1990 with Business Media, Inc. Business Media was named to Inc. 500 in 1994. Business Media, Inc., specializes in computer presentation equipment, graphics software, and computer supplies. Business Media has offices in Lincoln, Omaha and Kansas City.

University of
Nebraska
Lincoln

College of Business Administration

Nebraska Center for Entrepreneurship
1237 R Street, Suite 203
P.O. Box 880226
Lincoln, NE 68588-0226
(402) 472 3353

New Address
CBA 209
Lincoln, NE 68588-0487

April 4, 1995

Karen Dunning
Business Media, Inc.
300 Oak Creek Drive
Lincoln, NE 68528

Dear Karen:

Thank you for being a speaker at our Tenth Nebraska Conference on Productivity and Entrepreneurship. We were very pleased that you were able to attend. We know you have a very busy schedule, but we really appreciated your taking the time to speak at the conference.

We heard many positive comments about the conference, and your presence helped to make the conference a success. Thanks again.

Sincerely,

Robin D. Anderson
Director

Thank you again for your help!

"1995 Governor's CEO Roundtable Assembled." *The Courier* (Nebraska Department of Economic Development, Nebraska Diplomats) and Governor Nelson letter, December 1995.

"Working for a better Nebraska"

Front row (left to right): Ronald J. Burns, president, Union Pacific Railroad Co., Omaha; L. Dennis Smith, president University of Nebraska; Jeff Raikes, senior vice president, Microsoft North America, Redmond, Wash; C. Edward McVaney, chairman and CEO, J.D. Edwards & Company, Denver.
Back row: R. Craig Hoenshell, chief executive officer, RCH Enterprises, LLC, New York; Karen Dunning, CEO, Business Media Inc., Lincoln, Tony Raimondo, president & CEO, Behlen Mfg. Co., Columbus, Neb., Nebraska Governor E. Benjamin Nelson; Maxine B. Moul, director, Nebraska Department of Economic Development, Paul F Engler, co-founder & CEO, Cactus Feeders Inc., Amarillo, Tex.

1995 Governor's CEO Roundtable Assembled

the Courier

DECEMBER 1995

"Working for a better Nebraska"

Front row (left to right): Ronald J. Burns, president, Union Pacific Railroad Co., Omaha; L. Dennis Smith, president University of Nebraska; Jeff Raikes, senior vice president, Microsoft North America, Redmond, Wash; C. Edward McVaney, chairman and CEO, J.D. Edwards & Company, Denver.
Back row: R. Craig Hoenshell, chief executive officer, RCH Enterprises, LLC, New York; Karen Dunning, CEO, Business Media Inc., Lincoln, Tony Raimondo, president & CEO, Behlen Mfg. Co., Columbus, Neb., Nebraska Governor E. Benjamin Nelson; Maxine B. Moul, director, Nebraska Department of Economic Development, Paul F. Engler, co-founder & CEO, Cactus Feeders Inc., Amarillo, Tex.

1995 Governor's CEO Roundtable Assembled

Diplomats attended the Second Annual Governor's CEO Roundtable Conference on economic development, Sept. 29 as part of the annual meeting, banquet and Passport-To-Nebraska football weekend.

According to Diplomat President Tony Raimondo, the CEO Roundtable provided a unique opportunity for Nebraska business leaders to examine why specific business decisions are made and what the state can do to better develop its global economy.

"Nebraskans' greater understanding of opportunities and challenges have contributed to the creation of alliances which are making a difference in Nebraska's ability to be globally competitive," said Raimondo.

Approximately 250 Nebraskans attended the CEO Roundtable Conference.

More photos on page 4

On the Inside

"Four owners named Entrepreneurs of the Year."
©*Lincoln Journal Star*, April 15, 1996.

Four owners named Entrepreneurs of the Year

Four businesspeople were named Nebraska Entrepreneurs of the Year Saturday at the 11th Nebraska Conference on Entrepreneurship at The Cornhusker.

Honored were:

■ Dick Abramson, Prairie Systems Inc., of Omaha, a six-year-old telecommunications software and service company. It has successfully entered the international marketplace and its multiple-media, multiple-application MultiFlex architecture has been recognized as the only of its kind in the world. Abramson is chairman of the Nebraska delegation to the White House Conference on Small Business.

■ Gerald Schleich, Austin Realty Group of Companies, Lincoln. Schleich purchased Austin Realty Co. in 1964 for $3,000. Today, the company employs nearly 400 people and has combined assets totaling $25 million. Schleich is CEO of the holding company and president of the majority of the businesses held under Austin Realty.

■ Karen Dunning, Business Media, Lincoln. Since leaving IBM, where she worked for six years, she has owned and operated several small businesses. She has been named to INC. magazine's top 500 fastest growing privately held businesses in the country four times. Business Media specializes in computer presentation equipment, which allows the presenter to project computer images to large audiences.

■ Larry Schnase, Eagle Plastics Inc., Hastings. A founder of Eagle Plastics, now a wholly owned subsidiary of Eagle Pacific Industries. Schnase has more than 35 years of experience in the manufacture and sales of plastic pipe. As president and CEO, he led Eagle Plastics' growth from nothing to a $20 million company in just four years; it currently has 112 employees.

Winners named in the annual International Business Plan Competition, which drew 12 undergraduate entries and nine graduate teams:

■ Undergraduate division — 1. John Boucard, senior, Baker University, Baldwin City, Kan.; 2. Greg Carstens and Bill Scheele, seniors, University of Nebraska-Lincoln.

■ Graduate division — 1. Arizona State University team (Thomas Christensen, Christopher Dimes, Michael Luz, Bradley Repp); 2. San Diego State University (Kevin Dearing, Neil Greer, Cathy Simmons).

University of
Nebraska
Lincoln

College of Business Administration

Nebraska Center for Entrepreneurship
CBA 209
P.O. Box 880487
Lincoln, NE 68588-0487
(402) 472-3353

March 26, 1996

Karen Dunning
Business Media, Inc.
300 Oak Creek Drive
Lincoln, NE 68528

Dear Karen:

Each year a committee from the College of Business Administration selects entrepreneurs to be honored at our annual conference. It gives me great pleasure to inform you that during the Eleventh Nebraska Conference on Entrepreneurship. you will be announced as the winner of the Entrepreneur of the Year Award.

As a special honoree, we invite you to be our guest at this conference along with three or four other people you may want to bring along with you--family members or employees from your company. If you have more than four people that would like to join you for this event, we can give each additional person a special registration fee of $20 per person to help pay for meals. Please call us with the names of the people who will be attending the conference. We need this information for meal reservations and name tags.

Please send us a brief bio about yourself and information about your company by April 5. This information will be used for press releases after the conference and also when you are introduced as Entrepreneur of the Year.

We have enclosed a brochure about our conference. The award will be presented by Governor Benjamin Nelson at the awards luncheon. This is a very prestigious award which recognizes your significant contribution as a Nebraska business leader.

Congratulations on your success.

Sincerely,

Robin D. Anderson
Director

University of Nebraska–Lincoln University of Nebraska Medical Center University of Nebraska at Omaha University of Nebraska at Kearney

Women's Studies Awarded Endowment
Karen Dunning Fund for Women's Studies Established

The University of Nebraska Foundation announces that an endowment has been created in support of the UNL Women's Studies Program. Named the *Karen Dunning Fund for Women's Studies*, the endowment will help to maintain general Women's Studies activities, as well as for student and faculty support.

"The income from this endowment will allow us to do important things for the Program," says Barbara DiBernard, Director of the Women's Studies Program. "We appreciate the confidence in Women's Studies shown by Ms. Dunning."

Donor Karen Dunning of Lincoln is the owner of Business Media Incorporated, a company which specializes in multimedia presentation equipment and computer supplies. A 1978 graduate of the UNL Business School, Dunning worked for IBM before starting Business Media Inc. in 1988.

"I've been successful enough in my business that I believe it is now time to give something back," states Dunning. "It's important to support women. I wanted to give where it will go to good use."

Dunning is an active member of the Lincoln community. She has been a member of the Planned Parenthood-Lincoln board of directors for the last four years, and is currently Board Treasurer. As a local business owner, she is involved in the Lincoln Chamber of Commerce and in the Lincoln Rotary. Dunning is also a member of the newly formed Lincoln chapter of the National Association of Women Business Owners, which will be recognized at a national convention later this Spring.

"I feel that women have a powerful impact to make on our society," declares Dunning. "My goal for this Fund is to help women have more visible positions in Lincoln."

The *Karen Dunning Fund for Women's Studies* was created through a gift of an appreciated asset which will be managed by the NU Foundation. Each year the Women's Studies Program will be able to use the interest from the Dunning Fund in a way that will most benefit the Program during that academic year.

The Dunning Fund is the first endowment given to the Women's Studies Program, but it will be the second fund managed by the NU Foundation for Women's Studies. Since 1994 the Foundation has managed the *Women's Studies Development Fund* which accepts contributions from friends and alumni of the UNL Women's Studies Program. The Development Fund is used for a number of activities, such as to supplement Program curriculum, activities, and guest speakers.

For information on how to give for the benefit of the UNL Women's Studies Program through the NU Foundation, please contact Christine Scudder, Associate Director of Development at the University Foundation at 402/472-2151. Donations can also be made to the Women's Studies Development Fund by using the Development Fund coupon found in this newsletter.

Beutler, Patty. "Girls Just Wanna Have Funds." ©*Lincoln Journal Star*, March 15, 1997.

Women's Commission plans on more workshops for girls

Bringing Joline Godfrey and her "An Income of Her Own" program to Lincoln fits into the Lincoln-Lancaster Women's Commission decision to focus on women and economics, said Bonnie Coffey, commission executive director.

"While we may all wish to put on aprons and be June Cleaver again, changes in their lifetimes mean young girls are going to have to take care of themselves economically," Coffey said.

Karen Dunning, a commission member, spurred the group to bring Godfrey and her program to Lincoln, with financial help from the Friends of the Commission. Twenty business women volunteered to serve as facilitators at a Friday conference for girls.

But that's only the start, said Coffey. She and Dunning will head for California next month to learn how to run "An Income of Her Own" programs. They plan to have two more conferences here in the fall and next spring.

Also, the commission is planning to have its own "$tart-up" camp in 1998 to teach teen-age girls how to write a business plan.

Showing girls ways to be economically self-sufficient and encouraging them to have goals tends to lower teen birth rates and raise self-esteem, Coffey said.

"We have a chance to change what the face of welfare looks like in this town," she said, "and I don't think that's too lofty."

Todd, Daniel. "Enhanced graphics boost Business Media's sales." *Midlands Business Journal*, Spring 1997.

by Daniel Todd

Enhanced graphics and greater portability are the main features expected to boost Business Media's 1997 sales of electronic presentation products.

"Our sales for 1996 were $6 million," said Karen Dunning, CEO of the Lincoln-based business, which has offices in Omaha, Des Moines, Kansas City and St. Louis. "We probably did about $4 million two years before that. We'll probably increase sales by 30 to 40 percent this year."

Business Media sells liquid crystal displays and data-video projectors which are often used in company presentations and training sessions and in schools.

"When the industry started around 1988, all we had was a black and white $2,000 LCD panel which would hook to a computers, lie on an overhead projector and show a black and white image," Dunning said. "It was geared for very simple training before Windows came along. I remember showing the panel to 10 customers in 1989. They all thought it was really neat, but said, 'What would we do with it?' Within two months, nine bought the LCD panels."

Company representatives said they could train people twice as fast using the technology, Dunning said.

"They could see the exact image on the computer," Dunning said. "People used to make transparencies of what was seen on the screen and then flip to the next transparency. With LCD, the entire room could see exactly what the computer was going to do. It was much easier to follow."

Today, the company's projection devices can display information in full color and are bright enough to be shown in well-lit rooms, Dunning said. The projectors vary from nine to 50 pounds.

"You can project any image you create on a computer through our equipment," Dunning said. "It can be used for audiences of five people to 1,000 people. We have different price ranges based on what we're trying to accomplish.

"A lot of groups use them for computer training. Nebraska Wesleyan University hangs some of our projectors on the ceiling. They hook up to computers for training. They have a computer lab and an auditorium where they can project CD-ROM and video images. We've also done quite a few installations in business training rooms and boardrooms."

One of the more popular models is a 17-pound projector made by Epson, which projects a diagonal image of 20 feet. Often hung from a ceiling, these projectors have an advantage over overheads, which might block the view of some people in an audience, Dunning said. These projectors replaced three-beam projectors which came out in 1990.

"The three-gun projectors were very expensive to operate and not as reliable," Dunning said. "The first three-gun projectors go back 10 to 20 years. Some bars and establishments with big-screen television sets had three-gun projector systems. Sometimes the images would get out of focus and you might have to pay someone about $400 to calibrate the image."

Business Media was founded in December 1988 as a computer supply company. In 1990, the company changed its focus when it merged with Computer Products, which was an electronic presentation company selling LCD panels and data and video projectors.

Griess, Karen. "On the Waterfront." ©*Lincoln Journal Star*,
June 20, 1997.

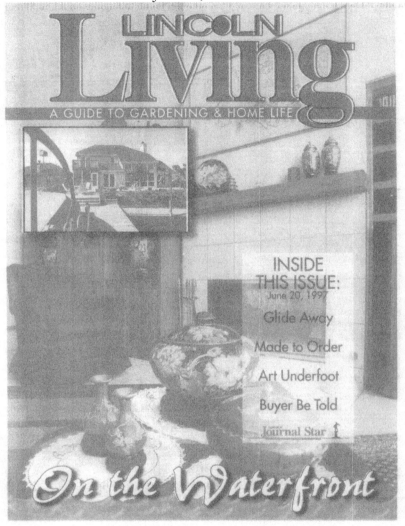

LINCOLN JOURNAL STAR, LINCOLN, NEB., FRIDAY, JUNE 20, 1997   8X

▲ A roomy whirlpool tub anchors one corner of the master bath.

▲ Cushy sofas are set at an angle to create a comfortable great room

▲ A cloisonné vase filled with budding tree branches becomes sculpture when displayed atop a low pedestal.

On the We

BY KAREN GRIEBS Lincoln Journal Star

Karen Dunning doesn't have to go far in search of a relaxing summer get-away. She escapes day-to-day demands and frustrations in the tranquility of her lake-front house in northwest Lincoln.

There, she welcomes purple martins into a martin house, watches yellow finches flutter about and gazes upon the evening sun setting across Capitol Beach Lake.

"I don't have to go anywhere," she said. "I can come home and relax. It's like being on vacation all the time."

Tranquil. Relaxing. Quiet.

The petite 46-year-old has lived at nature's door for four years in a 1½-story home that embraces guests with open spaces, warm light and big windows. "I wanted something really comfortable, casual, open and easy to entertain in, not stuffy," she said.

She found it by modifying a house plan to suit her narrow Capitol Beach lot in one of Lincoln's growing neighborhoods. "I like building from scratch and seeing things grow," Dunning said.

Her professional life follows the same path. She is co-owner of Business Media Inc., a company she founded in 1990 to sell electronic presentation equipment.

During the summer, Dunning prefers to vacation at home where she can garden, water-ski, grill and entertain friends in spacious surroundings. "I don't have to go anywhere. I can come home and relax."

She truly can. From her screened porch at 524 Pier One, Dunning has a front-row seat on the cottontail scampering across her yard or native grasses, scaring American cooks pecking at a neighbor's lawn.

Dunning spends much of her time in the combination living-dining-kitchen, three areas that flow together seamlessly and allow for easy conversation from any corner. The rooms face the lake and occupy nearly half of the first floor.

Soothing rather than showy.

The spacious living room is accented by a 13-foot ceiling and a north wall of windows that overlook the inlet. A lower ceiling defines the dining area.

The roomy kitchen, separated from the dining room by a peninsula, makes cooking a snap, thanks to built-in drawer dividers, a pull-out cutting board, roll-out drawers, a closet-sized pantry and a special tap for instant hot water. Tiny halogen lights set beneath the banks of oak cabinets spotlight the organized space and Corian counter.

Built-in speakers filter the sounds of Kelley Hunt, Bob Marley and Bonnie Raitt throughout the house, spilling over onto the lake-side patio where two finches nest above the outdoor speaker.

Dunning has an eye for details and "modern, simple, clean lines."

She also has a passion for ornate cloisonné vases, the oriental art pieces she's used to

▲ It's "like be Dunning says

highlight a hom and taupe.

Inviting. Wa

The floor pla neighboring hor by French door from the maste

...ting area, facing a wall fitted with display cases.

▲ The tiled entry is defined by a traditional oak balustrade and a softly curved console table.

screened porch. From there she watches children fish for carp and neighbors take paddle boats across the 9-foot deep inlet.

The master suite shares a see-through fireplace with the living and dining rooms. Its master bath features a double-sink counter, enclosed toilet and whirlpool tub off an L-shaped walk-in closet. The shower uniquely doubles as a steam shower.

Her house does not have a basement, but Dunning has compensated for that lack of storage space with a roomy double garage and a second-floor storeroom that accesses a large cedar closet.

An upstairs guest bedroom offers a glimpse of the State Capital between pitched roofs, and the second-floor office opens to a private balcony overlooking the inlet.

Dunning said she took advantage of the savings in building a smaller sized house to have "quality materials" and gadgets installed, such as ceiling fans throughout house, dimmer switches to alter lighting in seconds and a security system.

Without leaving home, the busy, single professional has created her own vacation house to entertain friends, family and nature's guests.

on vacation all the time," er lake-front home.

rash in blues, burgundies

Comfortable.
ke those of most is oriented to the water ening to concrete patios te, living room and

ON THE COVER: Cloisonné vases and bowls decorate Karen Dunning's stunning lakeside home at Capital Beach.
Photos by Robert Becker

▲ Artful furniture arrangement and a change in ceiling heights separate the living room from the kitchen (rear).

Griess, Karen. "On the Waterfront." ©*Lincoln Journal Star*, June 20, 1997. Enlarged Article for readability:

BY KAREN GRIESS Lincoln Journal Star

Karen Dunning doesn't have to go far in search of a relaxing, summer get-away. She escapes day-to-day demands and frustrations in the tranquillity of her lake-front house in northwest Lincoln.

There, she welcomes purple martins into a martin house, watches yellow finches flutter about and gazes upon the evening sun setting across Capital Beach Lake.

"I don't have to go anywhere," she said. "I can come home and relax. It's like being on vacation all the time."

Tranquil. Relaxing. Quiet.

The petite 40-year-old has lived at nature's door for four years in a 1½-story house that embraces guests with open spaces, warm light and big windows. "I wanted something really comfortable, casual, open and easy to entertain in, not stuffy," she said.

She found it by modifying a house plan to suit her narrow Capitol Beach lot in one of Lincoln's growing neighborhoods. "I like building from scratch and seeing things grow," Dunning said.

Her professional life follows the same path. She is co-owner of Business Media Inc., a company she founded in 1990 to sell electronic presentation equipment.

During the summer, Dunning prefers to vacation at home where she can garden, water-ski, grill and entertain friends in spacious surroundings. "I don't have to go anywhere. I can come home and relax."

She truly can. From her screened porch at 624 Pier One, Dunning has a front-row seat on the cottontail scampering across her yard of native grasses, scaring American coots pecking at a neighbor's lawn.

Dunning spends much of her time in the combination living-dining-kitchen, three areas that flow together seamlessly and allow for easy conversation from any corner. The rooms face the lake and occupy nearly half of the first floor.

Soothing rather than showy.

The spacious living room is accented by a 12-foot ceiling and a north wall of windows that overlook the inlet. A lower ceiling defines the dining area.

The roomy kitchen, separated from the dining room by a peninsula, makes cooking a snap, thanks to built-in drawer dividers, a pull-out cutting board, roll-out drawers, a closet-sized pantry and a special tap for instant hot water. Tiny halogen lights set beneath the banks of oak cabinets spotlight the organized space and Corian counter.

Built-in speakers filter the sounds of Kelley Hunt, Bob Marley and Bonnie Raitt throughout the house, spilling over onto the lake-side patio where two finches nest above the outdoor speaker.

Dunning has an eye for details and "modern, simple, clean lines."

She also has a passion for ornate cloisonne vases, the oriental art pieces she's used to

▲ It's 'like being on vacation all the time,' Dunning says of her lake-front home.

highlight a home awash in blues, burgundies and taupe.

Inviting. Warm. Comfortable.

The floor plan, like those of most neighboring homes, is oriented to the water by French doors opening to concrete patios from the master suite, living room and screened porch. From there she watches children fish for carp and neighbors take paddle boats across the 9-foot deep inlet.

The master suite shares a see-through fireplace with the living and dining rooms. Its master bath features a double-sink counter, enclosed toilet and whirlpool tub off an L-shaped walk-in closet. The shower uniquely doubles as a steam shower.

Her house does not have a basement, but Dunning has compensated for that lack of storage space with a roomy double garage and a second-floor storeroom that accesses a large cedar closet.

An upstairs guest bedroom offers a glimpse of the State Capital between pitched roofs, and the second-floor office opens to a private balcony overlooking the inlet.

Dunning said she took advantage of the savings in building a smaller sized house to have "quality materials" and gadgets installed, such as ceiling fans throughout house, dimmer switches to alter lighting in seconds and a security system.

Without leaving home, the busy, single professional has created her own vacation house to entertain friends, family and nature's guests.

ON THE COVER: Cloisonne vases and bowls decorate Karen Dunning's stunning lakeside home at Capital Beach.
                    Photos by Robert Becker

Karen Dunning

Karen Dunning's success as a businesswoman is so evident that she is now officially retired at the age of 40. Now, Karen says it's time to do all the things she's always wanted to do, but never had time for. These activities include traveling, scuba diving, obtaining a pilot's license, helping with young girls programs, and various business opportunities now available to her.

Karen is used to standing up for herself and reaching for her dreams. She attributes much of these characteristics to her upbringing, specifically her mother's influence. When she was five years old, her father died and her mother was left with four small children to raise. Her mother went back to college and received her teaching certificate to support her family. "She instilled in me that I could do anything I wanted," Karen reflects. "And that you need to know how to take care of yourself; always be ready for the unexpected."

Karen always knew she'd have her own business someday. In high-school, when she was counseled to be a teacher, she instead followed a friend's advise and went into business finance in order to follow her own dreams: owning a bank. She graduated in December 1978 from the University of Nebraska-Lincoln with a bachelors of science in Business Administration with a concentration in Finance and a minor in Spanish.

Because she was a woman, she wasn't able to be hired as a loan officer at a bank, only as a teller or secretary. But Karen obviously had other plans and accepted a position with IBM as a systems engineer, installing computers at banks across the state. In three years, she switched to sales at IBM and continued to enhance her computer knowledge through learning various specialties in the industry.

In 1984, Karen bought into a computer supply company and went from selling $200,000 computers to selling $3 ribbons. The business did extremely well and immediately became a success.

Then in 1988, Karen started the business, Computer Essentials, selling computer electronic equipment, such as LCD panels and data video equipment. Again, the business kicked off and jumped right into success. "I have a natural talent in starting businesses," Karen says. "I can tell what a business needs to do to be a success." In 1991, she merged Computer Essentials with Business Media. "It was fun to be in the Midwest and to be such a big player in the industry," Karen says. She sold her share on August 7, 1997.

Still adjusting to life without business, Karen has already picked certain areas she wants to focus some attention to in her new found "free time." She plans on focusing a lot of her attention now to helping young girls get the support and encouragement she had from her mother to be whatever you want to be. She serves on the Lincoln-Lancaster County Women's Commission and founded the Karen Dunning Fund for Women's Studies endowment for the UNL Women's Studies Program. In 1995, Karen served on Governor Nelson's CEO Roundtable Conference as the small business representative, and in 1996, she received the Entrepreneur of the Year Award from the College of Business Administration at UNL.

Kaiser, Rebecca. "Focus on 4: Karen Dunning." *Strictly Business* magazine, October–November 1997.

Dunning, Karen. "Power Presentation and When to Use Them." *Strictly Business* magazine, November 1997.

Power Presentation and When to Use Them

By Karen Dunning

So, you're thinking about giving a huge presentation. How is your presentation going to stand out in the crowd, have a positive impact and make a memorable impression?

Multimedia!! The buzzword that we've all heard has as many meanings as you can imagine. Multimedia is evolving. Multimedia used to mean 35-millimeter slide projectors and color transparencies. Remember those overhead projectors in high school?

Today, multimedia can be as simple as using a laptop computer while you page through a complicated slide show, such as Power Point. Or as complicated as using a Data/Video projector with up to 25-inch screens using full-blown audio, video, interactive digitized images and controlling the presentation with your remote laser pointer.

You've probably seen a presenter who stands at the side of a large screen image so overwhelming that you are mesmerized by the visual effects, but totally miss the presenter's message. Or the flustered presenter who is having so much trouble with their equipment that they forget their own message. This is really painful!

Don't let this happen to you!

First, remember in any presentation situation, you are the main focus. If the visuals don't enhance your message, you probably don't need them.

Before you do your presentation ask yourself the following:

What is the message you want to convey? Is it information only or persuasive? Are you trying to convince your audience to do something, or to buy something? Are you presenting your product in competition with other presenters?

How many people will be in your audience?

What size is the room you will be in? Is it an auditorium, or a small conference room?

What is the room layout?

How is the room lighted? Can you control the lighting or do you have large windows that would cause your visuals to appear faded? Would using multimedia presentation devices enhance your presentation? If so, use them, but be sure to spend most of your time practicing your presentation...you want to be polished

When used correctly, Multimedia should make your presentation memorable, and should set you apart from your competitors. You will create the perception that you are an expert.

Dunning, Karen. "Women: Flex Your Economic Power."
Lincoln–Lancaster Women's Commission Quarterly, Winter 1997/98.

Women: Flex Your Economic Power

By Karen Dunning

How many times have you met a woman who is intelligent, talented and energetic but struggling financially to make ends meet? Some of these women are caught in a catch-22 of being underemployed.

Underemployment is the phenomenon of being in a job for which you are so overqualified that you aren't using your full talents and are not earning what you could if employed at your level of talent and ability. Underemployment happens to both men and women, and sometimes it's by choice.

I don't want to imply that money is the most important aspect of a career. We all need to be doing something we truly enjoy, and sometimes we get paid well for that. It may be too late for some of us to get out of the rut of being underemployed, but we can all help to prepare our daughters so they will be able to utilize their talents.

Karen Dunning

Reality is that by the year 2000, two out of three new entrants into the labor force will be women. While most school-age girls plan to work, they do not plan for careers that could sustain themselves and their families. Women and girls continue to be enrolled in education and training programs that prepare them for low-wage jobs in traditionally female occupations.

In my own personal experience working in sales and owning businesses for the past 20 years, I have witnessed many women who were struggling financially. The following statements are my personal opinions based on my experience.

If you are able to build wealth, you will have many more life choices open to you. You are able to use your wealth as a tool to accomplish things important to you, and to donate to causes that you believe in.

I think the best way to create wealth is to work in a job that pays based on performance, such as sales or owning your own business, and to learn to manage the money that you do have. Women-owned businesses are the fastest-growing sector of the economy. The women who are taking risks and owning their own businesses, or who are good at sales, are the ones who are creating wealth for themselves and their families, and who will be able to impact issues that are important to them.

Karen Dunning is a Lincoln entrepreneur and a member of the Commission.

3C-8C

LIFE

TRENDS ■ PEOPLE ■ ISSUES

Monday C
March 29, 1999
Questions, comments? Call Linda Olig, 473-7210
Page design: Vicki S. Reynolds

Aiming for the

S T A R S

Former Lincoln woman gave up multimillion-dollar business to pursue acting career in L.A., where she hopes to make a difference

■ View master: Dunning has a good view of Los Angeles from her 24th-floor balcony.

■ The doctor is in: "Chicago Hope" star Mark Harmon directed the episode in which Dunning appeared.

BY JEFF KORBELIK
Lincoln Journal Star

When Karen Dunning watched a movie or TV program, she was appalled at how women were portrayed.

So the 42-year-old former Lincoln businesswoman decided to do something about it.

"The rules didn't seem realistic to me," she said. "I thought maybe if I went out there and learned the industry, I could make a positive impact."

That's what she's intending to do. Two years ago, Dunning sold Business Media Inc., her multimillion-dollar projector/computer supply company, to pursue a career in entertainment. She moved to Los Angeles last May.

■ What's up, doc?: Dunning meets up with "Chicago Hope" star Hector Elizondo outside the makeup trailer.

"I know it's kind of risky to give up everything," she said. "I had a for-sure salary, a lot of benefits and, of course, my own schedule. But this was something I had to do."

It's easy to believe Dunning will succeed because she's proved herself already. She still remembers when a business executive laughed at her when she left IBM Corp. after six years to start her first company.

Data Source Media had only three employees, including herself, when Dunning opened the doors in 1986. Her tiny company was responsible for developing business plans and marketing computer supplies.

In four years, sales grew from $150,000 to $3 million annually. Data Source Media was named to Inc. magazine's top 500 fastest-growing, privately held companies list three straight years. Dunning opened offices in Omaha, Des Moines and Davenport, Iowa,

■ IV league: Karen Dunning checks out the "ER" set, where she was an extra on the TV series.

before selling the company in December 1988.

She then founded Computer Products Inc. with offices in Kansas City, Mo., and Lincoln. CPI marketed electronic presentation equipment and computer supplies in Nebraska, Iowa, Kansas and Missouri.

In 1991, she merged her company with Lincoln's Business Media Inc. and became

president, chief executive officer and stockholder. Sales were $6 million in 1996 and $10 million in 1997.

Then she left it all behind.

"I'm used to skepticism," she said. "I've had people tell me I'm too old to start (acting). But I've met 75-year-old women who started two years ago and are already in

commercials. There's really no age to start, and I think people like to see all ages on TV."

Her acting experience is limited. She did plays in high school and college, but nothing else. She auditioned for Lincoln Community Playhouse's "Once on This Island" last spring

More on STARS, Page 3C

PHOTOS COURTESY KAREN DUNNING

LIFE

Stars/Former Lincoln woman made some acting contacts in Los Angeles

Continued from Page 1C

and got a callback but wasn't cast.

Before Dunning left Lincoln, her friends and peers gave her some Los Angeles contacts, including actor Ed Asner. A Lincoln friend who knew Asner told Dunning to call him. She did and he agreed to lunch with her. She also hooked up with Lincoln actress Harley Jane Kozak, who took Dunning to a fund-raiser at Jay Leno's house.

"All of the people who have met with me have been really nice," she said. "It was amazing."

Dunning already has made great strides. She landed her first part as an extra on "Chicago Hope" in August. Since then, she's been an extra on "ER," "LA Doctors" and "Maggie." She also was an extra in upcoming films starring Steve Martin, Eddie Murphy, Bruce Willis and Michelle Pfeiffer.

In December, Dunning was accepted by the Screen Actors Guild.

"I'm one little baby step in a very long process, but I'm looking at the big picture," she said. "I have a good altitude, which I think helped me get in the Screen Actors Guild so quickly. Normally, it takes people about a year and half. It only took me three months."

She's also taking acting classes and voice lessons.

"My big goal is to become a singer, but my big, big goal is to see if I could produce projects that put people into realistic roles," she said. "I'm really interested in putting women in realistic roles."

Dunning then recalled a recent experiment. She asked her acting professors whom they would cast her as in a production. All of them told her they could see her as a mom or a wife. She has been neither.

Then she asked them about casting her as a business person. Lower to middle management, maybe, they said, but nothing higher.

"They don't know I ran a multi-million-dollar company for 14 years," she said. "The perception of what a woman business owner looks like is different than what it really is because they think I've got too friendly a face. Friendly people aren't business people."

Midwestern stereotypes are just as bad, she said. She was asked to bring sweaters for a recent movie shot with a Midwest setting. She had several sweaters she had brought from Nebraska.

But "they told me my sweaters were all too nice," she said. They told me people in the Midwest don't have clothes like that, and so they gave me a really ugly brown sweater that had lint all over it."

She thought it was funny.

"They said, 'Now you look like the perfect football mom,'" she said.

Dunning became a regular extra this season on "Chicago Hope," the CBS doctor drama produced by David E. Kelley of "Ally McBeal" and "The Practice" fame. The show stars Mark Harmon, Emmy winner Christine Lahti, Hector Elizondo, Adam Arkin and Peter Berg.

"Hope's" first assistant director liked Dunning's look. "If they like the way you look, you're in," she said.

And because she's around so much, the crew allowed her to observe and ask questions.

"They really treated me like an intern," she said. "Most of the time, the extras are way in the back, and when they need you, they pull you in, so you don't get to know anybody."

She became more popular when she brought former Nebraska Gov. Ben Nelson on the set. Dunning spoke at Nelson's CEO Roundtable in 1995 and attended an International Trade Mission to Asia with him in August 1996.

"He met the producers and the high-up people, which meant I got to meet them because I brought the governor on the set," she said. "After that, my status elevated on the set because I knew the governor.

"It's a funny system out there," she added. "It's who you know and the perception. You start out as this lowly extra, but if you know someone and they find out, then all of a sudden you're better. It's really kind of sad, but true."

Dunning is now trying to make the transition from extra to actor.

As an extra, "all I do is float around," she said. "They tell you, 'When (Mark Harmon) says this, you walk over there.' If you don't have any speaking parts, you're really not noticed."

She's pining for that first line. But before she gets it, she needs an audition. Before she gets an audition, she needs an agent, and before she gets an agent, she needed to be in the guild. Now she's in the guild and working on getting an agent.

"I didn't realize how hard it is, but you don't get lines that easily," Dunning said. "You have to audition to get lines, or you have to know someone. If you knew the director of that show, they might let you have a line."

Knowing Dunning's tenacity, it's just a matter of time before she's speaking on screen and before she's producing work with realistic parts.

"I have an abundance theory," she said. "There's room for everybody to be successful. There's no reason why you shouldn't help other people be successful, too."

Karen D. Dunning M.D.
Cardiology
23-78786
CHICAGO HOPE
hospital

Typed version of "Aiming for the Stars", By Jeff Korbelik ©Lincoln Journal Star March 21, 1999 for readability:

When Karen Dunning watched a movie or TV program, she was appalled at how women were portrayed.

So the 42 year-old former Lincoln Business woman decided to do something about it.

"The roles didn't seem realistic to me," she said. "I thought maybe if I went out there and learned the industry, I could make a positive impact."

That's what she's intending to do. Two years ago, Dunning sold Business Media Inc., her multimillion-dollar projector/computer supply company, to pursue a career in entertainment. She moved to Los Angeles last May.

"I know it's kind of risky to give up everything," she said. "I had a for-sure salary, a lot of benefits and, of course, my own schedule. But this was something I had to do."

It's easy to believe Dunning will succeed because she's proved herself already. She still remembers when a business executive laughed at her when she left IBM Corp. after six years to start her first company.

Data Source Media had only three employees, including herself, when Dunning opened the doors in 1984. Her tiny company was responsible for developing business plans and marketing computer supplies.

In four years, sales grew from $100,000 to $3 million annually. Data Source Media was named to Inc. Magazine's top 500 fastest-growing, privately held companies list three straight years. Dunning opened offices in Omaha, Des Moines and Davenport, Iowa, before selling the company in December 1988.

She then founded Computer Products Inc. with offices in Kansas City, MO., and Lincoln. CPI marketed electronic presentation equipment and computer supplies in Nebraska, Iowa, Kansas and Missouri.

In 1991, she merged her company with Lincoln's Business Media Inc. and became president, chief executive officer and stockholder. Sales were $6 million in 1996 and $10 million in 1997.

Then she left it all behind.

"I'm used to skepticism," she said. "I've had people tell me I'm too old to start (acting). But I've met 75-year-old women who started two years ago and are already in commercials. There's really no age to start and I think people like to see all ages on TV." Her acting experience is limited. She did plays in high school and college, but nothing else. She auditioned for Lincoln Community Playhouse's "Once on This Island" last spring and got a callback but wasn't cast.

Before Dunning left Lincoln, her friends and peers gave her some Los Angeles contacts, including actor Ed Asner. A Lincoln friend who knew Asner told Dunning to call him. She did and he agreed to lunch with her. She also hooked up with Lincoln actress Harley Jane Kozak, who took Dunning to a fund-raiser at Jay Leno's house.

"All of the people who have met with me have been really nice," She said. "It was amazing."

Dunning already has made great strides. She landed her first part as an extra on "Chicago Hope" in August. Since then, she's been an extra on "ER," "LA Doctors" and "Maggie." She also was an extra in upcoming films starring Steve Martin, Eddie Murphy, Bruce Willis and Michelle Pfeiffer.

In December, Dunning was accepted by the Screen Actors Guild.

I'm one little baby step in very long process, but I'm looking at the big picture," she said. "I have a good attitude, which I think helped me get in the Screen Actors Guild so quickly. Normally, it takes people about a year and half. It only took me three months."

She's also taking acting classes and voice lessons.

"My big goal is to become a singer, but my big, big goal is to see if I could produce projects that put people into realistic roles," She said. "I'm really interested in putting women in realistic roles."

Dunning then recalled a recent experiment. She asked her acting professors whom they would cast her as in a production. All of them told her they could see her as a mom or wife. She has been neither.

Then she asked them about casting her as a business person. Lower to middle management, maybe, they said, but nothing higher.

"They don't know I ran a multi-million-dollar company for 14 years." she said. "The perception of what a woman business owner looks like is different than what it really is because they think I've got too friendly a face. Friendly people aren't business people."

Midwestern stereotypes are just as bad, she said. She was asked to bring sweaters for a recent movie shot with a Midwest setting. She had several sweaters she had brought from Nebraska.

But "they told me my sweaters were all too nice," she said. "They told me people in the Midwest don't have clothes like that, and so they gave me a really ugly brown sweater that had lint all over it."

She thought it was funny.

"They said, 'Now you look like the perfect football mom,' " she said.

Dunning became a regular extra this season on "Chicago Hope," the CBS doctor drama produced by David E. Kelley of "Ally McBeal" and "The Practice" fame. The show stars Mark Harmon, Emmy winner Christine Lahti, Hector Elizondo, Adam Arkin and Peter berg.

"Hope's" first assistant director liked Dunning's look. "If they like the way you look, you're in," she said.

And because she's around so much, the crew allowed her to observe and ask questions.

"They really treated me like an intern," she said. "Most of the time, the extras are way in the back, and when they need you, they pull you in, so you don't get to know anybody."

She because more popular when she brought former Nebraska Gov. Ben Nelson on the set. Dunning spoke at Nelson's CEO Roundtable in 1995 and attended an International Trade Mission to Asia with him in August 1998.

"He met the producers and the high-up people, which meant I got to meet them because I brought the governor on the set," she said. "After that, my status elevated on the set because I knew the governor.

'It's a funny system out there," she added. "It's who you know and the perception. You start out as this lowly extra, but if you know someone and they find out, then all of a sudden you're better. It's really kind of sad, but true."

Dunning is now trying to make the transition from extra to actor.

As an extra, "all I do is float around," she said. "They tell you, 'When (Mark Harmon) says this, you walk over there.' If you don't have any speaking parts, you're really not noticed."

She's pining for that first line. But before she gets it, she needs an audition. Before she gets an audition, she needs an agent , and before she gets an agent, she needed to be in the guild. Now she's in the guild and working on getting an agent.

"I didn't realize how hard it is, but you don't get lines that easily," Dunning said. "You have to audition to get lines, or you have to know someone. If you know the director of that show, they might let you have a line."

Knowing Dunning's tenacity, it's just a matter of time before she's speaking on screen and before she's producing work with realistic parts.

"I have an abundance theory," she said. "There's room for everybody to be successful. There's no reason why you shouldn't help other people be successful, too."

Dunning, Karen. "Company History."
©*Lincoln Journal Star*, **March 16, 2002. Editorial**

This letter is in regard to your recent business profile of a company called Business Media Inc. (LJS, March 14) and is an attempt to fill in some gaps in the article. I founded the projection equipment company in 1998 that merged with the computer supply company Business Media in December of 1990, and ran the projection equipment side of Business Media from 1991-1997, serving as CEO and president. When I chose to sell my part of Business Media in 1997 to my former employee [redacted] the projection equipment made up more than 90 percent of the business.

I was named Entrepreneur of the Year of Nebraska in 1996 by the University of Nebraska, and served on Gov. Nelson's CEO roundtable in 1995.

In December of 1988, I founded Computer Products, with offices in. Lincoln and Kansas City (dba Business Media), to distribute computer supplies and projection equipment.

Computer Products was one of the first Proxima brand resellers in the country, and became one of the largest resellers in the United States by working with H&R Block, Hallmark Cards, AMC theatres, Mutual of Omaha, Offutt, etc.

In December 1988, Vicki Lund (president) and a former employee of mine [redacted] when I was president and co-owner of Data Source Media, co-founded a computer supply company called Business Media in Lincoln.

In December of 1990, I merged Computer Products with Business Media, to enable Business Media to become a 3M dealer. We sent letters to our clients that the companies had merged, but the actual legal paperwork took longer to complete.

Karen Dunning, Fairfax, Calif.

KAREN DUNNING

E. BENJAMIN NELSON
NEBRASKA

720 HART SENATE OFFICE BUILDING
WASHINGTON, DC 20510
(202) 224-6551
FAX: (202) 228-0012
www.bennelson.senate.gov

United States Senate

December 17, 2008

The Honorable Barack Obama
President-Elect of the United States of America
Obama-Biden Presidential Transition Project
Washington, DC 20270

Dear President-Elect Obama:

I am writing this letter to recommend Karen Dunning for a senior managerial position in your administration. She has a particular interest in the Small Business Administration, but her qualifications would also extend to any position dealing with entrepreneurial development. What sets Karen apart from others is the fact that she has experience at many different levels – with private enterprise, government agencies, and nonprofit organizations alike.

Karen's business skills were formed at IBM, where she specialized in the finance industry, and were later honed by running and growing her own multi-million-dollar businesses, Data Source Media and Business Media, Inc. These companies were named to *Inc.* magazine's 500 Fastest Growing Privately Owned Businesses on four separate occasions.

Named Nebraska Entrepreneur of the Year in 1995, Karen was invited to attend a meeting at the Clinton White House with other business owners. She was also the only Nebraska business owner invited to attend a White House Summit held in Chicago the following year. When I served as Governor of Nebraska, she was a member of my CEO Roundtable. She also participated in a trade mission to Japan, Hong Kong and China.

Karen has helped many nonprofit organizations, including the Nebraska Arts Council, Lincoln-Lancaster Women's Commission, Planned Parenthood, and RSAC (Rape and Sexual Abuse Center), in addition to raising funds for entrepreneurial training workshops for young girls.

Upon selling her business interests and moving to California, Karen then worked as a consultant for two Bay-area dot.com companies. She has been politically involved for many years and sings for charity and political events.

I believe Karen Dunning is an individual who would help make our federal government more efficient and responsive. She has the passion and long-range vision necessary to evaluate a situation, build a consensus, and implement a plan for improvement and results. If you need further information, please do not hesitate to contact me at 202-224-6551.

Sincerely,

E. Benjamin Nelson
United States Senator

EBN:lh

440 NORTH 8TH STREET
SUITE 120
LINCOLN, NE 68508
(402) 441-4600
FAX (402) 476-8753

FIELD REPRESENTATIVE
POST OFFICE BOX 2105
KEARNEY, NE 68848
(308) 293-5818

FIELD REPRESENTATIVE
POST OFFICE BOX 1472
SCOTTSBLUFF, NE 69363
(308) 631-7614

FIELD REPRESENTATIVE
POST OFFICE BOX 791
SOUTH SIOUX CITY, NE 68776
(402) 209-3596

7602 PACIFIC STREET
SUITE 205
OMAHA, NE 68114
(402) 391-3411
FAX (402) 391-4725

Pohlman, Marty. "Hunter's Screenwriters Colony in full swing." *The Superior Express*, September 27, 2012.

> Karen Dunning, late of Los Angeles, Calif., and the owner of one very bribable canine with the name of Dancer, owned a music store in Lincoln, Neb., for 14 years. She sold the store and took off to southern California. She is a singer-songwriter. Her path is somewhat different from the other attendees. She is writing a screenplay with the ultimate goal of scoring the music when the film goes into production. Her project is entitled "Newlywed at 70," based on her mother's remarriage to an older man.

©Lincoln55+ Seniors, Fall 2016 (on Next Page).

Grace, Service Therapy Dog, Reporting for Duty - by Karen Dunning

by Karen Dunning

Grace, my service therapy dog for the past 3 years, accompanies me to numerous places in Lincoln. She brings love, laughter, delight and healing.

Children usually exclaim in joy, "A Puppy!" when they spot her.

Grace is a gray non-shedding 5 1/2-year-old Shih-Poo dog. She is a crossbreed between a Poodle and a Shih Tzu. We adopted each other August 1, 2013, my late Grandma's birthday. She is a cute and gentle diplomat and loves people, children, other dogs and cats. She patiently waits and is happy when people pet, hold or cuddle her. She likes to chase squirrels, and her squeaky tennis ball.

I met Grace at the Seattle Humane Society in Bellevue, WA on August 1, 2013, and immediately fell in love with her. I learned she had been lost on the streets of Los Angeles and spent several weeks in 2 different kill shelters before being flown with 35 dogs from LAX to Seattle Humane Society, a No-Kill Shelter. She weighed only 7 pounds and her ribs stuck out. Today she weighs 10 pounds.

The Seattle Humane Society had her microchipped, bathed, spayed, and cleaned her teeth. She was professionally evaluated

My medical doctor told me I qualify for a service animal to help me with complications from long term Lyme Disease, and PTSD resulting from being strangled and punched by 2 abusive men in Lincoln, NE. Grace was trained in Seattle, and became my service therapy dog.

She has made herself at home both in Seattle and Lincoln where I have spent half time helping my mother (93) and my late stepdad. She has been to Madonna Home, Bryan Hospital, Tabitha Home, and Legacy Estates.

Grace rides in the child seat of the grocery cart and brings mostly smiles from other shoppers. On a few occasions someone not familiar with service animals will make a negative comment. One time this happened while I was checking out at a local grocery store. The clerk came to Grace's defense immediately.

Grace flies with me from Omaha to Seattle on Alaska Airlines. The Alaska employees in Omaha welcome her with a smiley "Hi, Grace!"

Grace sits on my lap and

sometimes puts her head on the airplane seat armrest. On one such flight the attendant with the refreshment cart paused, smiled, and asked Grace, "Could you please move your cute puppy head?"

Wherever Grace goes I notice people are smiling and sometimes surprised. Some think she's a toy dog and are startled when she moves. One woman had a rabbit purse that matched Grace's fur so we took a photo of Grace by her matching bag. Several people have asked to take her photo.

Grace sits with me when I sing with the choir at First United Methodist Church. She has listened to sermons, attended events at the Lied Center, attended Nebraska Diplomat events, and cheered on my Salt Dog pitcher who lived with us for a season. She attended a music workshop with me in Nashville, TN. She has met Nebraska's Governor and a Senator. She has ridden Lincoln buses, and attended Leadership Lincoln, and Rotary meetings.

When I came to Lincoln from Seattle to help my mom and stepdad, I rented a U-Haul and towed my car. I drove and Grace rode shotgun. Other travelers asked if me if I felt safe traveling alone. I smiled and said, "I am safe. I am traveling with Grace."

and found to get along with children, cats, dogs, women and men. There was another woman who had already reserved Grace, but when she saw how much Grace loved me, she insisted I should adopt her instead, and she gave Grace several small dog vests, too.

Dunning, Karen. "Escape cycles of abuse."
©*Lincoln Journal Star*, March 2, 2015 Editorial

The recent Ray and Janay Rice violence brought back feelings of my own silent victim traumatic experience of being abused, punched and strangled by men who said they loved me. Through professional counseling, I was able to learn and understand the insidious cycle of violence and leave my abusers. I was too afraid and ashamed to report my first abuser. My second abuser was charged. I was too afraid and ashamed to testify so his charges were later dropped. I failed to protect myself and others from possible future abuse by not speaking out sooner. These men both live and work in Lincoln and I pray they have received help and healing. I forgive them. I ask forgiveness from society for allowing my fear and shame to silence me. I thank Voices of Hope and Friendship Home for helping me and so many victims to heal, survive and thrive.

Karen Dunning

Beach, Natalie. "#USToo: The United Shame of America." *O* magazine, March 2018.

Karen Dunning Childhood photo 4 years old

Each person is born with a unique divine unwavering essence.

We each get to choose if we allow our essence to shine through, or if we cover it up with our actions and learned patterns.

My dream is for each person to rediscover their true essence and to find their own inner peace, which will expand to world peace.

ABOUT THE AUTHOR

Karen Dunning is an entrepreneur, philanthropist, musician, and international traveler. Born in Everett, Washington, and raised in Nebraska, she earned a Bachelor's of Science in Business Administration Finance from the University of Nebraska–Lincoln with a minor in Spanish, and later earned an Associate's degree in Music from the College of Marin in Kentfield, California.

Karen worked for IBM in Lincoln as a systems engineer and marketing representative specializing in the finance industry, then owned, started, and grew her own multi-million-dollar businesses, resulting in an Entrepreneur of the Year award in 1996. On three separate occasions, her companies were named to *Inc.* magazine's 500 Fastest Growing Privately Owned Businesses. Karen had one of the first commercial websites and sold a line of computer projection/presentation equipment internationally.

She served as a member and speaker of Nebraska Governor Ben Nelson's CEO Roundtable, was inducted into the Nebraska Diplomats, and participated in international trade missions to Japan, Hong Kong, and China. She founded the Karen Dunning Fund Endowment in 1995 for the University of Nebraska–Lincoln Women and Gender Studies department to provide scholarships to students. Today, Karen mentors and serves as a judge at entrepreneurial conferences at the University of Nebraska–Lincoln.

Karen moved to California and joined the Screen Actors Guild in 1998. She has acted and sung in many movies, TV shows, and live stage productions, most notably playing a doctor for one season of the TV show *Chicago Hope*.

Karen formed the Dunning Group, Inc./MENTORmania, which specializes in helping individuals and companies realize their potential. She has raised funds and hosted workshops to teach girls entrepreneurial skills, and she has also been active in Rotary Club and served on numerous nonprofit boards. In addition to her philanthropic work, Karen has been politically active for many years, advocating for causes that are important to her and singing for a range of charity and political events.

Karen lives outside Seattle, and in her spare time she loves to sing, play her piano, and go on hikes with Grace dog and her family. She is a proud survivor of domestic violence and a fiercely compassionate advocate of overcoming the odds and finding your own unique path in life.

Website: www.KarenDunning.org and www.KarenDunning.com